Madison Evans

Biographical sketches of the pioneer preachers of Indiana

Madison Evans

Biographical sketches of the pioneer preachers of Indiana

ISBN/EAN: 9783337305208

Printed in Europe, USA, Canada, Australia, Japan

Cover: Foto ©Lupo / pixelio.de

More available books at **www.hansebooks.com**

BIOGRAPHICAL SKETCHES

OF THE

PIONEER PREACHERS

OF

INDIANA.

BY

MADISON EVANS, A. M.

"I say the pulpit (in the sober use
Of its legitimate, peculiar pow'rs)
Must stand acknowledged, while the world shall stand,
The most important and effectual guard,
Support and ornament of Virtue's cause."

Philadelphia:
J. CHALLEN & SONS,
1308 CHESTNUT STREET.
1862.

"TO THEM
THAT ARE SANCTIFIED
IN
CHRIST JESUS,
CALLED TO BE
SAINTS,
WITH ALL THAT IN EVERY PLACE CALL UPON THE
NAME OF JESUS CHRIST, OUR LORD,
BOTH THEIRS AND OURS,"
THIS BOOK
IS RESPECTFULLY INSCRIBED
BY
THE AUTHOR.

L.

PREFACE.

ASIDE from the ordinary motives that prompt men to write books, the author has undertaken the present work as a sacred duty, which *some one* owed to those venerable pioneers who, by their labors, sacrifices, and sufferings, first promulgated in Indiana, the great principles of the current Reformation. Refusing to be called by any of the names assumed by the various religious parties, they took upon themselves the name given to the disciples "first in Antioch." Out of sheer devotion to the truth they denied the faith of their fathers, in which they might have enjoyed great popularity, and embraced a system "everywhere spoken against," as the advocates of which, they became in the eyes of many as "the filth of the world and the offscouring of all things." Yet loving the praise of God more than the praise of men, and in nothing terrified by their adversaries, they stood fast "in one spirit with one mind striving together for *the* faith of *the* gospel." As they belted the trees of the forest, converting the woodlands into fertile fields, so they *deadened*, at least, deep-rooted *errors*, and deposited the good seed which has already produced a glorious harvest.

It is not just that such men should be

"Thrust foully in the earth to be forgot,"

nor is it meet that those upon whom their mantles have fallen—or will soon fall—should be deprived of the bracing influence of their example. It is, therefore, a duty to perpetuate their memory by setting their portraits in the record of their noble deeds, "like apples of gold in a framework of silver."

The author's apology for not leaving the performance of this duty to some one of riper years, and more mature judgment, is his fear that those better qualified would neglect in the future, that which has already been neglected too long, and his conviction that it is better that *some* things should be done *imperfectly* than that they *should not be done at all*.

The materials for the work have been obtained, chiefly, from the surviving pioneers—to whom the author acknowledges his obligations—and the facts, incidents, and in most instances the dates may be confidently relied upon. That the facts have not always been presented to the best advantage, and that there are infelicitous expressions and imperfections of style it is highly probable, but it is hoped that such errors will be looked upon in the spirit of that charity which "thinketh no evil."

In the selection of those whose lives and services form the subject of this volume, the author has endeavored to avoid every appearance of partiality. In addition to a careful exercise of his own judgment, he has sought and obtained the advice of older disciples who, in this State, have known the Reformation from the beginning. If many good and useful preachers have been passed by in silence, it is because they have been candidly regarded as less prominent, and because there is not room in one small volume for even a *short* history of *every* good man. Others have been omitted, because it was impossible to obtain a sufficiency of *definite* and *reliable* information concerning them. In this class are Elders Thomas C. Johnson and Joseph Fassett, whose names are "written in heaven." They were men altogether lovely; and none are more worthy of a place in this humble work, from which nothing but stern necessity has excluded them.

The critical reader will not fail to discover much sameness in many of the sketches, especially in those parts relative to the conversion of the persons under the systems of religion then prevailing, and the means by which they were finally brought into the Reformation. It seemed impossible to avoid this without concealing facts, or deviating from the truth; for, in the words of an acute writer, "about the same amount of groping is necessary to make one's way out of an atmosphere clouded with the smoke that ascends from Mystic Babylon."

In the midst of the great events that are transpiring around us, some may conclude that the incidents herein related are trivial, that the stage of action is too narrow, and that the facts are only

>—" feats
>Of heroes little known."

Such critics are respectfully reminded, that there is always more "pomp and circumstance" in war than in religion. He who chronicles the deeds of Napoleon, may interest his readers with the bloody engagements of great armies, or with a shifting of the campaign from the sands of Egypt to the snows of Russia; but even the inspired historian, in his account of the immaculate Son of God, had to content himself with saying that he "went about all Galilee, teaching in their synagogues and preaching the gospel of the kingdom." His presence at the marriage in Cana; his entrance into the house of a publican; his visits to the quiet home of Mary and Martha; his conversation with the woman of Samaria at Jacob's well; his entering into a ship and teaching the multitude that stood on the shore; his journeyings to and fro along the shores of Gennesaret—such are many of the facts out of which was composed the most interesting and important of all histories.

It has generally been regarded as difficult to write the biography of one who is living. Faults frankly stated are apt to give offense, and praise justly bestowed is construed into flattery. With a firm reliance upon the good sense of the surviving pioneers, and at the risk of offending the critical eye, we have taken the liberty *to write of the living as though they were dead.* This course seemed the more reasonable in view of the fact that one pioneer has passed away since the work was commenced, and that, according to the course of nature, the others will soon be beyond the reach of praise or blame.

The strictures on certain views and practices current in the religious world may be deemed severe, and their author presumptuous. Yet they are believed to be true and just, and they are therefore submitted, not vauntingly, but "with meekness and fear." The writer did not forget that some of his most esteemed friends, as well as many other excellent persons, are in the fellowship of those who hold and teach the errors against *which*, only, the remarks in question are directed. Should they render the evil apparent to "any dear friend," he will perhaps renounce it with thankfulness; if they do not, it is hoped that he will pardon the weakness that vainly essayed to point out that which was clearly seen.

The engraving, and the brief history of the N. W. C. University, will not be considered inappropriate, as the Institution is frequently referred to in the sketches, and as it is the *ripe fruit* from the seed sown years ago by the venerable men whose deeds and characters are the main subject of this volume.

If the book shall prolong for a single day the remembrance of those holy men—if it shall inspire with fresh courage only one soldier of the cross who is about to falter in the long line of battle—or if it shall in any way contribute to the edification of the saints, and the advancement of the Redeemer's kingdom, the result will be altogether satisfactory to

THE AUTHOR.

CONTENTS.

JOHN LONGLEY	11
JOHN WRIGHT	29
ABSALOM, AND JOHN T. LITTELL	42
JOSEPH HOSTETLER	57
JOHN B. NEW	75
BEVERLY VAWTER	101
JOHN P. THOMPSON	126
MICHAEL COMBS	139
ELIJAH GOODWIN	158
JOSEPH WILSON	186
WILLIAM WILSON	247
LOVE H. JAMESON	262
JAMES M. MATHES	277
R. T. BROWN	300
GEORGE CAMPBELL	315
JOHN O'KANE	331
THOMAS LOCKHART	340
JACOB WRIGHT	349
B. K. SMITH	363
BENJAMIN F. REEVE	374
JOSEPH W. WOLFE	386
THOMAS J. EDMONDSON	400
SKETCH OF NORTHWESTERN CHRISTIAN UNIVERSITY	414

JOHN LONGLEY.

This most aged of Indiana's pioneer preachers is a native of the Empire State, born in New York city, on the 13th of June, 1782. It will be remembered that this was one year before the independence of the United States was acknowledged by Great Britain, and seven years before the first inauguration of Washington. He entered upon life, therefore, in the midst of a political revolution; and he will fall as a soldier in an ecclesiastical reform fraught with even greater blessings to mankind.

His grandfather, on his father's side, was a Welchman, and his grandmother was a native of old England. His mother's ancestors were Hollanders. Prior to his earliest recollection his parents were devout Baptists. His mother, especially, whose maiden name was Ann Floyd, was one of "the holy women of the old time who trusted in God." She assiduously strove to bring up her son "in the nurture and admonition of the Lord;" and, though the outlines of her dear face have well nigh faded from his memory, her religious instructions are still plainly written on his heart. When very young, he was taught the Lord's prayer, and required to repeat it every night; and it is as true of this silver-haired father as it was of the youthful Timothy, that "from a child he has known the Holy Scriptures." He remembers a sample of needlework wrought by his mother, on which were the following words:

"Ann Floyd is my name,
New York is my station;
Heaven will be my dwelling-place,
For Christ is my salvation."

This simple stanza he treasures up in his memory as an humble little monument commemorative of her ingenuity and faith in God.

His father, Thomas Longley, was a boot-and-shoe dealer in the great metropolis. But, in the year 1790, a Baptist preacher came to New York, and persuaded him to sell out and emigrate to Kentucky, representing the village of Washington, in Mason county, as a better location for one in his business. Perhaps the good but short-sighted divine was prompted to give this advice by the fact that, when he left his Western home, many of the people of Mason county were bare-footed; or he may have believed that Washington was "predestinated" to become a greater mart than New York. However this may have been, Mr. Longley set out early in the season with his family, consisting of his wife, four children, and their grandmother, then seventy-five or eighty years of age.

In that day—1790—a journey from New York to the West was something like a journey, now, over the plains to the Golden State; for in all the New World was to be seen no track of the iron horse. But at last they reached the head waters of the Ohio, and embarked, with their earthly possessions, in rudely-constructed boats. The passage down the river was long and perilous. They were once caught in a storm, in which they lost one of their boats and its cargo; and they were several times fired upon by Indians from the inhospitable shore. Thus, early in life, Elder Longley was "in perils of waters," and " in perils of the wilderness."

About the middle of June, they disembarked at the mouth of Limestone creek, where Maysville now stands. This point was some four miles from Washington, to which place they made their way, expecting to be received and entertained for awhile by the preacher who had induced them to exchange the blessings of civilization for the privations of frontier life. But, when they appeared before the preacher's cabin, he informed them that they could not be admitted—that they must pitch their tents as others had done, and dwell therein until they could erect a cabin for themselves. Finally, the hospitalities of a Mr. Cox were extended to them, and gladly accepted. He had a hewed-log house, with two small rooms, and a good puncheon floor. In this the two families lived, on terms of the *closest* intimacy, until Mr. Longley could select a site, and erect thereon a dwelling. Thus this pioneer family, like the Trojan hero, "having been tossed about much, both on land and water, suffered many things, until they could build"—not a "city," but—a *cabin*.

The Indians, at that time, were very troublesome in Kentucky; and, for a long while, property and life were in perpetual danger. Father Longley is perhaps the only man now living who saw the celebrated Major Simon Kenton, when, Mazeppa-like, he took his famous ride on an unbroken colt. The Indians had taken him prisoner, and, in order to amuse the *papooses*, had bound him upon the colt, to the tail of which they attached several cowbells. But, fortunately, the animal was one which they had stolen from the whites; and, when liberated, it fled home, carrying the doomed prisoner back, very unexpectedly, into the midst of his friends.

In the community in which such scenes transpired, Father Longley passed his boyhood. His educational advantages were therefore very limited. He had been sent to school a short time in New York, and he does not remember when he was unable to read. But, after his removal to the West, it was several years before an old Irish schoolmaster made his appearance in the neighborhood. In about five three-month terms of the common subscription schools of the eighteenth century, he completed his education; having pretty well mastered a *postdiluvian* arithmetic, which was the only text book in the mathematical department; and having passed several times through the *classical* course, which comprised the old-fashioned "Speller" and "Reader."

In his fourteenth year he lost his kind mother, whose influence over him had ever been talismanic. In a short time his father married again, and all went on smoothly enough for awhile; but, finally, the children of the first mother were scattered abroad to give place to the fruits of the second marriage. John went to learn the trade of a tanner, being then in his eighteenth year. Unfortunately this movement brought him under the seductive influences of wicked associates. The man to whom he was apprenticed was himself very passionate and profane. The others about the establishment were of like character; so when he walked it was in "the counsel of the ungodly," when he stood it was "in the way of sinners," and when he sat it was "in the seat of the scornful." Under such circumstances he soon became expert in the practice of sin.

Thus things went on for a year and a half. At length he was induced to reflect upon his condition, by hearing the remarks of a young woman who was relating her experience at a Baptist meeting. She quoted, with great feeling, the first psalm, and said many things which seemed to be strangely applicable to his case. By this means he was led to recall the admonitions and last request of his dying mother; and to resolve that he would endeavor to take the cup of salvation, and pay his oft-repeated vows to the Most High. He sought repentance with many tears and some doubts; for, under the unenlightened teaching of that day, he feared that he had grieved the Holy Spirit, and that it had departed from him forever. He prayed and agonized with God for many months, but could obtain no message of peace from the skies; neither could he find rest on earth because of the taunts and jeers of his companions.

They concluded, one day, that John was good enough to be baptized, and, with the proprietor at their head, they undertook to immerse him in a filthy tan vat. He resisted with all his might, but for awhile was like a helpless babe in the hands of pedobaptists. Finally, however, he fastened his hands in the hair of his "boss," and, by vigorous pulling, made him glad to release him.

After this occurrence, he avoided their society as much as possible. Having completed his day's work, he would repair to the house of some of his Baptist friends, there to find sympathizers, and to converse about the interests of his soul. When he asked them for advice, or inquired of them what he must do to be saved, they told him he could do nothing but "*pray on*, and wait the Lord's own good time." How similar this direction to that given by the apostles! How admirably calculated to fill his heart with love towards God, who, he was constrained to believe, was alone responsible for the delay of his pardon!

While observing this commandment of men, he one night had a fearful dream. He dreamed that his departed mother came to him, carried him away through the air, alighted with him upon a beautiful greensward in front of a magnificent palace, took him by the hand, and led him to the door, which was open. They entered; and as they passed along a large hall, he saw his Saviour, who, his conductor told him, was writing for him a commission. Finding themselves at the extremity of the hall, he looked into illimitable space, but could see nothing. "Look a little to the left," said his angelic guide. He obeyed; and lo! he beheld the wicked in torment—

>"A dungeon horrible, on all sides round,
>　As one great furnace flamed: yet from those flames
>　No light, but rather darkness visible,
>　Served only to discover sights of woe."

Sixty years have passed since that night; yet he affirms that he still shudders at the recollection of that terrible vision. When we remember that the religious teachings of those times exposed the sinner to an awful perdition, without disclosing any plain and sure way of salvation, it is not surprising that "in thoughts from the visions of the night, fear came upon him, and trembling, which made all his bones to shake."

Receiving no encouragement from religious teachers, being "plagued all the day long" by his shopmates, and having tried so often to lay hold on the hope set before him, which hope always eluded his grasp, he was *almost* persuaded to abandon forever the path of the just. He now looks back to that critical period with the feeling of the Psalmist, when he said, "As for me my feet were almost gone; my steps had well nigh slipped." To all this disquietude, to all these shafts of ridicule, to this imminent danger of giving up all aims at a holy and useful life, he was exposed simply because orthodoxy had sealed the lips of Peter that he might not instruct him—simply because a human creed had closed the door against Ananias, that he might not tell him that which was appointed for him to do. Under the gospel of Jesus Christ three thousand Jews sought and found pardon in a single day; under that gospel the persecuting Saul, whose hands were red with the blood of the innocent, obtained mercy within the space of three days; and had the same gospel, in its original purity and simplicity, been preached to this comparatively innocent youth, he would have arisen without delay, been baptized, washed away his sins, and gone on his way rejoicing.

But under the "other gospel" which was preached to him, and which is still advocated among men, he could only resolve, after a hard conflict in his mind, to persevere in penitence, in tears, and in prayer. In this extremity, he shut himself up in his room on Sundays, and spent the hours in reading the Bible and supplicating its Author. Being ignorant of the arrangement of the Scriptures and the design of each part, he sought the way of life as often in *Leviticus* as in the *Acts of the Apostles.* Like most persons of his and our day, he delighted most in the Psalms, and there he looked oftenest for the *commands of the Lord!* One Sunday, he happened upon the twenty-seventh Psalm, which greatly cheered his heart. Part of it supplied him with courage to withstand the gibes of his co-laborers, and part encouraged him to "wait on the Lord." This scripture also met his eye, and touched his heart: "Blessed are ye when men shall revile you, and persecute you, and say all manner of evil against you falsely for my sake. Rejoice and be exceeding glad, for great is your reward in heaven." This beatitude seemed to have been spoken expressly for his sake. Therefore he did rejoice as he contemplated the heavenly reward, and, the wish being father to the thought, he concluded that his sins had at last been blotted out.

He then determined to offer himself to the Baptist Church at Washington. His "experience" being satisfactory, as all experiences are, he was received; and in March, 1801, was immersed in the Ohio river by William Payne.

Such was his entrance into the kingdom of God. If any one thinks the account of it is long and tedious, how does he suppose *their* patience must be taxed who are compelled to pass over such a circuitous route to the kingdom? If any reader of this volume be disposed to complain of long accounts of conversion, let him thenceforth discountenance all systems of religion that subject men to the necessity of having such facts connected with their history. In the same space might have been recorded a dozen such conversions as that of the "eunuch," which fills only half a page of a common pocket Bible. But many are not taught to be converted in that short and simple way, lest both teacher and taught should be called "Campbellites." This fear is one chief obstacle in the way of the gospel of the Son of God.

In May, 1804, Father Longley was married to Miss Francina Hendrickson, of Fleming county, Kentucky. She had been brought up a Presbyterian "after the straitest sect." She was a woman of sterling piety; and, soon after their removal to their own house, she one evening placed the Bible and hymn-book upon the stand, and requested her husband to read and pray. He complied, with some trepidation, and from that day to this—over fifty-seven years—he has attended to family worship, save when circumstances have rendered it impracticable. The fact is recorded that her example may "teach the young women."

At the time of his marriage he was foreman in a tannery at Mt. Sterling. His employer proved to be dishonest, and withheld the most of his year's salary. On account of this misfortune, he returned to his father-in-law's in Fleming county. There he cast in his lot with the Emancipation Baptists, whose distinguishing feature, the name seems to indicate, was their hostility to slavery.

About this time he began to feel that it was his duty to preach, but he waited a long while for a *divine call*. Upon this point he had a long struggle, the particulars of which need not be related; suffice it to say, that in 1805 he was licensed, by the Baptist Association, to preach the gospel wherever God might open the way.

In the meantime a new church was organized in the

neighborhood, the members of which desired him to be regularly ordained, and to become their pastor. He hesitated to be ordained in that connection, because he had begun to call in question the doctrine of close communion. But upon this question the brethren agreed to allow him some latitude; and, with this understanding, he was formally set apart, and duly installed as preacher in charge.

It was not long, however, until his mind became unsettled upon some other matters. Especially did he distrust the doctrine of eternal and unconditional election. While this subject was under consideration, he had another vision, which claims to be inserted, by virtue of its novelty. He dreamed that he was preaching the gospel of *John Calvin*. His words were visible, and, like so many birds, went flying out at the doors and windows, without producing any effect on his hearers. He sat down perplexed, and left the audience in a state of suspense for several minutes; when he again arose, and began to preach *Paul's* gospel—that Jesus "tasted death for every man." His words then seemed sharp-pointed arrows, which flew straight to the mark, and pierced the hearts of those who heard him. Though it was but a vision, it left an impression on his mind that was not favorable to the Calvinistic theory. It helped him to realize the importance of the subject, and warned him to "take heed to his doctrine."

Not long after this he had an interview with Barton W. Stone, who had come into that neighborhood to hold a protracted meeting. The prejudices of Father Longley were strong, but he concluded to go and hear Elder Stone, expecting, no doubt, to find him a *hard* man. But, contrary to his expectations, that holy man of God stirred up no strife, but drew all hearts after him by the irresistible power of the meek, gentle, and loving spirit that dwelt within him. "He took me out," says Father Longley, "to hold a private conversation, and talked like a father to me, advising me not to give up preaching." After this interview he looked upon the Bible as he had never done before; indeed, he seemed to realize for the first time that it *is* the Bible, the only, the all-sufficient chart which God has given to guide his dear children from earth to heaven.

Unsettled in mind, he went to see his father, an unshaken Calvinistic Baptist, who, in their long interview, labored hard to prevent him from giving up the precious doctrine of predestination. Together they made a trip to Ohio, during which trip he preached the truth as far as he had learned it; and it is remarkable that, as soon as he began to approximate to the old gospel, he began to meet with success. On this tour he baptized four persons, who were the first fruits of his ministry.

When they were about to separate, his father said to him, "John, I believe it is your duty to preach; and as long as you preach Christ as you learn from the Bible, you cannot be far wrong. If they will not suffer you to preach what you really learn from that blessed book, you have a perfect right to go where you can enjoy this privilege."

His next preaching tour was to Georgetown, Ky. When about to leave home, a justice of the peace, by due legal process, seized upon his horse, in order to satisfy the claims of an impatient creditor. But a friend became his surety for the return of the animal within ten days, and he went on his way. At the meeting a collection was raised to enable him to pay the debt. This was the first money he ever received for preaching.

A short time after this, B. W. Stone and others held a protracted meeting at Cabin Creek, in Lewis county. This meeting Elder Longley and his father-in-law attended. On Sunday morning, Elder Stone informed him that he (Longley) was to preach that forenoon. No excuse would suffice; so at the appointed hour he preached to a large assembly, upon the words, "Behold what manner of love the Father hath bestowed upon us, that we should be called the sons of God." Comprehending not the Lord's plan of salvation, most of the preachers of that day discoursed chiefly upon the love of God, the wrath to come, the untold horrors of hell, and the ineffable joys of heaven. His theme, on this occasion, was the love of God, with which he proceeded, on the wings of imagination, until he came to the crucifixion. When he had finished the picture, he cried out with a loud, yet pathetic voice, "Behold the Lamb of God, that taketh away the sin of the world;" whereupon they all set up such a shout that he could proceed no further. This incident simply illustrates the style of preaching in the olden time, and goes to show that the speaker on that occasion was a *stirring preacher*, possessing superior descriptive powers. He could arouse the people to action, but, as yet, he could not tell them what to do to be saved.

From this time he continued to preach a good deal among the Christians, (called Newlights.) but he still retained his membership among the Baptists. In the year 1810, he removed from Fleming to Lewis county, taking with him a letter from the Baptist Church at Blue Bank Run. Upon this recommendation he united with the Church of Christ at Cabin Creek. This movement brought him to the Bible alone, and the name Christian.

Upon this platform, and under this name, he continued to preach with tolerable success, until the great union effected by B. W. Stone and Alexander Campbell. Into this union he entered heart and soul, and has ever since been an untiring advocate of the claims of the current Reformation.

In the year 1813—some twenty years prior to the union above mentioned—he moved over into Adams county, Ohio, and settled in a community of Shaking Quakers. He immediately began to proclaim the gospel among them, and such was his success that, within a single year, the Disciples bought out their "dancing-house," as Elder Longley called it, and converted it into a house of worship. In this house he organized a small church, which increased so rapidly that in a short time it numbered over one hundred and fifty members. They then built an excellent stone meeting house, which still stands a monument of the zeal of those early times. In the providence of God, Father Longley had the pleasure, not long since, of preaching in the old stone house, nearly half a century after its erection. Like the earthly house of his own tabernacle, it exhibited unmistakable signs of decay.

After laboring a few years in Adams county, he returned to Kentucky, advocating chiefly the claims of the Bible, to the exclusion of all human creeds.

About the year 1826 he removed to Cincinnati, which then contained a population of only about eight thousand. When he first saw the town, some years before, its more appropriate name would have been Zoar—"a little one"—and from that small beginning he has seen it expand into its present magnificent proportions. To him belongs the honor of having planted the first church of Christ in Cincinnati; and he has had the pleasure of witnessing a growth of truth almost commensurate with that of the city. He remained in that place some two or three years, during which time the Bible cause prospered in his hands, and his little flock increased to about sixty. In the meantime he was bereft of his first companion, who died at Cheviot, in the suburbs of the city, in the year 1826. The following is an extract from her obituary notice published in the October number of the *Christian Messenger.*

"Died, August 17th, the wife of Elder John Longley, Hamilton County, Ohio, after an illness of about three weeks. From the very day on which she was taken sick, she viewed death as certain and near, and without fear talked with perfect composure about it. * * * Just before she breathed her last, she said, 'All is peace—the victory is gained—O he is a God of all grace,' and yielded up her spirit to him who gave it, without a struggle." Thus with prosperity in heavenly things came adversity in earthly things, turning his joy into heaviness.

The next Spring after this sad event he once more returned with his children to Kentucky. Not long afterward he was married to Agnes Hendrickson.

In the Spring of 1830 he removed to Rush county, Indiana. Thirty-two years ago, therefore, he began to plead in Indiana, for the principles which he had already advocated for twenty-one years in Ohio and Kentucky.

In Rush county he toiled, arduously and under many disadvantages for several years. There being but few, if any, churches in which he could preach, he frequently taught the people from house to house; there being no railroads he travelled on horseback or on foot; and his preaching being considered heretical, he was looked upon by many as "the filth of the world and the offscouring of all things." As the ancient seventy, being persecuted in one city, fled unto another, so he removed from place to place, not transgressing the bounds of his Judea, the county.

Receiving but little or nothing for his preaching, he established a small dry-goods store, hoping by that means to make a support for his family without giving up entirely the work of the Lord. In this enterprise he was unfortunate and well nigh became a broken merchant.

While misfortune thus overtook him in business, death

entered into his dwelling and robbed him of his second wife, who died in March, 1834. Within the same year he was again married, to his present wife, whose name was Emily Huntington.

After his ill fortune in Rush county, he removed his family and the remnant of his merchandise to Yorktown, Delaware county, where he was entirely broken up in a second effort to maintain his family by selling goods. His heart and thoughts were engaged in the work of the ministry, and for this reason he was unsuccessful in his attempts to "buy and sell and get gain." His failure was but a verification of the Saviour's dictum, "Ye cannot serve God and Mammon." The great book of remembrance will doubtless reveal the fact that it has been verified many thousand times by failures *in the business of serving God*. Father Longley is one of the few comparatively who have chosen to fail in things temporal rather than in things eternal.

Though unsuccessful in his own affairs, the work of the Lord prospered in his hands. He built up, in Delaware county, a large and influential church, which still shines as a light in the world, holding forth the word of life. Among his co-laborers at that place, were Benjamin and Daniel Franklin, who were just then entering the field in which he had been reaping for thirty years.

In 1840 he removed to Noblesville, Hamilton county. At that point he preached, with good results, for about four years, receiving for his labor what was barely sufficient for the support of his family.

In 1844 he went to La Fayette, where he has resided ever since. For several years after his removal to that city, the church there was under his pastoral care; but for the last few years he has been too infirm to perform the duties of the pastoral office. Though he has almost completed his four score years, yet, at times, he enjoys tolerable health. At such intervals he still labors in word and doctrine, resolved to spend his remaining strength in the service of Him whom he has so long, so faithfully, and so usefully followed.

In the course of his long and eventful career he has immersed over three thousand persons, most of whom will stand "about the throne" with the "ten thousand times ten thousand and thousands of thousands," who, arrayed in white robes and with palms in their hands, shall proclaim with a loud voice, "Worthy is the Lamb that was slain to receive power, and riches, and wisdom, and strength, and honor, and glory, and blessing."

Since his memorable vision of the winged words, he has preached a *free gospel*, almost gratuitously. At no time, perhaps, has his large family been amply provided for by the churches, and now, in his feeble old age, he is very poor and mainly, if not entirely, dependent upon the charities, or rather the *dues* of the Brotherhood. It will be a burning shame if that Brotherhood do not prove to him a "good Samaritan."

But, although he has received but little "of corruptible things, as silver and gold," he has been partly rewarded in beholding the glorious progress of the cause in which he has suffered and toiled. Looking back as he does even beyond the beginning, his view of the Reformation is like Ezekiel's vision of the Holy Waters.—(Ez. xlvii. 3-5.) The truth which had been hid for ages, at last burst forth, like a fountain, among the hills of Western Virginia. He looked upon the stream when the waters were but "to the ancles;" when they were "to the knees," he saw them; when they ascended to the loins he rejoiced; and now his dim eyes behold them swollen into a mighty river. Having swept away all barriers hitherto, the orthodox no longer attempt to impede its resistless flow. Like the ancient rustic, they patiently wait for it to pass by; but "it flows and will continue to flow, rolling on forever."*

Having witnessed the triumphant progress of truth thus far, he is content to have passed the time of his sojourning in battling for principles which he is confident will ultimately prevail. Though he has suffered much, sacrificed much, labored much, and received but little, in this life, he has laid up for himself, in heaven, an eternal weight of glory. There he has deposited his treasure; there are his friends and kinsmen, and there will he soon be also. He now tarries among us as one of a former generation, only waiting, like Job, until his "change come." May the God of all grace loose the "silver cord" with a tender hand, and grant him an abundant entrance into "the everlasting kingdom of our Lord and Saviour Jesus Christ."

Elder Longley was, in his palmy days, a good-looking, sinewy man, of medium height and slender form. He possessed remarkable strength and activity, and his great age attests the excellence of the physical constitution that has sustained him under so many burdens. He is among the best of the many noble specimens of manhood, produced in the age that is past.

His intellectual powers are above mediocrity, and proper cultivation would have rendered them decidedly superior. Though deprived of the advantages of education, yet he has been able to distinguish, for the most part, between good and evil in matters pertaining to doctrine, and to present with tolerable clearness the great facts of the gospel. In the sharp conflicts that attended the introduction of primitive Christianity in Indiana, he shrank from no engagement; and as the militia officer often eclipses the thorough-bred soldier, so he was more successful in

* Labitur et labetur in omne volubilis ævum.

the field than many who had emerged from theological seminaries.

Though never eloquent, he has been, on all occasions, a ready and impressive speaker; and now that he is so venerable—so near the confines of the invisible world—his tremulous voice affects his hearers almost like the voice of one "sent unto them from the dead." True, it does not so affect all, for many who assemble in the house of God only "to hear some new thing," have long since become impatient of his ministrations. He has never belonged to that class of speakers who

> "Fill the allotted scene,
> With lifeless drawls, insipid and serene;"

and he is quite as far removed from that other class—so numerous in the former days—who

> "Thunder every couplet o'er
> And almost crack your ears with rant and roar."

He moves about but little in the pulpit; his gestures are few and graceful; his delivery, calm, dignified, earnest, and, at proper periods, pathetic.

In the society of his friends he is companionable, though slightly inclined to sedateness. In the family circle he has been indulgent to a fault. It can hardly be said that he is remarkable for his administrative ability.

His sincerity in the sacred cause has never been rendered doubtful by any aberrations from the path of the just; but, during the whole of his long pilgrimage, his conduct has been, "as becometh the gospel of Christ."

Fearlessly may he look the people of his generation in the face, and say, with upright Samuel, "*I am old and gray-headed; and, behold, my sons are with you: and I have walked before you from my childhood unto this day:*

WITNESS AGAINST ME BEFORE THE LORD AND BEFORE HIS ANOINTED."

Having thus loved righteousness and hated iniquity, none can doubt that, when the saints shall ascend the throne, God, even his God, will anoint him with the oil of gladness.

JOHN WRIGHT.

ELDER JOHN WRIGHT was born in Rowan county, North Carolina, December 12th, 1785. His mother was of German descent. His ancestors on his father's side came from England in very early times, and settled on the eastern shore of Maryland. From that place they were scattered abroad, some making their way to the Carolinas. His father was brought up among the Quakers or Friends; and, singularly enough, he turned away from that fraternity, who baptized *none*, to the Tunkers, who practiced *trine immersion*. He afterwards cast in his lot with the Dependent Baptists, among whom he became a preacher.

Elder Wright remained in North Carolina until he was about twelve years of age. His father then removed with him to Powel's Valley, Virginia, where he grew up to manhood.

The most of his education he received from an old English gentleman by the name of Hodge, under whose tuition he acquired a good knowledge of reading, writing, and arithmetic. He received from the schools no further preparation for either the business of the world or the work of the ministry; but, having obtained the key to all knowledge—namely, reading—he constantly increased his stock of ideas by his own unassisted efforts. He was tolerably well informed upon general subjects, and could write a very respectable article, as may be seen by reference to the *Christian Record*, to which he was an occasional contributor.

From Virginia the whole family emigrated to the West, and settled in Wayne county, Kentucky, where, on the 5th of January, 1803, Elder Wright was married to Miss Peggy Wolfescale. She accompanied him but a short distance on the journey of life, dying on the 12th of December, 1805, and leaving him with an infant daughter, which he entrusted to the parents of its departed mother.

After this bereavement, he engaged for two years in teaching school. At the expiration of this time he was again joined in marriage to Miss Nancy Pelcer, who, for many years, proved a most excellent helpmate, ever ready, with him, to make any sacrifice for the cause of Christianity. She also died, on the 29th of August, 1844; and the following extract is from her obituary notice, written by T. C. Johnson, and published in the *Christian Record* for November of that year:

"She diligently followed every good work. The servants of God were often refreshed at her house by her hospitality. Saints always found her house their home; and sinners were so kindly treated by her as to endear her to them all. In short, she was an affectionate wife, a tender-hearted mother, an obliging and kind neighbor, and a mother in Israel, whose death is felt, not only by her afflicted relatives, but also by the Church and the community in which she lived."

Late in the year 1807—which was very soon after his second marriage—he removed from Kentucky to Clark's grant, Indiana Territory.

In August, 1808, he and his wife were immersed in the Ohio river, by William Summers, of Kentucky. He immediately united with the Baptist Church, and in the latter part of the same year he began to preach. Be it observed that this was *fifty-four* years ago—eight years previous to the admission of the Territory as a State, and long before the current Reformation was heard of by the inhabitants of the West. He must, therefore, have been among the very first to break the stillness of Indiana's forests with the glad tidings of salvation.

In January, 1810, he removed to Blue River, four miles south of Salem, in what was then Harrison, but now Washington county. There he entered a beautiful tract of land; and, by much hard labor, opened an excellent farm. In a short time his father moved into the same neighborhood; where, in 1810, they organized a congregation of Dependent or Free Will Baptists.

About this time they experienced serious trouble with the Indians; and, while the energies of the nation were directed against Great Britain, in the war of 1812, they were compelled to protect themselves by forts from the tomahawk and scalping-knife.

When peace and safety were restored, he entered again with increased zeal into the work of the ministry. He was assisted by his father, and a younger brother, Peter, who was beginning to preach with considerable success. The three Wrights exerted quite an influence in favor of Christianity, and it was not long until they had organized ten Baptist churches, which they formed into what was called the Blue River Association.

From the very first, John Wright was of the opinion that all human creeds are heretical and schismatical. He was perhaps the first man in Indiana that took his position on the *Bible alone;* and there has not come after him a more persistent contender for the word of God as the only sufficient guide in religious matters. He labored to destroy divisions, and promote union among all the children of God; and in this difficult yet most important service he made his indelible mark. Though at first he tolerated the term "Baptist"—it being natural to condemn ourselves last—yet he afterwards waged a war of extermination against *all* party names. This war was declared in the year 1819, when he offered, in the church at Blue River, a resolution in favor of discarding *their* party name, and calling themselves by some name authorized in the Scriptures. As individuals, he was willing that they should be called "Friends," "Disciples," or "Christians;" and, as a body, "the Church of Christ," or "the Church of God." He opposed the term "Christian," as applied to the Church, because it is not so applied in the writings of the apostles.

The resolution was adopted with more unanimity than was expected; and the *Baptist* church has since been known as the Church of Christ at Blue River. Having agreed, also, to lay aside, as far as possible, their speculative opinions and contradictory theories, they presumed that they were prepared to plead consistently for Christian union, and to invite others to stand with them upon the one broad and sure foundation. They then began in earnest the work of reformation, and with such success that by the year 1821 there was scarcely a *Baptist* church in all that region. They all took upon them "that worthy name," and converted their Association into an Annual Meeting.

About this time a spirited controversy on the subject of Trine Immersion, was going on among the Tunkers, of whom there were some fifteen congregations in that section of the country. The leading spirits in opposition to that doctrine were Abram Kern of Indiana, and Peter Hon of Kentucky. At first they contended against great odds, but so many of their opponents came over to their side that they finally gained a decisive victory in favor of one immersion.

At the close of the contest, while both parties were exhausted by the war, Elder Wright recommended to the Annual Meeting that they should send a letter to the Annual Conference of the Tunkers, proposing a union of the two bodies on the Bible alone. The letter was written, and John Wright, his brother Peter, and several others, were appointed as messengers to convey it to the Conference and there advocate the measures it proposed. So successful was the expedition that at the first meeting the union was permanently formed, the Tunkers being persuaded to call themselves Christians.

At the same annual meeting Elder Wright proposed a correspondence with the Newlights, for the purpose of forming with them a more perfect union. He was appointed to conduct the correspondence on the part of his brethren, which he did with so much ability and discretion, that a joint convention was assembled near Edinburg, where the union was readily formed. Only one church in all the vicinity refused to enter into the coalition, and it soon died of *chronic sectarianism.*

A few years subsequent to this, the work of Reformation began to progress rapidly among the Regular Baptists of the Silver Creek Association. This was, remotely, through the influence of Alexander Campbell, but directly through that of Absalom and J. T. Littell, and Mordecai Cole, the leading spirits in that locality. Through their teaching hundreds of individuals and sometimes whole churches were renouncing all human creeds and coming out on the Bible alone; yet a shyness existed between them and those who had previously done the same thing under the labors of John Wright. The former, having held Calvinistic opinions, stood aloof through fear of being called *Arians;* while the latter feared to make any advances lest they should be stigmatized as *Campbellites.* Thus the two parties stood, when Elder Wright, braving the danger of being denounced as a Campbellite, established a connection between them by which the sentiments of each were communicated to the other. By this means it was soon ascertained that they were all endeavoring to preach and practice the same things. The only important difference between them was in regard to the design of Baptism, and on this point Elder Wright yielded as soon as he was convinced of his error. Through the influence of himself, his brother Peter, Abram Kern, and others, on the part of what was called the Annual Meeting of the Southern District, which was composed of those who had been Baptists, Tunkers and Newlights; and through the efforts of Mordecai Cole and the Littells, on the part of the Silver Creek Association, a permanent union was formed between those two large and influential bodies of believers. In consequence of this glorious movement, more than *three thousand struck hands in one day*—not in person, but through their legal representatives, all agreeing to stand together on the one foundation and to forget all minor differences in their devotion to the great interests of the Redeemer's kingdom. This was, perhaps, the greatest achievement of Elder Wright's long and eventful life; and he deserves to be held in everlasting remembrance for his love of *truth* rather than of *party*, for his moral courage in carrying out his convictions of right, and for the meek and affectionate spirit which gave him such power in uniting opposing sects and cementing them in love.

To the happy effects of this obliteration of party lines he testified a few years afterward. In a communication to the October number of the Christian Record for 1845, he wrote as follows:

"Beloved brethren in the Lord:—Through the permission of our kind heavenly Father I have travelled through many of the churches in the south part of the State, and have been abundantly comforted in the society of our good brethren in Christ. For many years we have seen many who, like the Jews and Samaritans, had no religious dealings: but when the gospel was preached by Peter to the Jews according to his broad commission, about three thousand joyfully received and obeyed the truth. And when Philip, the evangelist, preached to the Samaritans, they 'believed and were baptized both men and women.' And when the same gospel was preached to the Gentiles by Peter, they also believed and obeyed from the heart the same divine form of doctrine. Thus we see believers from all the sectarian parties of that age united in one body in Christ: having laid aside their former prejudices and hatred, together they put on Christ according to the constitution of his kingdom; there was no longer Jew, Gentile, or Samaritan as formerly, but they were now all partakers of the divine nature, were all made to drink into one spirit, in short they all became children of God—Christians.

"So it was in Southern Indiana: formerly we had Regular Baptists, separate baptists, German or Dunkard Baptists, free will Baptists, christian connexion, or Newlights. These societies in some respects were like the Jews and Samaritans of old; but the old gospel was preached among *these* warring sects with great power and success. Much of the partyism that existed was removed, and most of their party names were done away. * * * Formerly we all had in our respective churches much that was purely *human;* but now, in the church of God, we have no need of the 'mourning bench,' 'the anxious seat,' or any other institution of man's device; but in the church is the place where the solemn feast of the Lord's body is celebrated, and sincere worship is offered to the Father in spirit and in truth."

It was not with the pen but with the tongue that his influence was chiefly exerted. The preceding extract is, perhaps, a fair specimen of his composition. The style, the capitals, and the punctuation, indicate that it is a genuine production of the unlettered pioneer.

At first it was prophesied that such a union could not

continue. This prediction grew out of the fact that the materials had been collected from many different denominations:—Baptists, Newlights, Tunkers, Methodists and Presbyterians. But a quarter of a century has passed away, and the prophecy is not yet fulfilled. On the contrary, those who were young when the union was formed, have, in their old age, almost forgotten that they ever were divided.

Alas for the interests of Christ's kingdom, that race of prophets is not yet extinct! There are still those who tell us that "men cannot all think alike, or belong to one Church;" and who give thanks to God that there is a variety of Churches, *so that all may be accommodated.* If, in the consequent confusion, thousands of our fellows should stumble over us into skepticism, and finally into destruction and perdition, it is no matter, if only we can all be "accommodated!" If Christ died for all, as the apostle affirms, then all *can* belong to one Church; otherwise he would have built two or more. The Lord, by the pen of his apostle, commands "all that in every place call upon the name of Jesus Christ," to "all speak the same thing, and to have no divisions among them." By this and every other positive commandment stands the Reformation, firm as the lone Elijah by the worship of the living God. As it fearlessly advances, sectarianism confronts it, saying, in the language of the wicked Ahab, "*Art thou he that troubleth Israel?*" It answers, in the bold words of Elijah, "I have not troubled Israel, but *thou* and thy father's house, in that *ye have departed from the commandments of the Lord.*" All the day long, as did those of old, these latter-day prophets have called upon God to convert the world in their way, but he has been deaf to all their cries. Now, therefore, in the *evening,* the advocates of reform desire to call upon him according to *his* will, confident, as was Elijah, that he will hear their cry and accept their sacrifice.

Besides his efforts to effect a union of all God's people, Elder Wright did much, in his lifetime, for the cause of the Redeemer. By means of his farm in Washington county he was able, without much labor, to make a comfortable living; and, as he sought to lay up no treasure on earth, he devoted the greater part of his time to the work of the ministry. Through lack of records it is impossible to follow him from year to year, giving a detailed account of his labors and successes in the gospel. Suffice it to say, that for more than forty years he preached much, and with good results, in Washington and several other counties of southeastern Indiana. The people had unbounded confidence in his piety and judgment, and wherever he went they were to a great extent under his influence.

On the death of his second wife, in 1844, he sold his farm to his son Ransom, reserving one room of the house for his occasional use during the remnant of his days. Afterwards he spent nearly all his time among the brethren, comforting, establishing, strengthening them.

In addition to his *labors*, he also *sacrificed* much for the support of the gospel. In the good providence of God, his father, step-mother, all of his brothers, sisters, and children were zealous members of the Church of Christ. His father and his four brothers—Peter, Levi, Joshua, and Amos—were all preachers of the "repentance and remission of sins" that began at Jerusalem. His youngest son died on the 19th of November, 1843; and Christianity had made bright his pathway to the tomb. He therefore felt that he could never give too much in support of that gospel which had given so much peace, and joy, and hope to his family. Often did he borrow money to defray his expenses to his appointments; and sometimes, through the illiberality of the brethren, he was compelled to resort to the same expedient in order to get home. He used to purchase wine at high rates, and carry it forty or fifty miles in his saddle-bags, in order that he might show forth the Lord's death with his brethren.

During the first years of his ministry, he never so much as expected any remuneration for his services; for it was a prominent article in the unwritten Baptist creed that the preacher should do nothing for filthy lucre. By this doctrine the generosity of the brethren was so stifled that it has not yet recovered the healthy action it possessed in apostolic times. Money was never the object for which he toiled; but he thankfully received, with an enlightened conscience, whatever was offered, believing that, as *he* loved to contribute, every other brother, who had the cause near his heart, should enjoy the same privilege. As heart and flesh failed him, the liberality of the churches increased; and, after his family had all begun life for themselves, or passed away to the spirit land, he received for his preaching what was amply sufficient to supply all his earthly wants.

He enjoyed excellent health until very near the close of his pilgrimage; and it was a saying with him that he "never had a pain as long as his little finger." But, though he lived many years, and rejoiced in them all, the days of darkness were in reservation for him. In the spring of 1850 he was seized with acute inflammation of the stomach. The disease readily yielded to medical treatment, and in a short time he resumed the Master's work. In the fall of the same year it returned upon him in a more violent and obstinate form, and he expressed the conviction that his race was almost run.

He passed the winter with his son Jacob, at Salem, and by the coming of spring he had so far recovered as to be able to return home to his son Ramson's. Immediately afterwards he grew worse, and began to sink rapidly. His brother in the gospel, Dr. H. T. N. Benedict, was called in; but he could do no more than to comort him in his afflictions by pointing him to his eternal weight of glory.

His living children were all near him except his son Jacob, who was preaching at New Albany. He was summoned; and when he came his father said, "My son, I am just waiting for my discharge." He seemed more like one preparing to start on a long journey than one about to experience the agony of death. He first spoke to his family relative to some pecuniary matters. These being disposed of to his satisfaction, he requested Dr. Benedict to write his obituary notice, and also expressed his desire that J. M. Mathes should preach his "Christian farewell," from Rev. xiv. 13. He observed that he had lived in Washington county over forty years; that if he had in it an enemy he did not know it; and that he thought he could make *one more* successful appeal to the citizens, through "little Jimmy," as he called Elder Mathes. In a few moments he said to J. L. Martin, "Brother Lem, you will see to making my little house" —meaning his coffin. He then remarked that he believed he was ready to go—that he did not think of any thing else. Presently he said to his son Jacob: "There is one thing I had forgotten. Abram Kern and I were appointed as messengers to write and convey a letter to the Annual Meeting of Silver Creek District. I want you to write the letter, and go with Brother Kern to introduce him, for he will be a stranger there."

As he approached his dissolution, he conversed more and more, exhorted those present to be faithful, and repeated several passages of Scripture—among them the fifth of Corinthians, commencing, "For we know that if our earthly house of this tabernacle were dissolved we have a building of God, a house not made with hands, eternal in the heavens." After taking his final leave of his family and friends, he placed his hands across his breast, closed his own eyes, and breathed softly and still more softly until he fell into his last long sleep, without the movement of a muscle, his lips remaining compressed, his eyes closed, and his hands just as he had placed them. Thus passed away from earth Elder John Wright, at eight o'clock in the evening of May 2d, 1851—aged 67 years, 6 months, and 26 days.

"Had the skeptic," says an eye-witness, "been privileged to behold the triumphant exit of this man of God, his skepticism would have been blown away by the dying breath of this aged, this devoted servant of our Divine Redeemer."

Elder Wright was a tall, square-built man, of excellent constitution and great physical power. Many were the giant oaks that he felled to earth by the sturdy strokes of his axe.

His mental powers were as good by nature as his physical: the disparity in their development was a necessity of the times in which he lived. He possessed an iron will, tempered even to flexibility by the spirit that was in Christ.

His character was a most happy combination of "whatsoever things are true, whatsoever things are honest, whatsoever things are just, whatsoever things are pure, whatsoever things are lovely, whatsoever things are of good report." He was an uncompromising advocate, a bold and fearless defender of the truth; yet he usually employed the "soft answer" that turns away wrath, rather than the "grievous words" which stir up strife.

As a speaker he was unpolished, not logical, but very sympathetic. His own heart being full of love and fealty to God, he induced the same feeling in the hearts of those who heard him; for, " as in water face answereth to face, so the heart of man to man."

Uneducated and untaught in the art of speaking, his useful career is a demonstration of *the power of a holy life.* May his brilliant success in the gospel stimulate all evangelists, of this more enlightened age, to combine with their intellectual acumen the godliness of this departed pioneer.

ABSALOM, AND JOHN T. LITTELL.

The subjects of this sketch were both born in Fayette county, Pennsylvania—Absalom in the year 1788, and John T. in 1790. Their parents were poor, and both members of the Presbyterian Church.

In 1799 their father, Absalom Littell, who was a soldier in the Revolution, emigrated to what was then the far West, and settled on the west side of Silver creek, in Clark's grant, Northwestern Territory; or, in what is now Clark county, Indiana.

At that date there were but few "pale faces" in the Territory, and no settlements between them and the Rocky mountains, except a few French stations, or forts, containing a small number of Americans. The great West, that is now shaking the earth with its giant tread, was then in its infancy, eager for new ideas, and more susceptible than now of religious impressions. The influence of the Christian preacher in that day was, therefore, like that of the parent over the child.

Before the advent of the school-teacher to that part of the world, both Absalom and John T. had almost attained to their majority; hence they received but little instruction save that which was imparted in the domestic circle. Yet, by their own exertions, they became tolerably well informed; and of the Holy Scriptures especially they acquired a thorough and ready knowledge. Absalom, being more fond of literary and scientific pursuits, became the better scholar. He was well versed in parliamentary rules, and none was more frequently called to preside

over religious meetings. Though his own life was regulated by the "perfect law of liberty," yet he had a respectable knowledge of the civil law; and his judgment in legal matters was as decisive as it was gratuitous. He peaceably settled many controversies between his neighbors, adjusting their differences with far more candor and fairness than a fee-hunting attorney would have done.

As there were no schools, so there were no churches. North of the Ohio river, and west of the Miami, not a single Protestant spire was to be seen. With a few exceptions there were no songs save the savage chant that led on the war-dance; no prayers, save those offered to the Great Spirit under the shadows of the tall oaks.

> "Then was the time
> For those whom wisdom and whom nature charm,
> To soar above this little scene of things;
> To tread low-thoughted vice beneath their feet;
> To soothe the throbbing passions into peace;
> And woo lone quiet in her silent walks."

It was not until the year 1798—a twelvemonth previous to the immigration of the Littells—that the first Protestant congregation was organized in Indiana Territory. This was a Regular Baptist church composed of *four members*, and established on the Philadelphia Confession of Faith.

The organization was effected a few miles northeast of the Littell settlement, but the first house of worship was subsequently erected on the east bank of Silver creek, near Mr. Littell's farm, where it became widely known as the Regular Baptist church at Silver creek. There it still stands, the oldest Protestant, and, perhaps, the first Reformed, church in the State.

Immigrants arriving constantly, brought with them their respective religious views, and it was not long until the people were favored with preaching by the representatives of the several leading sects.

Absalom Littell, sen., being an elder in the Presbyterian church, usually went with his family to that place of worship. Yet he was comparatively liberal in his views, and, in the absence of the Presbyterian minister, he attended, without partiality, the meetings of the various orders by which he was surrounded. By this means his sons acquired some knowledge of all the doctrines taught thereabout. Absalom was disposed to walk, if at all, in the steps of his father's faith, while John T. soon became much inclined toward the Baptists.

During the Indian troubles of 1811 and '12, Absalom and his eldest brother, Amos, served in the army of General Harrison; while John T. and others rendered no less important service as home-guards. Block-houses were built, sentinels posted, and every precaution taken to protect the women and children in the absence of their husbands and fathers. Amos was in the memorable battle of Tippecanoe, and Absalom was among the forces that marched to the relief of Fort Harrison, then in command of Lieutenant—afterwards President—Taylor.

The return of peace found them all alive; and, the weapons of war being cast aside, they turned their thoughts gratefully toward Him who had safely led them through so many dangers.

On the 27th of November, 1813, Amos united with the Baptist church and was immersed in Silver creek. On the 23d of July 1814, his example was followed by John T. Absalom, being at that time more disposed to see the world than to enter into the kingdom, travelled pretty extensively in Indiana, Kentucky, Ohio, Pennsylvania, and Virginia. He was present, however, at the baptism of John T.; but being greatly prejudiced against immersion, he stood afar off.

In the summer of 1816, John T. began to preach; and such was his natural ability that he very soon became a popular and most effective speaker.

Soon after his engaging in the work of the ministry, he removed to the muddy fork of Silver creek where he, with a few others from the old congregation, organized what is still known as the Muddy Fork church.

In April, 1815, Absalom, having become tired of rambling about, married, and settled down upon a small farm which he had acquired means to purchase.

Though he had been a young man of unexceptionable morals; and although he had been *a member of the church from his earliest infancy;* yet, strange to say, he had never made a profession of religion! It was this very question of Infant Church-Membership, that caused him to linger so long without the door of the kingdom. In vain he read the Bible to find a firm support for the doctrine on which alone was suspended his hope of a glorious immortality. In vain he searched through subtle disquisitions on theology, in hope of finding a demonstration of the validity of Infant Baptism. No writer, either sacred or profane, satisfied him of the truth of that which he desired most of all to believe, namely, that *baptism came in the room of circumcision.* Loth as he was to abandon this popular tradition, he was compelled to do so after a careful re-examination of all the premises.

This stumbling-block being removed, he immediately went forward in the plain path of obedience, and, on the 27th of October, 1816, united with the Old Silver Creek Church, being immersed at the same spot at which, a few months before, he had witnessed, with so great mortification, the baptism of his younger brother.

At the first approach of the ensuing winter, the icy hand of death was laid upon his first-born. This sad dispensation, as it may have been designed, drove him nearer the cross. Observing that every thing beautiful goes down to the grave—that all things seen are temporal—he began to direct his mind to those things which are eternal. Anxious to devote his energies to the accomplishment of *permanent* results, he thought seriously of preaching; but, for a while, he was discouraged by the feeble efforts of illiterate preachers whose only excuse for their ignorance was the pretension that they were "called and sent."

On the 21st of the following April his wife also departed this life, leaving to his care a helpless babe.

This second affliction disarranged all his earthly plans. In a short time he removed from his farm to New Albany, where he engaged in mercantile business which proved to be very profitable. He also began to preach in the city and vicinity; and his first efforts were more acceptable than he had hoped.

In September, 1818, while passing through Washington county, he called by a house at the road-side to make some inquiries as to his route. A young lady, whom he had never seen before, having intelligently answered all his questions, he took his leave. On the 18th of the next November that same young lady, the daughter of John Martin, sen., was Mrs. Littell. He was not a man who halted long between two opinions respecting any matter.

Returning to New Albany, he continued to devote a portion of his time to the work of the ministry; and, in January, 1820, he assisted in the organization of the first Baptist (now Christian) church in that city. It seems that on this occasion he departed from some of the landmarks, regarded as sacred by his Baptist brethren. For, being appointed to write and convey a letter to the Blue River Association, asking for fellowship with the same, and appearing before that body, as directed, he was sharply questioned by those official guardians of the interests of Zion. After a solemn conference, the assembly asked him if he would, in the name of the church he represented, renounce its faith, as embodied in the letter which he had brought, and accept that of the Association as set forth in its Articles of Faith? This he refused to do, and the infant church at New Albany was, therefore, left to take care of itself. *Such was the happy result produced by supreme devotion to creeds.*

However, the little flock in New Albany steadily grew in number and in grace, visited as it was by several of the more liberal Baptist preachers; but most of all by John T. Littell, whose efforts on its behalf were unremitting.

On the 13th of June, 1820, a severe thunder-storm passed over the city. The house of Elder A. Littell was struck by lightning, by which his wife was felled to the floor, and his only surviving child, the last of his first family, was instantly killed.

This stroke of Divine Providence quite overcame him. The face of the Lord seemed to be against him. Perhaps— he thought—it was because he was not more completely devoted to his service. Therefore he closed out his stock in trade, and returned to his farm in Clark county; and from that time his labors were far more abundant, in the Lord.

The little congregation in New Albany was cordially received into the Silver Creek Association (formed in 1812) on the fourth Saturday of August, 1821. Then for a little season they all dwelled together in unity, and their Christian fellowship was "like the precious ointment upon the head."

From that date, Absalom and John T. Littell were the leading spirits in that portion of Indiana. Like Saul, the son of Kish, "*from their shoulders and upward they were higher than any of the people.*"

For many years they annually, and by turns, wrote the "circular letter;" preached the "introductory sermon;"

presided over the Association; and served that body in the capacity of scribe.

In the year 1826, the Baptists having been greatly multiplied, Elder A. Littell proposed the formation of a new Association. As chairman of a committee he reported a line of division; which was agreed to; and the new Association was accordingly formed.

A little subsequent to this, southeastern Indiana was liberally supplied with some pamphlets written by the Rev. Daniel Parker of Illinois, in support of what was called the "two-seed doctrine." For a while these documents created great excitement and drew away many disciples after them. Absalom Littell sought several opportunities of hearing Mr. Parker, who also travelled preaching—and having made himself well acquainted with the gentleman's position, and having examined well the different texts by which it was fortified, he determined to bring on an engagement, and if possible, drive the enemy from his intrenchments.

The parties soon met at Corydon, Indiana, at which place the Blue River Association had convened. It pleased the Assembly to select A. Littell, Daniel Parker, and a minister from Kentucky to fill the pulpit on Lord's-day. The Kentuckian having spoken first, Elder Littell followed, basing his remarks upon Peter's declaration that "in every nation he that feareth him and worketh righteousness is accepted of him." With this and many other texts on his side, he felt that he went forth, like David, "in the name of the Lord of hosts;" and feeling thus, he dealt a heavy blow upon the two-seed Goliath.

The meeting was held in a grove; and just as he had concluded his sermon a shower of rain dispersed the multitude, and he was thus delivered from the shafts of his adversary. By this attack, however, he lost favor with many of his brethren, who had imbibed the two-seed doctrine.

About this time the light of the Reformation began to dawn upon that portion of the State. The terms "Campbellism" and "Campbellite" began to be heard frequently from the sacred desk, as well as in the family circle; and it was evident that a revolution in religious matters was near at hand. It was soon apparent, also, that hostilities were to commence in the old Silver Creek church—that there the first stone was to be cast at the old systems that were doomed to destruction.

Many of the brethren, as the eyes of their understanding were opened, manifested less and less respect for the Articles of Faith, until the creed party, unable longer to brook such contempt of the authority to which they bowed their willing necks, ventured to ask, in the public assembly, "*What was the faith of this church when it was first organized?*" By reference to the church record it was ascertained that it (the church) was established upon the Philadelphia Confession of Faith. Having given this plain hint as to the object to which all owed allegiance, the orthodox party permitted a brief season of rest. But seeing the joints of the old system opening wider and wider, they determined once more to tighten the screws.

To this end they proposed *that submission to the Confession of Faith should be strictly regarded as a condition of fellowship.* This proposition met with strong opposition, and disturbed the peace of the church for a long time.

Finally, a resolution was offered, demanding "*to know from this church whether she is governed by the Old and New Testaments or by the Articles of Faith?*" (Church Record.) This question, after a warm debate, was answered as follows: "*The church say, by the word of God.*" (Church Record.)

This decision produced great excitement. Many of the more zealous opposers of reform left the church, but their places were soon filled; for the community, generally, approved of the action by which the seceders were so greatly offended.

Thus the Silver Creek church exchanged its human for the Divine creed. But Elders Littell and their co-adjutors had not yet clean escaped from the thraldom of error. Though they had adopted the Bible as their rule of faith and practice, they were still subject to the *rule* of the Association; and they still adhered to many *practices* for which they could not have produced a "thus saith the Lord."

One would suppose that they would not have been long in *being freed*, if they did not free themselves, from the authority of the Association; for, under ordinary circumstances, that body would not have tolerated such an act, on the part of a congregation, as the open renouncement of the Confession of Faith. As it was, however, the Littells held the reins; and, by the exercise of discretion and a spirit of forbearance and conciliation, they easily thwarted the efforts of all such as desired their excommunication. The subject was brought before the Association at its next session in New Albany; but the excitement passed away for that time without any serious consequences.

The exercises of that session were also enlivened by a revival of the two-seed theory. An aged brother from the Blue River Association being appointed to preach, began his discourse, very properly, with an apology for his ignorance, adding, for the encouragement of his hearers, that *as the Lord would give to him so would he give to them.* He (or he and the Lord, as he would have people believe) then proceeded to elucidate the two-seed doctrine! His speech had a powerful effect on the large audience,—so powerful, indeed, that it moved many into the streets and to their homes.

After it was all over, an old brother, whose speech betrayed the dialect as well as the penetration of the Yankee, observed, that "all preachers of that kind would soon die off, and that the *Lord would make no more on 'em.*"

The prediction was in a measure verified; for from that time the favorite dogma of Elder Parker gradually waned, until it was no longer a matter of controversy.

For a few years subsequent to this, matters went on peaceably, being conducted in the spirit of compromise. The Baptists tolerated the abnormal views of those who were almost Reformers; and the Reformers, in turn, yielded to some of the peculiar views and practices of the Baptists. But each party became more and more positive in the advocacy of their respective tenets, until a final separation could no longer be averted. This took place first in the congregation at New Albany, in the year 1835; and soon afterwards in all the churches throughout that portion of the State.

The Reformers, in all cases, opposed division; and did all in their power to persuade their disquieted brethren to accept the word of God as their only rule of faith and practice. This the Baptists would not do; but, as soon as they found themselves in the minority, they chose rather to withdraw themselves, and have no further fellowship with what they regarded as "the unfruitful works of darkness."

With respect to those who continued in the "perfect law of liberty," the Association of 1835 was the last. From that time they held an Annual Meeting, not to form or amend constitutions; enact laws for the government of the church; or, in any way, to "lord it over God's heritage;" but to hear encouraging reports from the various churches; to worship the Lord in the "beauty of holiness;" and to consider how they might most promote the interests of the Redeemer's kingdom.

Such was the introduction of primitive Christianity within the bounds of the old Silver Creek Association; and such was, briefly, the part taken by the Elders Littell in that important movement.

All the elements of discord having been eliminated, the disciples dwelt together in unity under the mild sceptre of the Prince of Peace; and, on every hand, they were greatly multiplied.

John T. Littell, with unflagging zeal, continued to evangelize for many years, baptizing a great number of disciples, of whom he kept no record. Among the number were eleven of his own children; and, since his decease, the remaining one has entered into the kingdom. Two of his sons—Milburn and John T., jr.—are successful preachers; and a third son—Maxwell—is an occasional laborer "in word and doctrine."

Returning indisposed from one of his tours, on the 11th of February, 1848, he observed to his family that he had *filled his last outstanding appointment*—a thing which he had not done before in thirty years. It was a singular fact, in view of the sad event which so suddenly followed. Always punctual in filling his appointments, it seems that even death itself was not permitted to infringe upon so good a habit.

Having taken some refreshments, he lay down before the fire to rest. In a few minutes he made a sudden effort to rise; rested a moment on his elbow; exclaimed "I am dying;" and almost instantly expired. Thus he illustrated the great truth which he had so often endeavored to enforce, namely, that "*in the midst of life we are in death.*"

The following short extract is from his obituary notice, which appeared in the *Christian Record* for March, 1848:

"This good brother and affectionate elder has labored hard for his Lord and his numerous family for about forty years. I have thought that I never knew a man who loved the Bible more ardently than he. He has endured many hardships for the truth's sake. He plead the cause of the *Bible alone* in all matters of religion, and of the union of all Christians on the Bible, for some twenty years. But he has gone to 'rest from his labors; and his works do follow him.'"

Elder John Thompson Littell was a great man, physically, intellectually, morally. Had his mental been developed like his physical and moral powers, he would have been almost "perfect, thoroughly furnished unto all good works." His stature exceeded six feet; and his weight was more than two hundred pounds. He had dark hair; a large, well-shaped head; keen, blue, speaking eyes; a prominent nose; a mouth that seemed made for noble speech; and a broad, open face, expressive of every quick sensation.

He was a natural orator—clear in argument; powerful in exhortation; in manner positive, if not dogmatical. Education was all he lacked to make his name as familiar to the nation as it was to the little circle in which he lived, moved, and died. He was of a gentle and affectionate spirit, full of vivacity and most excellent humor. Seventy times seven, if his brother sinned against him, seventy times seven could he forgive him, on the legitimate condition of repentance. This trait of his character, as well as the severe and peculiar manner in which he sometimes put to shame the enemies of truth, was clearly exhibited in an incident which certainly occurred at or near Salem.

He was preaching to a large congregation in the presence of a certain minister whose name and order shall be mercifully concealed. In discussing some point relative to

Baptism, he made a quotation from Wesley's Doctrinal Tracts, remarking—as if fearful he had not given it *verbatim*—that if he had not quoted fairly he hoped he might be corrected. The unsuspecting preacher instantly cried out, "I unhesitatingly affirm that the passage does not read that way." "Well, well," said Elder Littell, with the greatest *sang froid*, "we will read it as it is." Suiting the action to the word, he drew from his pocket a copy of the "Tracts;" and read the passage which, as he knew very well, was precisely as he had quoted it. Nothing daunted, the preacher took the book; and gave the audience a different reading. At the request of Elder Littell a small boy then came forward; and again read the passage as it was. This settled the controversy; and the discourse was resumed as if nothing had happened.

When the speaker concluded, the convicted preacher asked leave to make a few remarks. Being politely assured that he should have perfect liberty, he arose and spoke substantially as follows:—"I confess," said he, "that, under the excitement of the moment and the bad feeling that then possessed me, I read the passage wrong; and I pray God to forgive me." "Amen," said Elder Littell; and those who knew him did not doubt that the response came from the bottom of his heart.

Though on all occasions he occupied a conspicuous place among his brethren; yet he never thrust himself into the highest seat; but was always meek and unassuming.

Living in a controversial age, he was, necessarily, somewhat doctrinal; but, in the main, his discourses were eminently practical. When the occasion demanded it, he could wield the sword of the Spirit with a strong and skillful hand; but he was more inclined to provoke his brethren to love and to good works; and most successful in persuading sinners to lay hold on the hope which he eloquently set before them. *Christianity in practice*, was the great object for which he strove.

Like all other men he doubtless had his faults; but in most things he might well have said to his brethren, "be ye followers of me;" for he followed Christ. But

> " No further seek his merits to disclose,
> Or draw his frailties from their dread abode—
> There they alike in trembling hope repose—
> The bosom of his father and his God."

After the death of John T., his brother Absalom continued to labor in the gospel as in former years. Finally, however, the infirmities of advancing age compelled him to economize his strength; and during the last years of his life he accomplished comparatively but little in the work of the ministry. Yet the spirit was willing; though the flesh was weak. The sickle was still keen as ever; but the power that wielded it was failing.

The nearer he approached the grave the more ardently he desired the steadfastness of the disciples; and among the last words he ever wrote, were the following addressed to his "dear brethren."

" Permit an old brother in the 74th year of his age, to say to his younger brethren, and to all: Suffer no strife to rise up among you. Abstain from all appearance of evil. And the very God of peace sanctify you wholly; and I pray God your whole spirit and soul and body be preserved blameless unto the coming of our Lord Jesus Christ."

On the 11th of May, 1862, at 9 o'clock, P. M., he breathed his last. Conscious of his approaching dissolution, he assured those present that death had no terrors; and that he "died only to live." His remains were followed by a long procession to their resting place, in the quiet old church-yard near Hamburg, where they await, in peace, the "voice of the archangel and the trump of God."

In appearance and character, Elder Absalom Littell was much like his brother, John T. Born of the same parents; rocked in the same cradle; hushed by the same lullabies; sent to the same schools; baptized in the same stream; and preachers of the same gospel, which changes men into the same image; they could not well be so dissimilar as to afford materials for two separate and distinct sketches.

Absalom was, however, somewhat larger than his brother; and he was regarded by many as correspondingly superior in point of intellect. But the difference of ability was rather the result of education than of any partiality on the part of nature.

As an orator he was inferior, though he spoke readily, forcibly, and to the point. Their sermons were similar in character; and were usually directed to the same end.

Absalom always conducted himself with gravity becoming his office; yet he too was most richly endowed with the faculty of wit, and with that cheerful disposition which "doeth good like a medicine." In a little circle of old friends, he was as agreeable as he was happy.

In the church and before the world, they manifested the same spirit; for both had "the spirit of Christ."

, Such were those two distinguished pioneers; and such the part they acted in establishing the "ancient order of things" in the commonwealth of Indiana. It is necessary to add only two borrowed lines, expressive, no doubt, of the feeling with which every Christian reader will reach the end of this brief and imperfect sketch:

"Those suns are set,
O rise some other such."

In hope of Eternal life
Joseph Hostetter

JOSEPH HOSTETLER.

The subject of this sketch was born in Shelby county, Kentucky, February 27th, 1797. His father and grandfather were natives of Pennsylvania; but his great-grandfather was born in Germany, near the Rhine. His mother, Agnes, was the daughter of Anthony Hardman, about whose ancestry nothing is known.

About the year 1795 his parents emigrated from Pennsylvania, and settled in Shelby county, Kentucky. Though no longer in a German settlement, they still retained in their family the German language; and Elder Hostetler distinctly remembers the difficulties he encountered in acquiring the rudiments of the English.

When in his seventh year he entered a common school, kept by a queer little Englishman of strong Roman Catholic proclivities, though a member of the Episcopal church. Intoxicating beverages were then freely used by people of both sexes; and, in this particular, the school-master was wholly conformed to the world. Yet he maintained inviolate the *form* of godliness; and, on every Friday afternoon, required his pupils to form in a circle about him and repeat after him, with great solemnity, the Lord's Prayer and the Apostles' Creed!

To this school he was sent three months each year until he was twelve years old. By this means he acquired the arts of reading and penmanship; and also completed the arithemetical course, which extended only to "the Single Rule of Three." Except the medical lectures, which he subsequently attended, this was all the instruction he ever received at school.

His parents were both exemplary members of the German Baptist or Tunker* church, which, even at that early period, had adopted the New Testament as its only book of discipline. It was their chief care to bring up their children in the nurture and admonition of the Lord; and the mother, especially, spared no pains in teaching her little ones to pray; and in instructing them in what she conceived to be the doctrine of Christ.

Under her teaching, Joseph became greatly interested in reading the scriptural account of patriarchs and prophets; and often did he pray to be like little Samuel, or like faithful Abraham, who "was called the friend of God."

Along with these wholesome lessons, many superstitious notions were inculcated by an old German woman, who came frequently to his father's house and related frightful stories about ghosts, witches, hobgoblins, etc. Each of these served "to point a moral;" and all together deeply impressed him with the reality of a future state and the awful penalties visited upon evil-doers.

It was to be supposed that one brought up under such circumstances would readily walk in the way of the righteous. But he was naturally of a very mischievous disposition; at times highly passionate; and "as prone to evil as the sparks to fly upward." When, therefore, he grew older and became less in the presence of his parents, he often set at naught all their counsel to walk in the counsel of the ungodly.

In the winter of 1810-11 there occurred, in his native county, a great revival, which, beginning among the Calvinistic Baptists, soon extended to the Methodists and Tunkers. His grandfather and his uncle Adam Hostetler

---

* Commonly, but improperly, called "Dunkard."

were the principal Tunker preachers, the former speaking in German, the latter in English. Under their earnest preaching and the excitement that generally prevailed, his early religious feelings were revived; and, but for the intervention of his parents, he would have covenanted to walk in a new life. They, however, thought him too young; and prevailed upon him to postpone for a brief period his union with the church.

In the mean time he listened to the several surrounding sects; and his faith was not a little shaken by their contradictory teaching.

Finally he heard one of his schoolmates relate to the Calvinistic Baptists an "experience," which, it seems, ought to be incorporated in his history, because it exerted a powerful influence on his life, and because it is a valuable though sad exponent of the religion of those times. When asked to describe the work of grace upon his heart, the poor lad sobbingly replied, "I don't know as I has any works of grace to tell. I is a poor sinner." "Do you believe in Christ?" said the blind leader of the blind. "O yes, ever sence I can recollect," answered the boy. Being asked if, when he found himself a sinner, he had dreamed any thing remarkable, he proceeded to relate, in substance, the following:

He said that he had retired, *as usual*, in great distress of mind; and had dreamed that as he was going he knew not whither, the devil met him in the way, seized upon him, and was hurrying him off toward hell: that having been conveyed a great way, and thinking himself lost forever, a young man met them, and rescued him from the grasp of the destroyer; and that on being thus liberated he had awoke in a transport of joy. At this point a gray-haired deacon sprang to his feet with a shout. "Brethren," said he, "I've been a Baptist for twenty-five year, and ef ever I heerd a experience o' true grace this boy has giv' us one. So it is with all poor sinners—they are going they know not where tell the Lord meets 'em as he did this boy. I can interpret his dream—he's 'powerfully converted.' Glory to God." This was the opinion of the church, and they received the young candidate into their fellowship, without a dissenting voice.

Hearing this experience, and reflecting on the fact that such dreams were the only foundation of the hope of hundreds, he became skeptical; banished all thoughts of religion; and was soon regarded as a ring-leader among the "rude fellows of the baser sort." Among these he was a kind of clown, who, after attending a meeting, would, for the amusement of his companions, and with mock solemnity, reproduce the sermon in substance, tone, and gesture.

Subsequently, through the efforts of his uncle Adam, he was induced to "ponder the path of his feet." He grew more serious; read the Bible through; and became convinced that his skepticism was based, not on the Scriptures, but on the contradictory theories and absurd speculations of professed Christians.

This conclusion reached, he again became a seeker; but the "whisper of peace," as formerly, strangely delayed its coming.

Finally he discovered by his own reading what the believer must do to be saved. He revealed his discovery to his uncle, who at once accepted his views and on the next Lord's day taught the people openly that they should repent; confess the Lord Jesus; and be baptized in His name "for the remission of sins." On that day Elder Hostetler—then in his nineteenth year—made the good confession and was immersed into the "one body."

Though he took this one proper step, yet he by no means comprehended clearly the Christian system, nor did he at that time realize the importance of the difference he had discovered between it and the systems commonly taught. On this account he drifted heedlessly with the popular tide; until he was again borne far away from the faith of the gospel.

Immediately after his immersion he began to take part with his brethren in prayer and exhortation, and to labor for the reformation of his wicked associates, some of whom are indebted to him, under God, for their hope of eternal life.

About this time a wealthy speculator in lands, whom he attended during a protracted illness at his father's house, gratefully offered to give him a classical education, upon the single condition that, for one year immediately after his graduation, he should remain, as a tutor, in his patron's family. The proposition he gladly accepted, for from a child he had thirsted for "the Pierian spring." But to his great mortification his father positively forbade him from entering into any such arrangement: alleging that "high larnin" only fitted a man to be a villain; and that he might as well sell his soul to the devil at once, for no lawyer could ever gain admission to the kingdom of God!

This cherished design thus thwarted, he turned his thoughts into a different channel; and, on the 20th of July, 1816, was married to a pious sister who still survives.

Shortly after this event he was authorized, by the congregation of which he was a member, to preach the gospel and baptize believers according to the custom of the Tunker church. His uncle being absent for the most part, he at once assumed the principal care of the home church; and in a short time he accompanied his kinsman on a preaching tour through the counties of Nelson, Franklin, Washington, Mercer, Casey, Nicolas, and Fleming.

His ministry was fruitful from the very first, on which

account, as well as by the expressions of his friends, he was greatly encouraged.

In the fall of 1817, he removed to Washington county, Indiana. Settling upon a tract of uncleared land, he devoted the most of his time and energies to the opening out of a farm; yet on Lord's-days, and usually on two evenings each week, he proclaimed all he knew of the gospel. Being yet in his minority he was denominated "the boy preacher." This appellation usually attracted a large audience; and, even at that early period, his influence as a preacher began to be felt.

In the Spring of 1819, he removed to Orange county, near Orleans, and again settled in the woods. Here also he worked hard by day; and at night was equally diligent in the study of the Bible and an English dictionary, which two volumes made up the greater part of his library.

Though he occasionally went into Lawrence county, yet his labors were for the most part confined to Orange; and in the fall of 1819 he and Elder John Ribble organized in his neighborhood, and on the foundation of apostles and prophets, a church of some thirty members. This was the origin of what is now known as Old Liberty church—one of the oldest, firmest, and most flourishing in the state.

One night in August of the next year he dreamed that he saw on the farther side of a river, a large field of wheat and several persons importuning him to come over and help them harvest. As dreams were then of great significance in matters of religion, he inferred from this one that God had called him to preach the gospel in the region beyond White River. He was not disobedient unto what he supposed "the heavenly vision," but set out straightway for the field indicated.

The first man—a blacksmith—to whom he revealed the object of his mission, said to him, "Sir, you have come to a poor place for your business. I have not been to meeting in four years." Yet, commencing at that man's house he preached at several points in that imaginary Macedonia, everywhere relating his dream, which made a deep and solemn impression upon the people; because it led them to believe that God had been mindful of them and had sent his servant to warn them. Having immersed eight persons and left appointments to preach again at each point in four weeks, he returned home.

On his next visit he immersed about twenty, among whom were the smith's wife and daughter; and a short time afterward a church was organized near Abraham Kern's, in Lawrence county.

This year (1820) the Tunker churches in Indiana and Kentucky determined to form a separate Association, being unwilling to conform to all the rules observed by the brethren in Ohio, Pennsylvania and other states. On a specified day the delegates met, organized, and proceeded to enact new laws for the government of the church. Against this action Elder Hostetler, John Ribble of Salem, and Peter Hon of Kentucky, solemnly, but vainly, protested. "Old men for counsel, young men for war," said the venerable controllers of that ecclesiastical body.

The following year this Association met at Old Liberty, at which session Elder Hostetler was regularly ordained as a minister of the grace of God.

As a part of the ceremony his uncle Adam presented him a small Bible, saying, "*Preach and practice only what you find in this Holy Book.*" This remark, made at that solemn moment when he was on his knees before his Maker, deeply impressed him with a sense of his responsibility. Hitherto he had humbly submitted to the dictum of those who had the rule over him, and had felt that they were chiefly responsible for his ministerial action. But now he realized for the first time that it was his duty to *study* to show himself a workman approved *unto God*, and that to his own Master he should stand or fall. Hence he applied himself more closely than ever before to the study of the Scriptures; and he was not long in discovering radical differences between the church described by the apostles and the various religious organisms by which he was surrounded.

Pursuing the subject of creeds, he perceived that their number constantly decreased in each preceding age, until, arriving at the apostolic period, he found but " *one* Lord, and the *name one.*" By this fact his confidence in the popular systems of religion was greatly shaken; yet he quietly adhered to the church of his fathers for two or three years, during which period he baptized about as many hundred persons.

But the eyes of his understanding were being gradually opened; and his preaching was becoming more and more in accordance with the oracles of God; so much so, indeed, that, at the session of the Association in 1825, he was accused, by some of his brethren, of disseminating heterodox opinions. No decisive action, however, was then taken against him; and he continued to preach during another year, with more and more freedom from all human authority.

In the mean time, the first volume of the Christian Baptist fell into his hands. This he read with eagerness though not with entire approbation; for being yet identified with a sect he felt that the blows descended too fast and too heavily. But still the light entered; the faith once delivered to the saints and long obscured by the traditions of men, became more and more apparent; objections to creeds and sects continued to be multiplied; until he found it impossible longer to refrain from a full and public avowal of his sentiments. Accordingly in the spring of 1826, he gave notice that, on a certain day, he would preach at Orleans on the subject of primitive Christianity. The news was carried far and wide; expectation was on tip-toe; and on the appointed day about a thousand persons, including several of the preachers of that section, assembled to hear the promised discourse. He spoke for an hour and a half from that proposition which affirms that "the disciples were called Christians first in Antioch," discussing,

I. The Name.
II. The Manner of becoming a Disciple.
III. Creeds.

It was a day of great excitement. After he concluded the people were seen in groups earnestly discussing the merits of the anomalous discourse. Though many doubted, not a few were convinced that Elder Hostetler had shown them a "more excellent way." The preachers present attempted no reply; but adopted a policy which was then, and still is, more effective than a manly opposition. "Oh," said they, "what a great pity that one so young, so useful, and so promising, should thus destroy his influence by bringing in damnable heresies and attempting to change the customs of our fathers." "You ought," said they to his brethren, "to talk to him; and unless he recant you should bring him before the proper authorities and expel him." This advice was listened to; and he was accordingly notified that at the next meeting of the Association he would be required to answer to the charge of heresy.

In the mean time, desiring that all his brethren should understand clearly the things whereof he was accused, he visited all the churches that were to have a voice at his trial; proclaimed to them the ancient gospel; and baptized about a hundred, who gladly received the word.

Thus did God cause even the wrath of man to praise him.

When the day of this trial came he made an able defense, showing that he opposed no practice for which the word of God furnished either precept or example; that he had taught only what was clearly expressed in words which the Holy Spirit teacheth; that he had exhorted to no duty not enjoined by the apostles; and that he had only repeated to the people the exceeding great and precious promises of God, assuring them that He is faithful that promised. In conclusion he referred to the intolerance of all creed-makers, and to the long list of martyrs that have been "beheaded for the witness of Jesus," asking his brethren if, actuated by the same spirit, they were willing to give their voices against him. "No, no," was the audible response; and a vote being taken, all but five were found to be in his favor. Thus he escaped excommunication; and, in escaping, he made more proselytes to primitive Christianity than he had ever before done in one day.

So great was the confidence reposed in him that his brethren appointed him to deliver the annual sermon at the convening of the next Association. Seeing this, he said to himself, "This day death passed upon this ecclesiastical body. About this time next year it will breathe its last; and my discourse shall be its funeral."

Such was, indeed, the case. Public sentiment rapidly underwent a change in favor of the Bible as the only platform on which all Christians could and should unite; and when the Association came together there were present delegates from the Dependent Baptists and the Old Christian Body, or Newlights, duly empowered to co-operate with them, the Tunkers, in forming a union of the three parties upon the foundation of apostles and prophets.

In this important movement they were successful. With few exceptions, all the churches of each sect throughout south-eastern Indiana, came promptly into the Reformation. Party names, and unauthorized assemblies such as were their Conferences and Associations, were dispensed with; and Christ became "all and in all."

From this date (1828) Elder Hostetler is to be reckoned among the public advocates of the current Reformation.

The year 1828 was fixed in his memory by other and sadder events. He was brought to death's door by a fever which seized upon him while on a preaching tour to Kentucky. He recovered; but two of his brothers were suddenly cut down, each leaving a widow and three children who became, to some extent, dependent upon him.

Depressed by these afflictions of Providence, and to better provide for his family and, if need be, for the families of his deceased brothers, he turned his attention to the study of medicine. During the year, therefore, he travelled but little and enlisted but few soldiers in the army of the Lord.

During the summer of 1829 he and Elder Peter Hon travelled extensively and preached the gospel with great success. They visited Oldham, Nicolas, Bourbon, Montgomery, and Fleming counties, Kentucky; Highland county, Ohio; and Lawrence, Harrison, Clarke, and Jackson counties, Indiana. They were frequently engaged in protracted meetings and they closed their labors for that year with about four hundred additions to the rapidly-increasing number of the disciples.

The next year he and Elder Hon revisited nearly all the churches for which they had preached the year before; held meetings at several other points; and brought, in all, about five hundred persons to the obedience of the faith.

In the Spring of 1832 he removed to Illinois and settled not far from Decatur. There he performed hard labor as a pioneer preacher as well as pioneer farmer; for the public mind was in a worse condition to receive the "incorruptible seed" than was the natural prairie to receive the corruptible seed. During his first Summer in that place he immersed some fifty persons; and in October he organized, near home, a church of fourteen members, which included more than half of the adults in the neighborhood. The church still exists, having now more than one hundred communicants.

Among the first and principal points at which he preached was Decatur, where he encountered the Methodists and Cumberland Presbyterians in force. They bitterly denounced his teaching as Campbellism, Romanism, Infidelity, etc., yet the people believed and were baptized; and in 1833 he organized what is still the church of Christ at Decatur.

The same year he went into McLean and Sangamon counties, where he baptized a considerable number; organized one new church; and brought into the Reformation a small congregation of his former Tunker brethren, who were still clinging to the traditions of the fathers.

In the spring of 1834 he removed to Decatur and engaged in the practice of medicine, though he still continued to preach with tolerable success. Among his proselytes was a Baptist preacher by the name of Bushrod Henry, who has since established a number of flourishing churches in Moultrie and Shelby counties, and rendered other important service in the cause of the Reformation.

In May, 1836, he returned to Indiana and settled on another tract of unimproved land near Bedford, in Lawrence county.

In September following, he attended once more the Annual Meeting, held near Salem; and enjoyed a happy reunion with many of his former yoke-fellows. Hundreds of people were in attendance, many of whom camped upon the ground; and after several days of refreshing the meeting closed with some sixty additions to be saved. Among these were fourteen young ladies who, dressed in white, walked out together into the stream where they were immersed by Elder Hostetler.

Elder Jacob Wright stood on the shore, watch in hand, and when they had all come up out of the water, he announced with a loud voice that the baptizing had occupied just *fifteen minutes.* He added that he had never seen as many *sprinkled* in so short a time; and that he hoped the scene just witnessed would convince all present that it was not impossible for the three thousand to be immersed on the day of Pentecost.

Elder Hostetler, sometimes assisted by Elder William Newland and others, held additional meetings this year at White River Union, Salt Creek and other points, baptizing in all about three hundred persons.

From 1838 to 1842 he devoted a portion of his time to teaching classes in English Grammar, a respectable knowledge of which he had acquired from a book presented him by a friend. In this respect he may be honorably contrasted with most uneducated preachers who, all their lives, trample under foot the laws of syntax rather than address themselves to the work of self-instruction.

Teaching, however, was never permitted to interfere seriously with his duties as an evangelist; and during the greater portion of his time he continued to preach the gospel to the churches in Lawrence and the adjacent counties, baptizing never less than a hundred, and sometimes as many as five hundred per annum.

In addition to his other labors in 1842, he held two debates with Mormon preachers, which sect, about that time, made a strong effort to gain a footing in Indiana. With the assistance of Elder J. M. Mathes, he also wrote and published, that year, a small pamphlet entitled "Calumnies Refuted." This pamphlet was in reply to another, entitled "Campbellism Exposed," which other was published by a Methodist preacher by the name of

Holiday. Many copies of the two little works were stitched together by the Christians and circulated among the Methodists.

During the greater part of the year 1843 he labored as an evangelist in Clark and Scott counties, discipling some, but mainly endeavoring to revive and instruct the churches. It seems that in some of these were entertained singular views of Christian obligations, one of which was that it was the duty only of elders to pay the evangelists that came among them! The bishops, it was held, were commanded to "feed the flock of God;" and this they must do in person or provide food at their own expense. Under such circumstances he received but little support; and his services being required in other and more promising fields of labor, he left the brethren of that locality to eat the fruit of their own way. But this error, not being embalmed in a creed, soon vanished away; and the few that had held it, began to manifest proper zeal and liberality in behalf of the gospel.

The progress of the truth was greatly retarded by the political campaign of 1844, yet Elder Hostetler turned a few from the darkness of sin or of mystic Babylon to "the light of the glorious gospel of Christ."

In the Fall of that year he consulted his memoranda and notes of travel; and found that he had, in the course of his ministry, baptized over three thousand persons, and that he had spent more than a thousand dollars in the service for which he had received from his brethren less than half that amount. That he was able to do this is owing to the fact that his family as well as himself were industrious and economical; and that he was very fortunate in his business transactions. He has acquired the most of his earthly possessions—and they are amply sufficient for the wants of his old age—by buying wild lands, clearing them up; and selling them at greatly advanced prices. In all things he seems to have been the man of whom it was said, "whatsoever he doeth shall prosper."

In 1845 the even tenor of his way was again interrupted by a debate which took place near Fayetteville, in Lawrence county. His opponent was the Rev. Mr. Forbes of the M. E. church.

In 1849 he purchased two thousand acres of land in Wisconsin, to which state he removed and entered into the practice of medicine. But he still continued to preach as formerly, and, in a short time, established two churches, which were among the first in the far north-west.

In 1855 he returned to Salem, Indiana, where he continued to reside for several years, preaching the gospel with wonted success throughout Washington and the surrounding counties. Among other points he visited Sullivan county, where, in company with Elder Jos. W. Wolfe, he held several interesting and very fruitful meetings.

He also returned in 1858 to Old Liberty church (in Orange county), which he had established nearly forty years before. Time had wrought many changes; and as he strolled sadly through the old church-yard, he read, on the monumental stones, the names of many with whom he had labored and rejoiced in early life.

In the Spring of 1861 he removed to Lovington, Illinois, where he still resides. After an absence of twenty-four years, he is once more a member of the congregation on Okaw creek, which church he organized in 1832. He is at the present time employed as county Evangelist; and the pleasure of the Lord continues to prosper in his hands.

Presuming that this sketch will be read by many of his brethren, after his decease, he has furnished a short address to them, a portion of which is here inserted agreeably to his wish. He says:

"As I shall soon take leave of this world, and as all I can do must be done quickly, permit me, my dear brethren, very briefly to address you.

"When I, with hundreds of others, came out of Babylon, we were a praying people; a Scripture-reading people; a church-going people. Our sisters were not ashamed to talk about Jesus or to pray to him in the public assembly. Our brethren carried their Testaments into their fields, their workshops, their stores and offices. The word of truth was spoken in the love of the truth. There were then no choirs to monopolize the songs of Zion, but the word was, 'Let the *people* praise Him; let *all* the people praise Him.' All joined in the sacred song; and the unrhetorical, though fervent, prayer was responded to by all with hearty 'amen.'

"But how are we now? We used to read the holy word—comparing our *lives*, as well as our doctrine, with the doctrine and lives of the primitive Christians; but now, alas! we too often compare ourselves with one another or with the pious among the sects. We now have a great many learned preachers, who deliver elaborate discourses, but seldom rebuke sin except at a distance.* Thus *they* have many disciples. But, alas! if the favorite preacher is not to be there, only a few come out even on the Lord's day. If any old-fashioned preacher comes along, and talks about old-fashioned religion—such as 'To visit the fatherless and the widows in their affliction and keep himself unspotted from the world'—they say, 'Ah, this will never do—this is old fogyism!' Thus we are becoming more and more conformed to the world. In

---

* Elder Hostetler would not be understood as opposed to an educated ministry; and the fault which he justly finds with modern preachers no doubt appears greater when contrasted with the plain, blunt manner of the "former days."

theory we are right, but in *practice* how far do we fall be-
' the measure of the stature of the fullness of Christ !'

"The light of the world! The salt of the earth! ' If the light that is in us be darkness, how great is that darkness!' 'If the salt have lost its savor wherewith shall it be salted?'

"What else than unfruitfulness can we reasonably expect if we walk not habitually with God? If we have no pleasure in obeying him; no pleasure in his holy ordinances; but if we have pleasure in the things of earth—its goods, its honors, its fashions, its follies, its forbidden joys—whatever our professions of Christianity may be—we can never stand justified before the Judge of quick and dead in the great day of eternity.

"Long after I shall have gone to the grave, and, as I trust, to rest, these words may meet the eyes of thousands who have heard my feeble voice within the last forty-five years. Let me therefore, for the last time, and standing, as I do, near the brink of the grave, entreat them to live for Christ, for Heaven, for the success of the glorious cause in which they are engaged.

'Why should we love the things of time? This world is a Golgotha; and during every hour of the cycles of earth, thousands are breathing their last; and tens of thousands are weeping around their dying beds. Truly 'The world passeth away and the lust thereof, but he that doeth the will of God abideth forever.'

"Shall we not then so live that, when the coming of the Lord draweth nigh, each may say, with happy John, 'Even so, come, Lord Jesus.'

"In the hope of eternal life,
"Joseph Hostetler."

Elder Hostetler is about five feet eight inches high, heavy set, and weighs about one hundred and seventy pounds. He possesses extraordinary vigor of both mind and body. His years seem to press upon him lightly.

Though by no means a scholar, yet he has gleaned, by the wayside, a great deal of useful knowledge. He is well acquainted with history—especially the history of the church and of the religion of different ages and nations.

As a speaker he is of the "rough and ready" style—especially the "ready." Indeed he is particularly remarkable for the ability and apparent ease with which he can preach without previous preparation. His words are always at hand; his ideas clear; his gestures numerous and earnest.

In his daily walk he endeavors to live peaceably with all men; but in religious matters, he is fond of controversy; and indisposed to make any compromise that requires the sacrifice of one jot or tittle of the word of God.

He is a man that has many warm friends; and one, too, who has need to pray—as he no doubt does—for his enemies. He loves the truth of God, and jealously defends it at whatever sacrifice of ease or popularity.

If he has *fought*, it has been a *good* fight; and his character is such—take him all in all—that there is reason to believe there is laid up for him a crown of righteousness.

JOHN B. NEW.

Elder John Bowman New was born in Guilford county, North Carolina, November 7th, 1793. His father, Jethro New, was a native of Kent county, Delaware, born September 20th, 1757. He served as a soldier under General Washington, in the war of Independence; and was one of the guards over the unfortunate Major Andre, whose execution he witnessed. His mother, whose maiden name was Sarah Bowman, was also born in Kent county, Delaware, on the 25th of May, 1764. His parents were both Calvinistic Baptists, thoroughly orthodox on the subject of Predestination; and careful to instill into the minds of their children the traditions of the fathers.

In the Fall of 1794, they emigrated to Kentucky, and settled in Franklin county, in Dry Run, about five miles from Frankfort. This long journey through a rough, wild country, the mother and her infant son John B. made on horseback, the *iron* horse having not yet been created.

After a residence of five years in Franklin county, they removed to within fifteen miles of the Ohio river; entered three hundred acres of wild land in Owen county; and settled upon it, about three and a half miles from where the town of New Liberty now stands. Their nearest neighbor at that time lived at a distance of five miles. It was therefore several years before the settlement was sufficiently populous to secure the advantages of a school. The first one was taught by Willis Blanton, to whom, on the first day of the term, flocked stalwart youths and blushing maidens, all—or nearly all—in their A B C's. The first day, Johnny New—as he was then called—learned his alphabet plus a line or two of spelling; and throughout the term his progress was satisfactory to both teacher and parents. Subsequently his teachers were a Mr. Ward, Nathan Briton, and Henry Miller; under whose instructions he obtained a tolerable education, according to the standard of those times. The little one-story cabin in Owen county with its rude benches and puncheon floor, was the *highest* school he ever attended—to him it was both college and theological seminary.

The education of his heart began at an earlier period than that of his head. When only four years old he had learned, and could sing very well, a song of fourteen stanzas, relating to a Roman Catholic girl who had been burnt at the stake for joining a Protestant church. This little hymn inspired his young heart with devotion to the truth and hatred of religious intolerance. His parents, brothers and sisters were all good singers; and the family spent much of their time in singing the songs of Zion.

When seven years of age he attended, for the first time, a meeting for the worship of God. It was a prayer-meeting of the members of the Baptist church, not then organized, and was held in a log-cabin erected in the forest by James Blanton. At the close of the exercises they extended to one another the hand of brotherly love; and an old brother by the name of Moses Baker, warmly shook the hand of the little boy who was intently beholding their devotions. The little fellow was highly pleased with this expression of regard for him; and from that day to this Elder New has been a great lover of prayer-meetings.

Soon after this occurrence the first sermon he ever heard was preached by a Baptist named John Reece, a German who had been a soldier under General Washington. The next sermon he heard was by a Methodist preacher, by the name of Hardy. His text was, "Say to the righteous it shall go well with them, for they shall eat the fruit of their doings; but woe to the wicked, it shall go ill with them, for the reward of their hand shall be given them." Although he had never been disobedient to his parents or guilty of falsehood or profanity; yet he felt that he was classed among the wicked; and, desiring that in eternity it should go well with him, and not ill, he resolved to seek a place among the righteous. To this end he read the Bible daily, and prayed often and fervently; and for a while he thought he was making rapid progress in "the divine life." But one day while guiding an old-fashioned plow around a large tree that stood in the field, the point of the plow caught under a root, throwing up the handles with such force as to hurt him severely, and causing the horse, in his recoil, to plant his foot on a hill of corn. This threw him into a terrible passion, which destroyed in a moment all confidence in his righteousness. The accident has been of great service to him, admonishing him all along the journey of his Christian life to put away anger which "resteth in the bosom of fools."

The next discourse to which he listened was delivered by John Scott, a Baptist of more than ordinary ability. His subject, "The Cumberers of the Ground," was presented in such a manner as to cause young New to address himself again to the task of "seeking religion"—a search which was anxiously prosecuted for several weeks.

At length on a certain afternoon, as he rose up from prayer for the *fifteenth time* that day, he *felt* that his sins had been blotted out. But after a few moments' reflection he concluded that this peace of mind was not owing to the presence of the Holy Spirit—that it was only Satan whispering to his conscience "peace, peace, when there was no peace." He therefore applied himself again to the work of prayer, that he might obtain from God an evidence of pardon, or some *new revelation* of the divine will concerning him.

Finally, after struggling a long time in the Slough of Despond, he read in Romans:—" If thou shalt confess with thy mouth the Lord Jesus and shalt believe in thy heart that God hath raised him from the dead, thou shalt be saved." He read also in Mark:—" He that *believeth and is baptized* shall be saved." Though he did not then know that baptism, preceded by faith and repentance, is "for the remission of sins;" yet he determined to confess the Messiah before men; and be baptized in obedience to his command. At the next opportunity he did so; and as he walked out of the water he proclaimed with a loud voice, to the many spectators:—"*This is the way, walk ye in it.*"

At the next meeting of the Baptist church he united with them; and for the space of three years continued to walk in what he believed to be all the statutes and ordinances blameless, praying often in secret and reading the Bible and other books of a religious character, prominent among which were Pilgrim's Progress and Whitfield's Sermons.

About this time, being then sixteen years of age, he first conceived the idea of becoming, one day, a preacher of the gospel.

In May, 1812, he was drafted as a soldier for six months, to defend Indiana Territory against the invasion of the Indians. He was not called into service until the next August, on the 17th of which month he joined Colonel Wilcox's regiment at Louisville, where he was inspected by General Harrison, then on his way to Cincinnati to take command of the army of the north-west.

Having been armed and equipped at Jeffersonville, his regiment marched first to the defense of Fort Harrison, then commanded by Captain Zachary Taylor, subsequently

President of the United States. Afterwards they marched up the Wabash to a point near La Fayette, whence they returned in January, having passed the Winter thus far in the *flax-linen clothing with which they left home in August!* During the campaign he saw but one Indian, who was running at such a rate that he could not obtain a shot. Like Frederick V. in his dying hour, he could say, "There is not a drop of blood on my hands." Since his prejudices against that unfortunate people have worn away, he is exceedingly glad that he took not the life of one.

In the Spring of 1813 he entered the establishment of Matthew Craigmiles for the purpose of learning the trade of a cabinet maker. There he served out his apprenticeship; and afterwards opened a shop in the town of Cynthiana, Ky.

Toward the last of February, 1814, the weather, which had been very warm, suddenly became extremely cold, occasioning a fearful disease, which the physicians called Cold Plague — a malady similar in many respects to Asiatic Cholera.

After having lost a beloved brother and several other relatives, Elder New was himself seized with the swift destroyer. The attack was severe; the physicians decided that he must die; and his friends prepared for him his grave clothes. But while reflecting one day he came to the conclusion that he would not then die; that his work for the Lord was not yet all accomplished; and, perhaps, through the mysterious influence which the mind exerts over the body, or, it may be, through the providence of God, the long-balanced scale turned in favor of life; and he slowly regained his wonted health.

On the 2d of February, 1815, he located in Madison, then a small village in Indiana Territory. The cause of his leaving Kentucky was the same that has driven many a good citizen from her fertile soil—namely, the institution of human slavery. His object in coming to Indiana was to assist in making it a free State. His views of slavery may be most fairly given by an extract from an article written by himself. In his own peculiar style, he says: "I saw that a man in a slave State might possess twice as much property as his slaveholding neighbor; might have four times as good fare upon his table; might have eight times as much sense; and might manifest sixteen times as much honor in his business transactions; and yet the slaveholder would not regard him as his equal. The possession of a few poor, ignorant, debased slaves was a standard of respectability that I was unwilling for myself and my posterity to be measured by."

In April, 1815, he cast his first vote, as a citizen of Indiana, for delegates to form the first free State constitution. In the same month he looked upon the first steamboat that ever ascended the Ohio. When the six-pounder announced her approach to the port, every man, woman, and child in the village—in all about forty families—ran down to the river to see the great wonder, the Robert Fulton; while the cattle, differently affected, fled affrighted to the hills.

Soon after his arrival at Madison, he entered the cabinet shop of Henry Critz, where he worked as a journeyman for two or three years; during the greater part of which time he served as clerk of the Baptist church at Mount Pleasant, near Madison.

At this time and place the "great salvation" was generally neglected; and, falling in with the popular current, he too soon became "barren and unfruitful." But he soon repented of his folly, and with tears sought the favor and the forgiveness of God. In order to renew his spiritual strength, he determined to visit New Liberty, Ky., near which place protracted meetings were then being held with great success. He went in the spirit of David, praying God to create within him a clean heart, and restore unto him the joys of his salvation.

The people among whom he went most certainly had a zeal for God, though their knowledge of the truth was imperfect. Their doctrine was corrupt, but their lives were pure; and it is to be regretted that in many respects neither time nor the Reformation has produced their superiors in moral excellence. They were a praying people—in the family as well as at church; in secret as well as in public. They were a simple people, comparatively free from "the lust of the flesh, the lust of the eye, and the pride of life." They were a happy people, singing aloud the praises of God as they went to and from the house of worship. They were a patient people, never growing restless under a sermon sixty minutes long; but often assembling an hour before sunset, and protracting their worship until midnight. Among such a people it was good for a faltering pilgrim to go; for they that act thus "declare plainly that they seek a country." On the next day after his arrival there he delivered his first exhortation, at the house of a brother, Samuel Sneed; and, throughout the long series of meetings which followed, he took an active part in singing, prayer, and exhortation.

After several weeks, the meetings closed with about two hundred additions; and he reluctantly returned to Madison. On the first Saturday after his arrival, at the request of the pastor, Jesse Vawter, he gave the church at Mt. Pleasant an account of the Kentucky revivals; and exhorted them to diligence in the great work of saving a world that "lieth in wickedness." This address was quite unexpected to the brethren, causing them to partially open their eyes and awake from their sinful slumber.

On the next day—Sunday—after a sermon by the pastor, Elder New again arose, and began an earnest and touching exhortation. Many in the audience were soon weeping profusely; and, when he sat down, the pastor, with tears streaming down his face, began to go through the house, exhorting and shaking hands indiscriminately. The effect was electrical; and from that meeting the interest spread into the country on both sides of the Ohio; nor did it abate until great numbers were "added to the saved."

After his return to Madison, he endeavored to atone for past delinquencies by double diligence in the service of God. He quit all secular business, and entered upon the study of the Bible, with the aid of Scott's Commentary, resolved that, *if the Lord should call him* to preach the gospel, he would not be disobedient. He believed firmly in the doctrine of "a divine call" to the ministry, as did thousands in his day, who, while waiting to receive it, saw multitudes go by in the broad road to destruction, who, but for this grievous doctrine, would have been among those who shall ascribe "blessing, and honor, and glory, and power to Him that sitteth upon the throne, and to the Lamb forever and ever."

After studying and praying over this subject for several months, he finally compromised the matter by resolving that the church should assign him his sphere of action; and that he would endeavor to do whatever they might require at his hands. They decided that he should preach; and he accordingly began about the year 1818. But, having spent all his money while investigating the question of a divine call, he was obliged to betake himself again to manual labor. Yet, with characteristic order and economy, he reserved four hours out of the twenty-four for study.

On the 19th of February, 1818, he was married to Miss

Maria Chalfant, the third daughter of Thomas and Mary Chalfant, who resided in Kentucky, seven miles from Madison, on the Frankfort road. Her parents were from Pennsylvania; and both they and their daughter were Baptists, and opposed to the institution of slavery. The choice of his youth, and the sharer of his toils and trials in the gospel, is still the companion of his old age.

Soon after his marriage, he and several others were appointed a committee to amend and enlarge the rules of decorum of the Mt. Pleasant church. When the committee met, he inquired of them if, in their opinion, the church required rules to enforce any thing which the Lord had not commanded in the New Testament. They said, "Certainly not." He next inquired if they thought the church needed rules forbidding any thing which the Lord had not forbidden in the Scriptures. This was also answered in the negative. "Then," said he, "it would take much time, ink, and paper to write out all the Christian duties and privileges; and, on looking into the law of the Lord, I find that he has graciously relieved us from so much labor and expense, by enumerating them for us; I therefore move that this committee recommend to the church the adoption of the Holy Bible as their all-sufficient rule of faith and practice." Such a report was accordingly made and adopted by the congregation. It will be remembered that this was at a very early period. As yet no great reformer had clearly brought to light the evil of creeds; and he reached his conclusions by following the plain reading of the word of God.

In March, 1821, he removed to Vernon, Jennings county. In a short time Joel Butler, an orthodox Baptist preacher of Indianapolis, delivered a discourse at the house of Luther Newton, near Vernon; and called on brother New to close the meeting. In doing so he pressed upon the audience the duty of complying with the "conditions" of the gospel. After dismission, the chief speaker approached him, with an air of great concern, saying, "Brother New, are there any conditions in the gospel? If so, what are they?" In reply to this singular question he quoted Mark xvi. 16, Rev. ii. 10, and Heb. x. 38. Most of the Baptist preachers of that day were equally ignorant of the plan of salvation. They believed that God either would or would not have mercy, according to his own good pleasure; and that the sinner either should or should not be saved, according to his predestination to glory or to shame.

On this subject of predestination he had much controversy with his brethren, who stigmatized him as an Arminian because he was not a Calvinist. On one occasion, a Baptist from Kentucky preached in the court house at Vernon; and vulgarly announced to the audience that he was "a predestinarian up to his knees, with a steel hoop and an iron jacket." He and Elder New went to the same house for dinner; and at the table a controversy arose between them, which continued, with a short intermission for sleep, until nearly noon the next day. It is said that when Sir Orthodox went back to Kentucky, he unlaced his jacket somewhat, and did not wade quite so deep in the mire of predestination.

The first standard work on theology that he read was Gill's Body of Divinity. Finding that it advocated the doctrine of a partial atonement, he laid it aside, when finished, and christened it Gill's Body of *Humanity;* because it was, in his opinion, as unlike the Divinity of Christ as John Gill was unlike the Messiah. He next read Andrew Fuller's Gospel, which he found to be very different from Paul's; for, although it taught that Christ made an atonement for all, yet none could believe unless first regenerated by the Holy Spirit, which was effectually imparted "according to the determinate counsel and foreknowledge of God;" thus virtually attributing the loss of the non-elect to Adam and the Almighty, while Gill laid the blame upon Adam and the Redeemer!

As fast as he could condemn such doctrines of men by comparing them with the word of God, he threw them aside; for he had determined that, in matters of doctrine, he would reject every thing which was not as old as the New Testament; and that he would confine himself as closely as possible to the language of the Book, when speaking of Father, Son, Holy Spirit, faith, repentance, baptism, remission of sins, and whatever else is intimately connected with man's salvation—a practice which, if adopted by all preachers, would soon utterly destroy the worthless dogmas that distract the church and stay the progress of the gospel.

So numerous were these dogmas then, that it often happened that there would be several sorts of Baptists in one congregation. At one time the church at Vernon wished to prepare a letter for the Silver Creek Association. In carrying out their wish a difficulty arose as to the manner in which the said letter should be prefaced. Some desired that the adjective "United" should be prefixed; others preferred the prefix "Regular;" while some, for the sake of compromise, suggested the single word "Baptist." To this Joel Butler stoutly objected, and, in his turn, suggested that it be written: "*The Calvinistic Close-Communion Baptist Church*"—a name eminently commemorative of him who loved the church and gave himself for it! But, says the practice of the orthodox,

"What's in a name?
A rose by any other name would smell as sweet."

Soon after his removal to Vernon, he began to preach once a month in Ripley county, where he soon organized a church according to the word of the Lord. Among the

8

many additions to that congregation was old father Wiley, then seventy-five years of age—almost ready to descend into an earthy, instead of a watery grave. He had been a Methodist for *forty years*, and when he walked out into the stream he took hold of his coat with both hands and turning toward the large assembly he said, "Some may think that the old man is about to change his coat in his old age; but if I change it for the better I hope you will excuse me." His wife, who had been a Methodist for *thirty years*, preceded him into the kingdom. They both walked worthy of their vocation during the remainder of their earthly pilgrimage; and died in full assurance of faith.

A little prior to the immersion of father Wiley, a few of that congregation, through the influence of Baptist preachers, became greatly afraid that Elder New would lead the church into "Campbellism." They therefore summoned, from the neighboring churches, a council to assist them in placing their pastor on the iron bedstead. On a certain day the counselors came, and after a discourse by Elder New, the clerk of the church, who was one of the alarmists, asked permission to read *the Articles of Faith of the Silver Creek Association*. Permission being granted the articles were read; whereupon a brother James McClusky arose, and offered the following resolution: "Whereas the church of Christ at this place has lived together in peace and love, under the government of the Lord without any rules of man's device, therefore

"*Resolved*, That the said church continue to live by and under his laws alone, as revealed in the New Testament." This resolution was adopted by a vote of thirty-five to seven; and the "council" retreated in the direction of Silver creek!

About this time, it seems that others became alarmed at *Campbellism*. While the Association was in session at Shann creek, Bartholomew county, a brother Daniel Pritchard arose and delivered the following lamentation. Said he, "I expect to be compelled to live and die with Arminians, a thing which I can submit to, though it hurts my feelings to call them brethren; but to live in full fellowship with Campbellites (glancing at Elder New) is more than I can endure." Upon this Elder New stood up, and, with an air of great seriousness, observed that, if there were such persons about, it would be well to have them pointed out so that all *good* people might avoid them. The conscientious brother, who afterwards came into the Reformation, did not say any thing further, being no doubt in the condition of another opposer who said of a certain discourse, that he would have liked it very well if it had not been so full of Campbellism. "True," said he, "I do not know what Campbellism is, and God forbid I ever should know."

In April, 1830, there being much strife and disorder in the congregation at Vernon, he, with some eleven others, including his wife and his brother Hickman New, obtained from the church letters of dismission in full fellowship, designing to organize as a separate church. For the satisfaction of all concerned they requested that a council should be summoned from six adjacent churches, by the decision of which they pledged themselves to be governed. The council met and decided that they should postpone the new organization for one year, in hope that in the mean time Providence would indicate some means by which they might all dwell together in peace. He therefore waited until the next Spring, when he began to preach the Reformation in the Baptist church. In July following he immersed his brother Hickman's wife "for the remission of sins." On Saturday evening before his regular meeting in September, he preached at his own house, and Perry M. Blankenship, whom he had brought up and educated, confessed his faith in the Son of God. Brother Blankenship's entrance into the kingdom was strangely opposed by his relatives, especially by his mother, who, when she heard of his confession, declared that she would rather have heard of his death!—The next day she came post-haste to meeting to prevent his immersion. But her objections were finally overruled, and her son, through obedience, became a son of God. He afterwards studied theology, though compelled to labor at the *work bench;* and has been for many years an efficient evangelist.

In November, 1831, he organized the Church of Christ at Vernon, with about thirteen members, to whom were soon added several others, including the wife of P. M. Blankenship.

In the Summer of 1832, Colonel John King, the county surveyor, came to Elder New's house on Sunday morning with a change of raiment. After some conversation on the subject of religion, he confessed his faith in Jesus, and stated that he had come on purpose to obey him After the morning service at church he was immersed, and in a short time he became a zealous and successful preacher. Through his influence, his father, then a deist, profane and dissipated—was brought occasionally into the sanctuary. He had not long heard the word until he also believed; and one day, while Elder New was in the midst of a discourse, he rose up in the congregation and expressed his desire to confess the Saviour before men, and be buried with him by baptism into death. The sermon being discontinued and an invitation given, he, his son George, and several others came forward to the acknowledgment of the truth. His wife, who had been brought up a Presbyterian, soon followed him into the Reformation, as did others of the relatives, in all about twenty. The old man continued a faithful and devoted disciple until the day of his death, Christ and the cross being his constant theme.

In August, 1832, he attended a meeting at the Bluffs of White River, some fifteen miles below Indianapolis. There he first met John O'Kane, who agreed to meet him at Greensburg in September and go with him thence to Vernon to assist in a protracted meeting to be held there in October. They met according to agreement, and held their meeting at Greensburg on the last Saturday and Sunday in September. On the next day they set out for Vernon by way of Madison, preaching at New Marion, Hebron, Madison, and Franklin's school-house. At the last place David C. Branham was immersed—the first of that large family that came out in opposition to all human creeds. On Friday morning they arrived at Vernon, where they met with a sore disappointment. They found that the Baptist church, which had long been engaged for the occasion by the Disciples, was occupied by the Presbyterians of Hanover, who were holding in it their Presbytery. A Methodist Quarterly Meeting was in progress in the court house; and there was left no better place for holding their meeting than in Hickman New's cabinet shop. Previous to their arrival the brethren had set the shop in order, and, hoping that all things would work together for good, they began their meeting. It continued for about a week, and resulted in *forty-five* additions—the truth triumphing gloriously over its allied opposers. The Presbyterians had no accessions; the Methodists drew only a few to the anxious seat, the most of whom went away to the Christians' meeting, and obtained pardon by attending to what had been appointed for them to do; while the Baptists were rewarded for their faithlessness by the loss of ten of their members, who went over to the Reformation.

About this time he began to preach monthly at Coffee

creek, some twelve miles from Vernon. It was a Baptist community, and he held his meetings in the Baptist church. It was not long however until the chain and padlock—"the last arguments to which *errorists* resort"—were placed upon the door. At this crisis two of the Baptists, more noble than the rest, invited him to preach in their houses, at the same time addressing him as "*brother* New." For this act they were arraigned before the church, which had already agreed to be governed by the word of God. To that word they appealed, but were informed that they were to be tried by the Baptist rules. They then plead successfully that those rules did not forbid their calling a good man brother or inviting him to preach in their dwellings. It was then charged in the indictment that they had *hurt the feelings of the church.* On this charge they were excluded; but through the door, which was opened for *their* egress, about twenty others went out—so great a matter did a little fire kindle. He continued his meetings and organized a church there which soon numbered a hundred members, about half of whom were from the Baptists. In a little while they built a substantial brick meeting-house, which, to this day commemorates the victory at Coffee creek.

In November, 1832, he and Carey Smith organized the Church of Christ at Madison, which consisted at first of about a dozen members. Among the original members were Jessee Mavity and his wife. Elder Mavity had been preaching for a few years and was an educated and promising evangelist. To support his family he taught school in the basement of the Masonic Hall, assisted by his brother Henry Mavity. Prior to the organization of the church, he had preached with great acceptance for the several denominations of the city, all of whom were liberal patrons of his school. But no sooner was an effort made to build a church on the foundation which God has laid in Zion, than they induced him to change his common school to a High School, assuring him that he would thus make a better support with less labor. The change being made, they withdrew so much of their patronage that the High School proved a failure. He was therefore compelled to leave the city and retire into the country—a movement which deprived the infant church of a pastor. This seems to have been a strategic movement on the part of the allied sects to which they were no doubt prompted by the Scripture which saith, "*Smite the shepherd, and the sheep shall be scattered.*"

The stategy, however, did not succeed. Elder New went to the relief of the congregation, which he visited once a month gratuitously until they were able to sustain a preacher. Thus he not only planted, but also saved, the Church of Christ at Madison.

Having assisted in building a good brick meeting-house at Vernon, and having placed the cause upon a good footing, he determined to entrust the work, in that county, to his brother Hickman and several other young preachers. Accordingly in October, 1839, he removed to Greensburg, Decatur county, where there was a languishing church of some thirty members. His first meeting was on a beautiful Lord's day in October; but, the brethren had so far forsaken the assembling of themselves together, that there were but thirteen of them and three small boys present. After the discourse, he and his wife handed their letters to one of the bishops, and were received into what little fellowship the church possessed. The prospect was so dark that his wife wept bitterly; and his stouter heart was not a little discouraged. They had left their comfortable old home; were in debt for their new one; and without even the promise of a single dollar from the church at that place. But he looked upon the Lord's vineyard, all grown over with thorns, and also upon the field ripe for the harvest; he girded up his loins with truth; set his sickle in order; and resolved to labor, and wait for his reward until the resurrection of the just.

He appointed a protracted meeting to be held early in November; and obtained the assistance of George Caldwell of Rush, and Samuel Ellis of Decatur. At the first meeting on Saturday morning *eight* persons were present, one of whom had walked from Hartsville, a distance of fourteen miles. On Saturday night there were twelve present; on Sunday twenty-five; and the *big* meeting adjourned *sine die*. It was about four months before he could get a tolerable hearing; but he received as much pay, almost, from the empty pews as from the people, so he toiled on, preaching in town every Thursday night and five times on one Saturday and Sunday of each month, and holding meetings in school-houses and private dwellings throughout a district of ten miles square. Such persevering industry, accompanied with fervent prayer to the Giver of all increase, could not fail to produce some good results; and during the first year there were seventy-five additions to the church. He preached at Greensburg one fourth of his time for six years; and each year brought about fifty into the fold of Christ. Under his diligent culture, the small seed which he found there took such deep root that it has steadily grown into a great tree under whose shadow all other gospels enjoy but a sickly existence.

In December, 1839, he went to Cincinnati, where he preached five discourses and had twelve additions. This was the beginning of the great meeting, which lasted three whole months, and resulted in two hundred and fifty accessions to the cause of righteousness and truth.

In January, 1840, he organized a church five miles south of Greensburg; and continued to preach for them monthly until they reached a membership of sixty. In

June of the same year he held a meeting at Napoleon, Ripley county. At this point there was no Christian church, nor were there more than two or three disciples in all that region. After a meeting of four days' continuance, there was a church there of twenty-four members. The *twenty-two* additions were from *eleven* different religious parties! Hence it appears that the ancient gospel, which in the days of Paul made " of twain one new man," has not yet lost its power; for it has in this century made of *eleven* one new church. Notwithstanding their differences of opinion previous to their union, they afterwards stood together as one man ; and Christ became " all and in all." *So would all material differences of opinion perish, were they not embalmed, like Egyptian bodies, in the Creeds and Confessions of Faith.*

In May, 1841, he held a meeting at Milroy, in Rush county. The padlock being on the door of the M. E. church, he preached at the house of Austin Smith. There was then no Christian church at that place, and only one disciple, the wife of Dr. Samuel Barbour. On Monday morning the citizens said to him that if he would return in eight weeks they would have a house ready for his use. When he came, accompanied by Jos. Fassett, the house was ready. They preached in it a few days, and left there a church of seventeen members. Them also he fed with the sincere milk of the word, until they were able to take care of themselves. They are still a large congregation, and have a good house of worship.

In August, 1841, he and Joseph Fassett held a meeting of two days at Shelbyville, and immersed one. There were then but three disciples at that place, and the opposition was very strong. He returned in March, 1842; preached several days in the town and vicinity, and with great difficulty collected sufficient materials to organize a church, to which, in April following, he added some twenty disciples.

The same year, 1842, he organized two more churches —one at Milford, and the other at Blue River. He also held that year a number of protracted meetings, extending his circuit as far as Rising Sun.

On the first Lord's day in March, 1843, the weather being very cold, he began a protracted meeting at Edinburg, Johnson county. When he arrived at the church on Monday morning, a little before the hour for preaching, he found the door still locked. He hunted up the key, unlocked the door, and proceeded to examine the stove, which he found cold as the church, and nearly full of ashes. These he carried out, and began to cast about him for wood to make a fire. Finding none save some large hickory logs, he procured an axe, prepared wood, and soon had a comfortable fire. By this time a faithful few had assembled; and, being already "warmed up," he discoursed to them with unusual ease and fluency. Notwithstanding this sad beginning, he continued the meeting for several days; and closed with nineteen additions, most of whom were persons of wealth, intelligence, and moral worth.

In September, 1846, he held a meeting at Williamsburg, Johnson county. When he began, a certain brother observed that he would not be afraid to promise him a hundred dollars for every one he would immerse, there being much sickness in the neighborhood, and also a great sale of personal property, which attracted the attention of the people. He continued to preach to very small audiences until Thursday afternoon, at which time there were sixteen persons present—ten citizens of the kingdom, and six "foreigners." Of these six, he immersed, that afternoon, five; and the other waited only a few days, to obtain the consent of his mother. This circumstance fairly illustrates his perseverance and hope.

In October, 1846, he was appointed by the State Meeting as missionary to Fort Wayne, for a period of one year. He was to receive out of the treasury two hundred and fifty dollars, and the balance of his expenses he was to meet by the labor of his own hands. On the 7th of November he arrived at Fort Wayne, in which were then only two sisters and one brother. On the evening of the 15th he preached his first sermon, in the court house, all the churches being closed against him. Fort Wayne then contained eleven churches, and a population of about four thousand, of whom one thousand were Roman Catholics and nearly another thousand German Lutherans. The claims of the ancient gospel were firmly disputed by the "clergy," who spared no pains to prejudice the public mind against it. From any point of view the prospect was by no means flattering, if not absolutely discouraging. However he still persevered in the work, and it was not long until his efforts were rewarded by the conversion of an Episcopal minister by the name of Edward Hodgkins, who became an able advocate of primitive Christianity.

It was two full months before he could command a large audience; but, when he began to immerse believers in the canal, in which the ice was more than a foot thick, the inhabitants became anxious to know more of those people that were everywhere spoken against.

At the expiration of the first half of his year there was at Fort Wayne a Christian church of fifty members, with a well-attended and interesting Sunday-school. During the other six months he preached half his time at other points, including Auburn and Newville, De Kalb county; Ashland, Wabash county; and Huntington and Wabashtown, Huntington county. The result of his labors for the year was two churches organized, and one hundred and fifty-five accessions to the cause of primitive Christianity.

During the next six months he preached for the churches at Marion, Ashland, Wabashtown, and Huntington. In those days he usually travelled in a buggy, and was frequently accompanied by his wife. The roads were sometimes in such wretched plight that the horse could with difficulty draw the buggy containing sister New alone. In such cases the evangelist would be compelled to alight, and, with pantaloons well rolled up, plod his weary way through almost unfathomable depths of mud. Yet he patiently endured all for Christ's sake and the gospel's; and, on reaching *terra firma*, he would mount again into his carriage, with all the hopefulness of the poet, when he sang :

> "Come, let us anew
> Our journey pursue ;
> Roll round with the year,
> And never stand still,
> Till the Master appear."

In the Spring of 1848 he returned to Greensburg; and during the following Summer and Fall he visited most of the churches he had planted, confirming the brethren.

In January, 1849, he preached, by invitation, before the Co-operation Meeting then in session at Crawfordsville. In March following, he was employed for one year by the brethren at Crawfordsville, to which place he removed. The church was then in a sad state, owing to strifes and divisions. He labored long and earnestly in the capacity of a peace-maker, and finally succeeded in reconciling the most of them; but the influence of their example was such upon the world that he could accomplish but very little outside of the congregation.

At the close of his year he went back to Indianapolis,

where he fixed his permanent residence, perhaps for life. For about six months after his return to that city he was employed as agent and evangelist for the State Missionary Society. During this time he travelled extensively in various parts of the State; and his efforts were attended with good success.

During the year 1852, being again employed by the Missionary Society, he preached in the counties of Madison and Delaware; and with such success that he was continued in that field six months longer. Within the eighteen months he organized five new churches, and made one hundred and twenty-five proselytes.

In February, 1853, he held a meeting at Terre Haute, which greatly strengthened the church in that city. In March following he organized the church at Paris, Illinois, and left it with thirty-seven members.

About this time the great controversy with regard to the powers of elders and evangelists was sweeping like a tornado over Illinois, laying church after church in ruins. Perceiving that general destruction was inevitable unless the tempest could be stayed, Elder New made a tour through that State, preaching almost exclusively to the brethren, and exhorting them to "keep the unity of the spirit in the bond of peace."

At Jacksonville he addressed the State Meeting on the subject of Missions, on which occasion he presented the following as the essential elements of a successful missionary: 1st. *Godliness.* 2d. *A clear understanding of the Christian system.* 3d. *Aptness to teach.* 4th. *A thorough acquaintance with human nature.*

During the year 1860, he served the congregations at Mishawaka, South Bend, and Harris' Prairie, St. Joseph county. When he first visited those churches, some were weak and powerless on account of divisions. He succeeded in removing the most of these obstacles; and the gospel, in St. Joseph, now has "free course that it may run and be glorified."

During the past year he has continued to reside at Indianapolis; from which point he has gone in every direction, preaching the gospel wherever there has been a demand for his services.

Having thus reached the present, history can proceed no further; but if one had the gift of prophecy this sketch might no doubt be considerably extended. For, though old in years, the subject of it is still young in spirit, and there is reason to hope that he will yet do much that will redound to the glory of God and the advancement of the Redeemer's kingdom. But already, as he looks back through sunshine and shadow to the churches he has planted, the schisms he has healed, the opposers he has vanquished, and the hearts he has cheered, he may well rejoice that he has not run in vain neither labored in vain.

In the physical contour of John B. New there is nothing remarkable. He is a man of medium size, blessed by nature with more than ordinary activity. Altogether, he is a man of very good appearance; and one, you may be sure, who never appears to disadvantage through any neglect of his toilette. Every hair knows its inevitable position; which position his nicely smoothed hat is careful never to disturb. His snow-white cravat is always tied precisely *so*, and his large full shirt bosom is spotless as the soul of a saint. His boots are generally well blacked, and you might as well search for the philosopher's stone as for a grease-spot upon his clothing. Yet you must not think he is foppish, he is only neat—hardly ever up with the fashion, but generally dressed a little after the style of the olden time.

Not merely in dress, but in every thing, he is cleanly even to a fault. Should he see you enter your own house with a little mud adhering to your shoe, he would hardly hesitate to tell you to step out and remove the intruder; and if, in a house at which he is stopping, the children have *very* dirty faces—or if the window panes are so dusty that he cannot see out clearly—the good sister in charge need not be surprised to receive from him a gentle hint relative to the virtues of warm water. It is a matter of regret, therefore, that with some housewives he is not a favorite—yet he is "not a terror to good works but to the evil."

He takes care that every thing is done not only "decently," but also *in order*. Every book and paper must be in just the right place. When he writes every *i* must be dotted, and every *t* crossed; and, about the whole premises, every thing must be done just *then* and *so*. It is related of him that in one of his preaching tours he was tarrying on Saturday at the house of a brother, who to the neglect of his work had kept him company all the afternoon. Towards nightfall he observed to his host that if he had any chores to do, any wood to get, or *chickens to catch*, it was then the proper time to attend to such business. *If this be true*, there was not a particle of selfishness in the whole matter. It was not his *appetite*, but his *bump of order* that constrained him to offer the suggestion.

But with all these little faults, which lean to virtue's side, he is an agreeable, an amiable man. Deep down below these surface appearances he has a frank, generous nature; a pure, warm heart. He grasps your hand like a brother indeed; and when he says, "How do you do?" it is because he really desires to know that you are well.

His mind is well informed, though neither of the highest order nor thoroughly cultivated. He has a large share of the sound common-sense which Providence bestowed on the generation past in lieu of the colleges and universities vouchsafed to the generation present. He has a remarkably good memory, retentive of time, place, and event; supplying him promptly with chapter and verse; and reaching back almost to infancy.

In the pulpit, he is an eccentric, yet safe teacher—an earnest and effective exhorter. His gestures are quick, cramped, and rectilinear; and he utters bluntly whatever he thinks, whether it relates to friend or foe. He is mainly argumentative, proving all things and holding *very fast* that which is good. Owing to his highly nervous temperament, he thinks and speaks rapidly; yet he is not always brief; and it need not surprise you if in his enumeration of topics he ascend even to *thirteenthly*. True, he very often looks at his elegant watch; but he cares no more for its admonitions than he does for a Confession of Faith.

He enters with spirit into his subject; but it is said that he never becomes so excited in speaking, that he fails to notice a dog if one ventures into the house of God. It is said further, that, in such a case, he stops suddenly; indulges in a few significant looks and gestures; and if no one else restores order, he quietly descends from the pulpit; takes his cane; expels the intruder; and then resumes his discourse. No Jew could have been much more zealous in excluding the idolater from the Holy Temple.

Altogether he is a character worthy of the pen of a Shakspeare. He has done but little evil to live after him, and the good that he has accomplished can never be "interred with his bones." He may pass away, and his children in the gospel may lie down with him to sleep in dust; but the churches he has planted will flourish after his death; the principles he has helped to establish will survive even his memory; and the spirits of the just, made perfect through the gospel he has preached, shall live and rejoice with him forever before the throne of God.

BEVERLY VAWTER.

ELDER BEVERLY VAWTER is a native of Virginia, born on the 28th of September, 1789—the same year in which George Washington was inaugurated first President of the United States. In the same year also, Ethan Allen died, and thus the place of the celebrated infidel was supplied by the veteran Christian.

His parents, Philemon and Ann Vawter, were both born in Culpepper county, Virginia, and brought up in the Episcopal Church. Soon after their marriage they crossed the mountains and settled in Western Virginia, where their son Beverly was born.

In 1792 they emigrated to Kentucky, then a new-born babe in the sisterhood of States. They settled in Woodford county, and united with the Baptist church, in which faith they lived and died without reproach. Several years prior to his death, the father became a Baptist preacher.

In about three years after their settlement in Woodford county, they removed to a new home, on the bank of the Ohio, in Boone county, Ky. There Elder Vawter spent his boyhood, surrounded by savages and a few adventurous pioneers. Books were so scarce in those times that he was a full-grown man before he saw even an almanac! The best family library contained only a Bible and hymn book, while newspapers and religious magazines were not only unseen but almost unheard of.

Under such circumstances his education was necessarily very limited. He farmed, shivered with the ague, and went to what was called school, alternately; and if it were all summed up—lost time being deducted—his student life would amount to less than two years. To spell, read, write, and "cipher" a very little, was all he learned at school. He has not, by his own efforts, greatly multiplied his literary and scientific attainments; but by reading and observation he has, in the course of his long life, acquired a respectable stock of general information. When he entered into the Reformation, he was, in point of scholarship, one of the weak things which God has chosen to confound the things that are mighty.

His first attempt to draw nigh to God, was in harmony with the religious teachings of his times, and not unlike the efforts of others whose histories are contained in this volume. It was simply a blind feeling after God in places where he has never promised to be found, attended with alternate seasons of hope and despair. In view of the darkness of that day and the light that now shines upon the way of life, he may well say to the people of this generation: "Blessed are your eyes, for they see." But the darkness is not all dispelled. Some of the old errors still remain; and, in order that the world may have still further evidence of their pernicious influence, the history of his conversion must be given.

When he was about ten years old there was a great revival of religion in the only Baptist church then in Boone county. Every body seemed to be joining the church, under the stirring preaching of an aged minister named John Taylor. One day, after meeting, Mrs. Vawter took occasion to talk with her son in regard to his religious impressions, saying that he seemed to be affected by the preaching; that he ought to pray daily in secret; and, if possible, "get religion." Being a dutiful son, that never was chastised with the rod in all his life, he readily promised to follow her advice.

Soon after this, he again attended a meeting, at which a great many young persons—older, however, than himself—were uniting with the church. One day, after a large in-gathering, the preacher arose and inquired if there was not "another little boy wishing to join:" then, growing personal in his exhortation, he added, "Come, Beverly, and tell us how *you* feel." At the mention of his name, a certain Judge Watts took him up in his arms; carried him, *nolens volens*, over the benches; and sat down with him among the mourners. The preacher with great solemnity asked him a great many questions, all of which he was too much abashed to answer. His mother came to his relief; and testified that, although she could not get him to talk, she knew he prayed every day; and she thought that from a given period she *had noticed a change in his countenance!* This was regarded, by the preacher and church, as good evidence of a sound conversion! The next day they baptized him; and gave him the right hand of fellowship. About the same time the wife of a Major Kirtley, a most excellent woman, presented to him a nice suit of clothes as an earnest of the many "good deeds" she afterwards performed for him. Thus he experienced a change of *raiment*, instead of a change of *heart!* He suspected as much himself, but finally concluded that all was well, as the church seemed to think so; and they were certainly better judges than himself. Soon, however, he expressed doubts as to his conversion; but these *very doubts* were construed by his brethren into the most conclusive evidence that he was a child of God! This is one of the errors that remain, as the following incident will show.

About three years ago a Christian preacher was holding a protracted meeting in a strong Baptist community, in Warrick county, Indiana. He was accompanied by a young man, a disciple, who, some years before, had been "powerfully converted" at the mourner's bench in the same house in which the meeting was being held. At the close of a discourse which made some encroachments on that peculiar institution of pardon, the disciple above mentioned arose and made the following revelation: Said he, "It will do you no harm to go to the mourner's bench." "Amen, that's a fact!" responded the Baptists. "I am glad," he added, "to see one become so humble that he is willing to go to the mourner's bench." Here the voice of the Baptist preacher rose above all others, saying, "Amen, go on Brother J—!" "But," continued the speaker, "the *feelings* there experienced *must not be regarded as evidence of pardon*." (No response.) "I experienced such feelings at this very altar, and I shouted and praised God, believing that my sins were forgiven." "But," said he, addressing the Baptists, who could not question his integrity, "the next day I doubted my conversion; I expressed my doubts to you, and you said: '*O, never mind it, that's the way we all feel!*'" It is needless to say that this "most unkind cut of all" was received with profound silence.

Agreeably to this advice, Elder Vawter tried to "never mind it;" but the older he grew the more he was compelled to "mind it." He soon discontinued his prayers; but he remained in the church until he reached his twenty-second year; both because he feared to turn back, on his own account, and was unwilling to wound the feelings of his parents. At times he would renew his efforts to obtain a satisfactory evidence of his acceptance with God; but it was all in vain.

When in his twenty-second year, some disturbance occurred in the family of one of his brethren. He thought the brother was guilty of maltreating his wife; and he one day said to a neighbor that "such a fellow ought to be cowhided." This remark reached the ear of the church; and a brother was sent to obtain from him an acknowledgment of his fault. Desiring to be excluded, he refused to confess. Being threatened with excommunication, he replied that he had never "had religion;" and it was better for him to be out of the church than in it. This reply being reported, he was promptly excluded—a matter which troubled him only as it distressed his parents.

During the next five or six years of his life, he banished all religious impressions from his mind—God was not in all his thoughts. Within this time he volunteered twice in the service of his country; and, in the pioneer uniform, marched to the defense of the north-western frontier. At the close of the second campaign he exchanged the demoralizing influences of camp-life for the evil communications of river men. In the capacity of a flat-boatman he made a trip to the South, experiencing by the way the earthquakes which occurred near New Madrid in 1811.

On the 5th of March, 1812, he married Miss Elizabeth Crawford; settled down upon a farm; and, for a few years, devoted all his powers to the acquisition of wealth.

On a certain Lord's day, in June, 1816, he went to hear a Newlight preacher. The discourse made no impression on his mind; for he was strongly prejudiced against that people on account of the bodily exercises* prevailing among them. Returning home, he was passing through his field of corn, then gently swayed by a summer breeze. "This," said he to himself, "is God's blessing on a sinner, for which he receives no thanks." He instantly re-

---

* "The bodily agitations, or exercises, attending the excitement in the beginning of this century, were various, and called by various names—as, the falling exercise; the jerks; the dancing exercise; the barking exercise; the laughing, and singing exercise, &c."—*Biography of W. B. Stone.*

solved that he would once more "praise the Lord for his goodness and for his wonderful works to the children of men." While, therefore, his wife was preparing dinner, he stole away into a grove; and there offered thanks to God, beseeching him to grant unto him faith and remission of sins, if indeed he was one of the *elect*—for he was a firm believer in the doctrine of eternal election, and faith as the direct gift of God, through the secret operation of the Holy Spirit. He was a firm believer also in the Bible, if he had known it; but he had been taught to expect "some great thing" instead of "the simplicity that is in Christ."

In search of faith he opened his mind to the Newlight preacher; but he received from him no consolation. He informed his uncle, a Baptist preacher, that he "could not obtain that divine faith which proceeds from the throne of God." His uncle tried to persuade him that he already had religion; and offered to receive him into fellowship. He refused, observing that he would never rest until satisfied of his pardon. "*That*," said his uncle, "*is a hard thing to know in this life, but we hope on till death.*" How little better the consolations of such religion than the uncertain hopes of immortality cherished by the heathen philosophers! Again he applied to an aged and intelligent Presbyterian, whose only reply was: "A man cannot help what he believes." He attended the meetings of the sects within his reach, ever in search of one object, which he already possessed—that is faith.

At last he obtained light on this subject in the following manner: On going, one day, to the house of his brother-in-law, he found his wife's sister alone and engaged in fervent prayer. He sat down on the door-step that he might not disturb her devotions. When she arose from prayer she approached him with a face bedewed with tears, and placed in his hand a small pamphlet, with the request that he would read it. It proved to be "*Stone, on the Doctrine of the Trinity, Atonement, and Faith.*" He read with avidity the essay on Faith, which was short, pointed, and evangelical. Among the quotations introduced were Romans x. 17, and John xx. 30. These passages relieved his mind; for if faith is only to believe that Jesus Christ is the Son of God, on the authority of the written word, he was satisfied that he had it. But he did not yet enjoy the conviction that his sins were forgiven; therefore he continued his efforts to obtain pardon. The common methods of seeking it in those days were by prayer and by endeavoring to claim, in a special manner, some promise of the Lord. To both these expedients he resorted; and in search of promises he happened upon these: "He that believeth and is baptized shall be saved." "Repent, and be baptized every one of you in the name of Jesus Christ, for the remission of sins, and you shall receive the gift of the Holy Spirit." Upon these promises he rested, assured that they indicated the way of salvation; and, notwithstanding that he had been once baptized, he resolved to obey the commands afresh, and receive God's word as the evidence of his pardon. He communicated his intention to his wife, who expressed her determination to do likewise. The only question was to what church they should present themselves; her relatives being Newlights and his being Baptists, to whose views he was strongly inclined. They were not long in deciding. John McClung, a Newlight, was preaching once a month in the neighborhood; and they attended his next meeting. He presented the Bible alone as the only sufficient rule of faith and practice; and, with great earnestness, urged all who loved the Lord Jesus in sincerity to forsake all human creeds, and unite on the foundation of apostles and prophets. This turned the scale in favor of the divine creed; and on the first Lord's day in January, 1817, they were immersed by John McClung. It was a clear, bitter cold day, and their garments froze upon them as they walked from the icy stream to the nearest house. But they were in possession of a good conscience; and, by faith, they rejoiced in the assurance of the remission of sins and the hope of eternal life.

Thus, under the religious systems of those times, was Elder Vawter *eighteen years* in experiencing the joys of salvation! Yet the same systems, slightly modified, are still recommended to the people as the gospel of the Son of God! How long, O Lord, how long, till the minds of the people shall no more be "corrupted from the simplicity that is in Christ!"

A little subsequent to his immersion, a church was organized in his neighborhood. Elder Vawter was appointed deacon; they held social meetings weekly; and the first year there were a great many additions. He then began to think of preaching to others the gospel he had been so long learning. But to this procedure two things stood opposed. At the door of the ministry the doctrine of "a divine and effectual call" confronted him. At this he halted, reflected, and prayed, until finally his uncle Jesse Vawter convinced him that *a good opportunity to do good is the best call to the ministry.*

This difficulty being disposed of, another yet remained. He was so timid that he almost despaired of ever being able to speak in public. Of this weakness the following incident is a correct exponent:

Having two children, which he wished to train up in the nurture and admonition of the Lord, he set up an altar, and instituted family worship. He conducted the service very well while the family were left to themselves; but it was not long until his mother came to pass a night under his roof. Her presence was a cross which he felt unable to bear. After a long conflict, conscience prevailed. He read a chapter, and offered his sacrifice of praise; but so confused was he that, on kneeling down to pray, he felt that he "was spinning round like a top," and when he arose his mother observed, "I thought you were a good reader, Beverly, but you can scarcely read at all."

This diffidence he gradually overcame by singing, praying, and exhorting in the social meetings, of which they had many; and, being encouraged to preach the gospel, he finally gained the consent of his mind to make the effort. Accordingly he was ordained as an evangelist in the year 1819, by Elders J. Crafton and John Henderson.

In order to support his family, he determined to invest his limited means in a carding machine. As he designed this to be driven by water power, he removed to Indiana in March, 1819, and settled a few miles above Madison, on the west fork of a small creek called Indian Kentucky. There he united with a church organized the summer before by John McClung and Henry Brown, preachers full of zeal and love, who have long since entered into rest. For that congregation he preached regularly; and, aided by Truman Waldron and Joshua Loudrey, he held there a protracted meeting, which resulted in many additions.

In 1820, having got his machine in successful operation, and employed a hand to attend to it, he began to devote the most of his time to the proclamation of the word. About this time he began to travel, his first tour being into Monroe county, where he held some interesting meetings. The burden of his preaching at that time was the sufficiency of the Holy Scriptures for the government of the Church of Christ; and in his humble way he did much to weaken public confidence in human creeds, and direct the minds of the people to the Bible as the only authority in matters of religion. . Thus was he preparing the way for the Reformation, which was nigh at hand.

In the winter of 1821 he visited a brother-in-law, who lived on Laughery creek, in a community in which sin so abounded that a Methodist and a Baptist preacher had been driven away by a mob. His brother-in-law received him kindly; took him over his farm; and did all in his power to interest him with things temporal; but the preacher's thoughts were on things spiritual and eternal: he was considering how he might get an opportunity to declare unto them the gospel.

As his host was a staunch Seceder, he did not suppose that he would be permitted to preach in his house; but night came, and, somewhat to his surprise, he was invited to read and pray with the family. The next day was Sunday, and he retired to rest, longing to see the truth planted in that place. That night he dreamed that he was invited to preach; and, before the sun arose, his dream was realized. His host and hostess invited him to preach in their house; and the appointment was speedily circulated. At the appointed hour the house was crowded; and, to his great surprise, the auditors were respectful and attentive. At the close of the discourse, he said he would visit them again if they would signify their consent by rising; whereupon every person in the house rose up. Accordingly he preached for them occasionally for about a year, but with few indications of reform.

The next winter, aided by Elder Jesse Mavity, he held a protracted meeting at that place, which resulted in a great many additions; among whom were several—perhaps all—of the Seceder's children. These were all immersed without their father's consent, as they had been sprinkled in infancy; except two, who had never been thus christened. The father himself led them down to the water, while the big tears rolled copiously down his cheeks. Such was the fruit gathered, by prudent management, where violence was expected.

In August, 1822, he held a protracted meeting at the mouth of Turkey Run, on Laughery creek, in a house built for his use, mainly by citizens who had not yet obeyed the gospel. His first discourse, on Church Government, he closed with an invitation to all who were disposed to place themselves under the government of the Lord. Several persons presented themselves, among whom were two Baptists. Many others were added during the progress of the meeting, which gave a great impetus to the Bible cause in that region. There he organized a church, which he visited for several years with gratifying results.

Sometime in the year 1823 he was invited to preach to a Baptist congregation on Hogan Creek. He went; and by sound and discreet teaching turned them all over to the divine creed and Christian name; for be it remembered that they called themselves *Christians*, and were called Newlights only to distinguish them from others who *claimed* to be "Christians" also, but would not call *themselves* by that name. In addition to this flock and their pastor, Joseph Shannon, there were among the converted a Methodist class and their leader, together with many from the world. These were all united on the one foundation.

In the year 1824 he organized another church on Otter creek, in which stream he immersed a great many. At that place there came to him a woman, saying that she had long been seeking religion, but could not obtain it; and that she greatly desired to be immersed because the Lord had commanded it. He asked her if she believed that Jesus Christ is the Son of God. When she had replied firmly in the affirmative, he said, "On this profession I will immerse you. 'If thou believest with all thy heart, thou mayst,' is the language of the Book." "But," said she, "my husband has declared that he will whip any man who attempts to baptize me. Must I obey him or my Saviour?" He replied, "It is better to obey God than man; come to-morrow to the baptizing, and we shall see." She came, and while he was immersing others she was prepared by the sisters, and conducted down to the water. Casting his eye up on the bank, he saw her husband, looking calm and composed; but, having resolved to immerse her at all hazards, he proceeded at once to the performance of the dangerous task. When she came out of the water praising God, the husband walked down to the edge of the stream; took the preacher by the hand; and invited him to his house for dinner! He observed to others that the work had been so nicely done that he could say nothing against it; but there was, no doubt, a more serious reason.

On another occasion, he immersed a woman, and thereby so enraged her husband that, at his next appointment, he was barely saved, by a civil officer, from violence at the hands of a mob. At the next meeting, also, the offended man called him out, saying that he wished to speak to him, and that he would not, at that time, injure him. Though opposed by the brethren, he went out; and was addressed by the man as follows: "Did you know, sir, when you baptized my wife, that it was being done contrary to my will?" "I did," replied the preacher. "Then," said he, "if ever you pass through my farm, I will whip you; I am able to do it, and I have a bundle of switches and a pile of stones prepared for you." For several years he submitted to the inconvenience of avoiding the belligerent soil. But thinking the matter was all forgotten, he one day attempted to pass through the premises in company with two other brethren. As they neared the house, the proprietor leaped over the fence, and gathered up a handful of stones, saying, "Back out, sir, back out. You remember what I told you." Had he attempted to advance instead of making good his retreat, he would doubtless have shared the fate of Stephen!

Soon after the meeting at Otter creek, he organized a church at Vernon, Jennings county, and subsequently preached extensively in Jefferson, Switzerland, Ohio, Decatur, Scott, Clarke, and some other counties.

Up to this time, it must be borne in mind, he had not entered fully into the Reformation. He was with it on the one platform, and on the action of baptism. *Theoretically* he was with it on the *design* of baptism, and sometimes *practically;* but in the main he yielded to the views of his fellow-preachers who clung to the old system with its mourner's bench.

At a protracted meeting held in 1826, he conversed with a brother Daniel Roberts with regard to baptizing believing penitents, or "mourners." He related the several cases that had occurred in his abnormal ministry, and expressed his belief that such persons were proper subjects for baptism. "Brother Vawter," said he, "give me your hand on that: I will preach it if I have to be sawn asunder for it."

Two years after that, at a protracted meeting held at Pleasant meeting house, in Jefferson county, this same Daniel Roberts came to him, took him aside, and thus addressed him: "Brother Vawter, the brethren have solicited me to inform you that you must desist from preaching baptism for the remission of sins. They say you will ruin your popularity by this procedure." "Is the doctrine true?" inquired Elder Vawter. "Yes; we must confess that it is found in the Bible," was the reply. "Be assured, then," replied the faithful minister, "that I shall continue to preach it, whatever may become of my popularity." "Then," said the would-be martyr, "I give you up for lost; and will so report you to the church."

In a short time he held a meeting near Greensburg, Decatur county, assisted by his true yoke-fellow Joseph Shannon, and a Baptist preacher named Daniel Douglas. On Lord's day his subject was the Kingdom of Heaven; and in the course of his remarks he, for the first time, boldly and publicly taught the "strangers and foreigners" how they might obtain citizenship in that Kingdom. Among his quotations was Acts ii. 38. By repeating this text he greatly offended his good brother, Douglas, who met him at the foot of the stand with the observation: "You preached rotten doctrine, to-day."

Vawter.—What did I teach that is wrong?

Douglas.—It is not "wrong;" it is *rotten*—rotten as a pumpkin, sir. You preached baptism for the remission of sins.

Vawter.—Did not Peter preach the same?

Douglas.—Yes, but he did not mean it. He meant "because of."

Vawter.—How do you know that? His words do not convey that idea, and if he meant "because of" why did he not say so? In the conversation that followed, the Baptist preacher stated that a man had recently passed through Kentucky, preaching that doctrine and thereby doing great mischief in the Baptist churches. That "man" was Alexander Campbell, never before heard of by Elder Vawter. He is not, therefore, a "Campbellite:" he obtained his views from Peter, and must at least be acknowledged as a *Peterite.*

Mortified by the difference of opinion between him and his senior co-laborer, he took his Bible; stole away into the forest; prayed God to guide him in the way of truth; and then read again and again the offensive passage: but he could not ascertain why Peter did not say what he meant, or why he should not be understood to mean what he said.

The next morning they met at the water. His friend Douglas preached on the all-engrossing theme, Baptism, and gave a synopsis of Campbell's views. Unlike many of his successors, he did it fairly; for he had sufficient sense to understand an argument when clearly stated; and such were his powers of memory that he could repeat almost *verbatim* any discourse he had ever heard. He then labored long to refute the doctrine stated; but when he descended from the pulpit, Elder Vawter said to him:—"Brother Douglas you did not refute it. You have been of great service to me to-day in telling how Campbell presents that subject." This discourse dispelled from his mind every lingering doubt on this important subject; and from that day he began to proclaim, with all boldness, the gospel as it was declared by the inspired apostles. Here the glorious light of the Reformation beamed directly upon him; he saw clearly the great first principles of Christianity; and all the mist and fog engendered by tradition and philosophy vanished away forever.

Returning home from Greensburg, he held a meeting near Thomas Jameson's, on Indian Kentucky. On Lord's day an orthodox preacher occupied the pulpit, and two persons "got religion" at the mourner's bench. On Monday Elder Vawter preached the more excellent way, from Peter's second discourse; Acts iii. 19. At the close of the sermon two persons professed their faith in Jesus; and were straightway immersed. As he went to the water he heard much complaint as to his novel procedure. A colored preacher, named Aaron Wallace, observed in the crowd, that brother Vawter "*had cut a new road to Heaven.*"

Returning to the house, he was rejoiced to find that

brother Jameson and his wife agreed with him upon the new doctrine; and a brother Samuel Humphreys also, met him in the yard, and handed him three dollars, saying, "That's the doctrine, brother Vawter. You will meet with opposition, but it will give way before the truth." This was the first money he ever received for preaching; and about the first encouragement to preach the plain word of God. The opposition did give way so rapidly that in a short time the majority were on the side of reform. Elder Vawter, being absent much of his time, advised the church to select three elders to preside over the congregation and administer the Lord's supper on every first day of the week. This proposition was agreed to, and John Eccles, William Guthrie, and Thomas Jameson were appointed elders. After this they, in all things, imitated the order of the churches in apostolic times.

In July, 1828, a conference was held near Edinburg, in Bartholomew county, for the purpose of effecting a union between the Newlights and the Dependent Baptists, who were represented on that occasion by that able and earnest union advocate, John Wright, sen., and other prominent preachers. Sectarianism had done its work so well in that community that, out of fifteen preachers present, Elder Vawter was the only one whose preaching would probably be acceptable to all parties. Being therefore pressed into the service, he discoursed to them on the government and unity of the primitive church, and with such effect that the contemplated union was speedily formed on the Bible creed and Christian name.

During the remainder of this year and the next, he was engaged in many remarkable meetings. Sometimes the tide of controversy would rise high; for the opposing currents of truth and error would meet in the same house. The Baptist and Newlight preachers would bring the people to the anxious seat to plead for pardon; and Elder

Vawter would approach them like Ananias, saying, "Why tarriest thou? arise and be baptized and wash away thy sins calling on the name of the Lord." With many other words would " he testify and exhort them, saying, Save yourselves from this untoward generation." Many of them would gladly receive the word; and the same hour of the day or night, would obey from the heart the form of doctrine delivered unto them, with an intelligent understanding that they were *then* to be made free from sin and become the servants of righteousness.

In the Spring of 1830 he was invited to Kent—then called White River—to preach at the funeral of a brother Ramsay. At the close of the services he was requested by Samuel Maxwell to deliver, immediately, a sermon on Primitive Church Government; and make an effort to organize a church. He complied with the request without leaving the house; and warmly exhorted the people to unite on the God-given foundation. Nine persons presented themselves, and the Church of Christ at Kent was then organized. With the exception of one serious and shameful disturbance it has enjoyed a peaceful and prosperous career, and is now one of the principal churches of south-eastern Indiana.

In the Summer of this same year, he was invited to attend the monthly meeting of a Separate Baptist church near the forks of Indian Kentucky. Their preacher and elder was a man by the name of Levitt, who was bitterly opposed to what he was pleased to denominate Campbellism. At the meeting on Sunday Elder Vawter preached, and four persons made the confession. The Baptist elder, being requested to attend to their immersion, replied indignantly, " No, sir, they are your converts—I will have nothing to do with them." The next day the elder came to meeting with Walker's Dictionary, which he thrust into the face of Elder Vawter, exclaiming, with an air of triumph, "There's what will refute your doctrine." But the Bible withstood even Walker's Dictionary, which gives "because of" as the only definition of "for." The meeting closed with good results; and Elder Vawter was invited to be with them at their next monthly meeting, at which time they proposed to examine their creed in the light of divine revelation. The meeting came on; the invited preacher was present; the creed was weighed in the balance and found wanting; and the Bible was accepted as their only rule of faith and practice. This was the origin of the Church of Christ, now known as Milton Church, which still yields the peaceable fruits of righteousness under the pastoral care of Charles Lanham.

In 1831 he visited Barton W. Stone at his residence near Georgetown, Kentucky. He arrived on Saturday evening, too late to attend a meeting then in progress. The next morning Elder Stone admonished him to prepare to preach that forenoon. At this juncture his subdued timidity revived again and plead for him many excuses, which were all unavailing. Just as he had consented to preach, a fine looking young man was ushered in, whom Elder Stone introduced as Elder John A. Gano. The presence of this strange and apparently polished preacher, greatly increased the weight of the cross that had been laid upon the brother from Indiana. On arriving at the place of worship he met Elder Frank Palmer, to whom also he was introduced as the preacher of the day. Despairing of being able to proclaim the gospel in the presence of so many superior workmen, he renewed his request to be excused. This being kindly denied, he ascended into the pulpit with a feeling of fear and trembling akin to that of Moses on the Holy Mount. He preached as best he could under the circumstances; the other two preachers made some remarks also; and Elder Stone closed the meeting with a most beautiful and touching exhortation. Nor was it a fruitless meeting; on the contrary some six or eight were added to the saved. He remained several days with brother Stone, whom he represents as so meek and affable that his presence was to the stranger as the society of old friends.

He returned home by way of Lexington, where he made the acquaintance of Dr. Fishback. On the way home he also met, for the first time, Elders Marshall and Paterson, with whom he made arrangements for holding a series of meetings, the next year, on both sides of the Ohio river, above Madison. These meetings were held; were largely attended; and resulted in great good.

Prior to the meetings above mentioned he made a tour through Switzerland county, where the light of the Reformation was just beginning to dawn. On one occasion, having preached to a large audience in which were many Methodists and Baptists—the dominant sects at that time—an aged Methodist minister arose in defense of the doctrines contained in the creeds This led to a sharp discussion, from which the Methodist soon withdrew in high dudgeon declaring that he would never again listen to such a preacher, and hoping that his brethren would close their ears and their *house* against him. Whereupon a Baptist by the name of John Buchanan invited Elder Vawter to leave another appointment, promising that he would procure for him the Baptist church. The appointment was left; but when he came to fill it, he found the door firmly secured by chain and padlock! He was therefore compelled to retire to an humble school-house; the only place, save the open air, in which even certain quotations from Holy Writ could find expression. But, although the rude doors of the orthodox churches could shut out the preacher, they could not exclude *all the light.* A sufficiency of rays gained admission to enable all who *would* see to discover their errors. Such as these gladly received the word, together with many who were wedded to no creed; and, even in the midst of such united opposition, a church was established on the foundation laid by the "wise master-builder." This result was effected, not by any extraordinary excitement, but by a plain, earnest declaration of the whole counsel of God. The "incorruptible seed" was sown indiscriminately, with a liberal hand, and, whenever it chanced to fall upon "good ground," it germinated and yielded its fruit as quietly as do the seeds deposited in the earth. The following incident will illustrate the influence of the simple truth in that community:

Once while Elder Vawter was waiting, at the house of a brother, for the return of night, at which time he was to preach, the wife of a Mr. Harvey entered the room where he was sitting, and, after the usual salutations, informed him that she wished to obey the gospel. Agreeably to the precedent established by the ancient evangelist, he replied, "If thou believest, thou mayst." She assured him of her faith in Jesus, the Son of God; was immersed the same afternoon; and to this day is a burning and shining light in the Church of Christ at that place. He had preached to her the word, on some previous visit; during his absence it had germinated; on his return it brought forth fruit.

In the year 1832, he travelled and preached, in company with Love H. Jameson, through the counties bordering on the Ohio, above the city of Madison. At Vevay they preached in the school-house; and from them the people of that village heard, perhaps for the first time, the repentance and remission of sins which began at Jerusalem. As they went from the place of worship to the spot where they had hitched their horses, they reflected on the unpleasant fact that they were in a strange land without a cent of money with which to procure food for themselves and their horses. While indulging these reflections their old friend Buchanan, the Baptist previously referred to, took them them to an inn, where both horses and riders were duly cared for. After dinner they again set out, neither knowing nor caring whither they went; for they sought only the lost sheep to bring them back to the Shepherd's fold. Wherever a door of utterance was opened there they set forth Christ crucified; and exhorted the people to receive and obey the truth. Upon this journey they were not *reapers* gathering into the Master's barn what was already ripe for the harvest, but *sowers* rather, removing the obstructions of sectarianism, and depositing, in the simple and candid hearts of those times, the incorruptible seed, which, through the labors of other men, brought forth abundant fruit to the glory of God and the advancement of the Redeemer's kingdom.

Soon after his return from this tour he so far lost his health that for several years he was unable to enter into the sanctuary of God. On his recovery he found the home church on Indian Kentucky in a bad condition, through indiscreet management and lack of regular preaching. His first effort after his recovery, was to deliver this flock from spiritual famine. In this he was entirely successful. Under his teaching and the wise rule of Elders Jackson and Halcomb, the church soon revived, and became stronger than at any past period in its history.

About the year 1850, the subject of Co-operation began to be agitated in southeastern Indiana; but it was a great while before there was much action in that direction. In the meantime Elder Vawter kept the field as in former years, making numerous proselytes; organizing here and there a church; warning the people against the delusion of Millerism; and endeavoring to turn them from all other *isms* to the faith of the gospel.

In the year 1853, a mass-meeting was held at North

Madison to devise a system of co-operation for the counties of Jefferson, Switzerland, Ohio, Ripley, Jennings, and Bartholomew. Of said meeting W. C. Bramwell was chairman, and Elijah Goodwin secretary. After due deliberation they appointed Beverly Vawter as an agent to raise funds, at a salary of $0.00 per annum; and his son Philemon Vawter as an evangelist, at a salary of six hundred dollars per annum. He accepted this agency, and was far more successful in raising money for others than he had ever been in his own behalf. In the course of fifteen months he payed into the treasury over one thousand dollars; and obtained pledges for as much more. He also made some fifty proselytes; and re-united a scattered flock at New Marion, Ripley county. His success so encouraged the Board that they voted him a compensation of two hundred dollars. At the expiration of the fifteenth month, his resignation, which had been several times tendered, was accepted by the Board; and, as the public predicted, the system of co-operation soon failed through lack of means.

After his resignation of the agency, he in a measure retired from the field, until some two years ago, when he preached a good deal while paying perhaps his last visit to his friends, relatives, and brethren in various portions of the country.

He is now in his seventy-third year; and what he may yet accomplish will not materially change the sum of his life-work. We may therefore present a brief summary of his labors in the Lord's vineyard.

He has organized thirteen churches on the apostolic basis; and immersed more than twelve hundred disciples, very many of whom are scattered throughout half the States of the Union, dispensing, wherever they go, the principles of the Reformation. He has also been instrumental in sending into the field several other preachers, whose labors have added many a living stone to God's building. Prominent among those whom he has set on Zion's walls is Love H. Jameson, his son in the gospel. He has faithfully preached *during forty-two years,* for which service he thinks he has received from the churches only eighty-seven dollars, plus a few presents, amounting in all to about one hundred dollars, or less than *two dollars and fifty cents per annum.* The church at Liberty, where he began to preach, and where he still officiates occasionally, is said to have paid him, for the services of nearly half a century, the sum of twenty-five dollars, or a little more than *fifty cents a year.* He could truthfully say to his brethren, in the words of the self-sacrificing Paul, " I have coveted no man's silver, or gold, or apparel. Yea, ye yourselves know that *these hands* have ministered unto my necessities and to them that were with me."

But his hands are now growing tremulous and feeble; and it is to be hoped that the brethren, among whom he has gone preaching the kingdom of God, will soon learn —nay, have already learned—" that so laboring they *ought to support the weak;*" and to remember the words of the Lord Jesus, how he said, "*It is more blessed to give than to receive.*"

———

Physically considered, Elder Vawter is of medium size. His frame is well proportioned, and it moves about with the easy, graceful, and dignified air of an old Kentucky gentleman. Stoutly compacted by nature, and carefully preserved by life-long habits of temperance, it seems to bear along easily the weight of three score years and ten. His sallow face is but slightly furrowed; his keen black eye gleams almost as of old; and the light of the other world, fast dawning upon him, has not yet chased *all* the dark shadows from his hair.

In mind, as in body, he is not a giant; but a man of

moderate ability, possessing a sound judgment, a clear perception, and an excellent memory. His head is best developed in the moral department; but his reasoning powers were worthy of a better cultivation than it was possible for them to receive.

He is a man of great firmness; of strong determination; and is at times, perhaps, a little self-willed—as are most men who accomplish any good in the world. There is not a little combativeness in his mental organism; and therefore he has never refused to take up the gauntlet when thrown down to him—never hesitated to assail whatever stood opposed to the glory of God, or the spiritual interests of man.

In the pulpit he is the impersonation of candor and of love to God and man. His plain address and the earnest expression of his honest face impress the hearer no less than what he says. He argues with considerable force, and speaks with tolerable fluency; but he is not an orator either born or made. He is a *documentary man*, always giving chapter and verse; and succeeding more by engaging the intellect than by storming the citadel of the heart.

In the church he is faithful, peaceable, liberal; having given far more for the support of the gospel than he has ever received for preaching it. So much of his means has been invested in heaven that he has but little treasure laid up on earth; yet he is *rich* in good works, ready to distribute, willing to communicate.

In society he is universally regarded as a man fearing God and following after righteousness. Though some may find fault with him as a *preacher*, all esteem him highly as a *neighbor* and *friend*. Much of his usefulness is owing to the fact that in every place he has possessed "a good name," which, by the evangelist especially, is rather to be chosen than great riches, or great learning, or great eloquence.

His value to the church of Christ and to the community in which he lives, will scarcely be realized until after his departure. This event cannot be far distant—his course must be almost finished. Like Bunyan's Pilgrim, he has passed, after a long and severe struggle, through the strait gate; traversed the Slough of Despond peculiar to the gospels which are of men; surmounted many Hills of Difficulty; and encountered lions in the persons of violent opposers of the truth. Soon will he cross the river of death; and press with his weary feet the golden pavements of the celestial city.

JOHN P. THOMPSON.

Elder John Philips Thompson was born in the city of Washington, D. C., March 6th, 1795. His grandfather on his father's side was a native of Scotland, born in Edinburg, in 1749. About the year 1770 he came to America, suffering himself to be sold for a season to pay the cost of his transportation. He subsequently married Nancy Perry, who is said to have been a distant relative of the hero of Lake Erie. They were blessed with six children, James, the father of John P., being the eldest of their four sons.

Elder Thompson's grandfather served in the Revolution; and an uncle on his mother's side lost his life in the struggle for independence. His father also served eighteen months in the war of 1812, and participated in the bloody and disastrous engagement at the river Raisin. Having survived the awful slaughter of that day, he afterwards joined an artillery company, and applied the match to the guns at the defence of Fort Meigs. He died in peace when almost eighty years of age.

Jonathan Philips, the grandfather of Elder Thompson, (on his mother's side,) was of English descent, and a member of the Church of England. He lived on the eastern shore of Maryland, where his daughter Mary, the mother of Elder Thompson, was born, bred, and married. She was of age at the time of the Revolution; and saw the French army on its march to Yorktown to assist in capturing the forces under Lord Cornwallis. In after years she often described to her children the stirring

events, and sang to them the patriotic songs of that era of heroism. By such means she inspired them with the love of liberty, and with an undying devotion to the flag of their country. She attained to the remarkable age of ninety-five years.

In the year 1800 James Thompson removed with his family to Kentucky, and settled near Germantown in Bracken county; whither his father had previously emigrated. The Thompsons were a religious people; and the most of them were members of the Baptist church. The grandfather of John P. was a preacher of that order, noted for the facility with which he could quote Scripture.

As Elder Thompson was only five years old when he came to the West, he claims to be a Kentuckian. His habits, as well as many of his political and religious opinions, were formed and confirmed in that renowned State which contains the graves of his ancestors. There too, he acquired his education, which was not better than that ordinarily received by the children of the West in that day.

Vice, especially in the forms of drunkenness, gambling, and profanity, prevailed all around him; yet through the influence of his pious parents, and in that quiet Baptist retreat, he formed habits of temperance, honesty, and piety, which have successfully resisted all the temptations incident to his long life. He naturally inclined to virtue's side; and he had also a laudable pride which would not permit him to do any thing that would have sullied the good name of his family.

It is perhaps natural, rather than remarkable, that in the midst of scenes of oppression he learned to sympathize with those in bonds; and became a firm believer in the doctrine that "all men are created equal; and are endowed by their Creator with certain inalienable rights;

among which are life, liberty, and the pursuit of happiness."

About the year 1805, a division on the subject of slavery took place in the Licking Locust church, which was a member of the Bracken Association. The said Association, in attempting to suppress the anti-slavery element, inflamed the other churches within its confines, and similar divisions occurred in the congregations at Ohio Locust, Lawrence creek, Mayslick, Mt. Sterling, New Hope, Gilgal, and several other points.

This new sect called themselves Friends of Humanity. They differed from their late Baptist brethren only on the slavery question; and proposed to return to their spiritual allegiance provided the Baptists would join them in a petition to the Legislature, praying for the gradual emancipation of the slaves. This proviso not being acceptable to the pro-slavery party, the Friends of Humanity formed an independent Association; and were subsequently among the first to embrace the current Reformation.

Mr. Thompson, though a small boy, imbibed the emancipation views of those people; which views he has held fast to the present day.

It was in the year 1812, and under the ministry of Jeremiah Vardemon, that he was first led to reflect upon his spiritual condition and his obligations to God.

Then came the usual long period of seeking and supplicating; of hoping for the mercy of God, and fearing that he was one of the non-elect.

At last, by a certain train of reflection—not by the knowledge that he had complied with the terms of pardon—he was brought to *feel* that his burden of sins had been removed. Soon afterwards (being then in his seventeenth year) he united with the Baptist Church, and was immersed by his grandfather.

When in his nineteenth year he was employed as a

country school-teacher; and so acceptable were his services in that profession that he was retained in the same neighborhood for a period of six years. While thus employed he acquired, by diligent self-instruction, the most of his own education.

When in his twenty-third year, he was married to Miss Priscilla Gregg; all of whose ancestors, as far back as known, were staunch members of the Society of Friends. At the time of their marriage both parties were very poor, their united fortune consisting of only a horse, a cow, and the essential articles of log-cabin furniture. But "better is a little with the fear of the Lord, than great treasure and trouble therewith."

In August, 1819—forty-three years ago—he began to preach the gospel in the community in which he lived. He would have commenced preaching at even an earlier period, but for the fact that he waited a long while for a special call from heaven.

The commencement of his public ministry was attended by a considerable revival of religion; and he at once became a preacher of some prominence. He preached regularly, once a month, for the home church, (Ohio Locust,) and also for the congregation at Lawrence creek. In a short time he began to travel abroad, visiting the churches in Mason, Nicholas, and Montgomery counties.

In the fall of 1819, while on his way to the Baptist Association, held that year in Butler county, Ohio, he stood for the first time upon the soil of Indiana. The following fall he again came to this State on a visit to some of his relatives, who urged him to settle near them. Accordingly he borrowed money, entered eighty acres of land in Rush county, and removed to it on the 22d of March, 1821.

Here he lived for several years in a log-cabin, working hard at the carpenter's bench and in the forest with handspike and axe. At log-rollings, clearings, house-raisings, etc., he was always on hand; and through his influence mainly a rule was established in the neighborhood, prohibiting the use of intoxicating liquors, on all such occasions. He has always been a zealous advocate of the temperance cause.

Very soon after his removal to Indiana he united with the Flat Rock (Baptist) church and began to preach for the same once a month. He also preached monthly at Franklin, near Connersville; and occasionally at Ben Davis Creek, Pleasant-Run, Blue River, and Antioch.

In 1822 he organized a church in Rushville, and had the pastoral care of it during his connection with the Regular Baptists.

In those days he travelled altogether on horseback or on foot, and received but little pay for his services. Ten dollars would perhaps cover all his cash receipts during his stay with the Baptists. Yet he does not complain of their treatment. They too were very poor—so poor that each could almost say with Peter, "Silver and gold have I none." They esteemed him very highly for his work's sake. The busy-fingered sisters occasionally presented him a homespun coat or vest; and the strong-armed brethren met together, prepared his firewood, split his rails, and made his fences.

In the Fall of 1821 he went as a delegate from the Flat Rock church to the White River Association which met that year at Franklin. Finding that body divided into two parties—some being ultra Calvinists who called the others Arminians—he sided with the latter; took an active part in the discussions, and at once became a leading spirit in the assembly. He was subsequently elected clerk of that body, and more than once had the honor of writing what was called the "circular letter."

One of his letters on the subject of Predestination was

printed by the Association; and it did much to modify the views of his ultra Calvinistic brethren. He was at this time very popular as well as influential among the Baptists, to many of whom he, in turn, was ardently attached. But the period of their separation was drawing nigh.

In June, 1826, he became a subscriber for the Christian Baptist. In that he read accounts of remarkable meetings held in various parts of Kentucky by Elders Walter Scott, John Smith, and other pioneer Reformers. Ere long he learned that the tide of reformation had reached his old home in Kentucky: and that many of his friends and relatives were worshipping God in the way which was generally called heresy. Anxious to discover the means which seemed so effectual in turning people from the old paths, he resolved to revisit the scenes of his childhood, and listen to the teachers of the strange, subversive doctrine.

Arriving upon the spot he found the reports true—that those who were turning the world upside down had indeed come thither also. He listened to the views of his friends without losing much of his former faith. He went to hear Elder Abernathy, the chief Reformer in that locality: but even he did not convince him of any superior excellence in what he regarded as the new way.

At the close of his sermon the speaker gave notice that John Smith would preach at that place on the next day. Though Elder Thompson was on the eve of returning home as he had come, he resolved to remain one day longer in order to hear the discourse of one as renowned for his acumen as for his eccentricity. Elder Smith was accompanied by a young brother Payne, who spoke first, presenting the facts and conditions of the gospel with great force and clearness. When he concluded Elder Smith arose; and in his peculiar manner said, "I have no doubt that while my brother was speaking you were thinking as I was, of that passage of Scripture which saith, "The natural man receiveth not the things of the Spirit of God; for they are foolishness unto him; neither can he know them, because they are spiritually discerned." This very passage had been in the mind of Elder Thompson; and he had employed it to rebut many of the texts introduced by the first speaker. It was, indeed, the key-stone of his whole theological system. After listening to the profound exposition of the passage, he seriously doubted the correctness of his former teachings; and without revealing his thoughts to any one he resolved to examine carefully the whole ground.

He entered upon this investigation with fear and trembling; for he had a presentiment that he would find himself in error; and he foresaw the estrangement, the strife, the schism that would result from any attempt to change his position. He spoke of all this to his wife; and with her full consent, he resolved to open his understanding to every ray of light and to follow the truth of God at whatever sacrifice of property, friends, or reputation.

The next time he met with the congregation at Flat Rock, he felt but little inclination to preach; for the old landmarks had been removed, while others had not been firmly established in their stead. However, he took for his text John v. 1, because he could discourse upon that without revealing his new views or his doubts relative to his old ones; and the brethren were well pleased as usual with his teaching.

The next meeting was at a brother Elias Stone's house, an humble cabin with a puncheon floor and a rude porch on one side. A large congregation for that day were seated in the house and on the porch; while Elder Thompson, who by this time had a tolerable knowledge of the Christian system, took his position in the door to declare once more to his humble neighbors "the unsearchable riches of Christ." He did not intend at that time to bring any "strange things" to the ears of his brethren; but his mind was full of great ideas recently acquired, and his heart was swelling with unfeigned devotion to God and sincere desires for the welfare of his fellow men. When, therefore, he was about half through his sermon, his spirit overleaped all barriers that creeds and traditions had thrown around it; and, as if suddenly inspired, he proclaimed to his astonished hearers the fullness, the freeness, the simplicity of the gospel of Christ.

That morning's service was the beginning of a great reformation in eastern Indiana. Hitherto the people had taken but little interest in the study of the Bible, having been taught that it was designedly incomprehensible to the unregenerate mind. But now all was excitement, searching the Scriptures, animated private discussions, and flocking to the house of worship to hear the public teachers and compare their views with the word of God. The preacher's dixit was no longer profitable for doctrine, nor was the Confession of Faith an end of all controversy. The people were beginning to demand for every tenet a "thus saith the Lord."

There were at that time but three houses of worship in Rush county; and these were merely closed in—not finished. The uncovered sleepers served for pews; a rude box, filled with clay, on which glowed a heap of charcoal, constituted the warming apparatus; and a clapboard, nailed to the top of a couple of great pins or posts inserted in the sleepers completed the substitute for a pulpit. To these houses, when the private cabins would no longer hold the increasing audiences, the worshippers resorted; and they were frequently filled with anxious inquirers after truth, many of whom came a distance of ten or twelve miles, and returned home the same day or night.

Elder Thompson was, of course, the chief speaker. He travelled over the whole county, inculcating the doctrine of the apostles so far as he had learned it. The most of the converts of that day have remained steadfast; and the church called Boundary Line, in Wabash county, has now within its pale many of the fruits of the early reformation.

Elder Thompson was still a nominal Baptist. The more orthodox of his brethren had perceived with regret the change that had taken place in his preaching; but they esteemed him very highly as a brother, and on that account were disposed to say to one another, "Let brother Thompson alone : it is owing to the excitement that he fails to inculcate the received doctrines; and when the revival is over he will teach the converts " experience and doctrine"—a phrase which simply meant that he would return to the traditions of the fathers.

Thus matters went on until about sixty members—all Reformers—withdrew from the Flat Rock church with its consent; and, at a more convenient point in Fayette county, were organized as a separate church on the foundation of apostles and prophets.

But he did not long enjoy the blessedness of such toleration. The leading orthodox preachers having given their voices against him, many of his nearest neighbors and most intimate friends could no longer listen patiently to his teaching. At first they endeavored to dissuade him from his course; but he continued witnessing to both small and great, and appealing to the Scriptures as proof that he taught none other things than those which he had learned and received from the apostles. All other means having proved ineffectual, they determined to cast him out of the synagogue. They arraigned him before the congregation, and both prosecution and defense were conducted in the presence of a large and intensely excited audience.

It was finally agreed that the church should decide by a vote whether or not his teaching was heretical; and the vote being taken it was decided by a majority of seven that he taught according to the oracles of God. It being a well established law of the church that the majority should rule in every case, he immediately turned the tables upon his prosecutors; and had he been so disposed, *he might have excluded every one of* THEM *for heterodoxy!* But he was unwilling to attempt, himself, what he had so recently condemned in them; so the proceedings were discontinued and the *Inquisition* adjourned.

At the next official meeting it was agreed by the two parties that they should occupy the house alternately for one year. A short time afterward Mr. Thompson and those whose views coincided with his own, formed a separate organization called the Church of Christ; and gave to one another the hand of *Christian* fellowship.

Thus did he enter fully into the Reformation; and thus did he bring with him out of the Flat Rock church, the nuclei of what are now two large and flourishing churches of the living God.

On the next Lord's day after their organization, an eccentric Baptist preacher by the name of Thomas (commonly called the White Pilgrim, on account of his white raiment) was present, and, by request, preached. A great many "Newlights," of whom there was a large congregation about two miles to the north, were present on that occasion, and they became greatly offended because not specially invited to the Lord's table. Out of this circumstance there arose a great controversy on the subject of communion, which warfare was zealously participated in by Elders Thompson and John Longley, then a member of the Newlight congregation mentioned above.

At last the difficulty was amicably adjusted. Elder Longley with the majority of his brethren soon came over to the Reformation; and he became also a zealous advocate of the ancient gospel.

In the mean time the congregation was greatly strengthened by accessions from the world, and by immigrant disciples from Kentucky, among whom was Elder Benjamin F. Reeve. He, having already commenced preaching, was soon associated with Elder Thompson in the eldership of the congregation, which they directed and edified with the most perfect unanimity for nineteen years.

So great was the prosperity of the new church that within one year after its organization a new house of worship was erected. None were more liberal or zealous than Elder Thompson in the prosecution of this enterprise.

In the Fall of 1832, John O'Kane first visited Rush county, where he was employed to evangelize for one year. He and Elder Thompson travelled together over the counties of Rush, Fayette, and Decatur, being the first at almost every point to publish the doctrine of the Reformation. When they arrived at Greensburg, O'Kane rang the court-house bell; a small audience collected; Thompson preached; and one came forward to confess the Lord. This was the first evangelical sermon and the first disciple at that place, which is now the centre of a powerful influence in favor of primitive Christianity. O'Kane followed, and three others made the good confession.

At night they preached at a point four miles northwest of Greensburg; and two were added to the saved—one of them a daughter of a brother North Parker, who is believed to have been the first person that embraced the ancient gospel in Eastern Indiana.

From that point they continued their journey, the people everywhere gladly receiving the word. Though sectarian opposition was very strong; and though there was much ill-feeling toward O'Kane, growing out of his active participation in the Presidential campaign; still the disciples were multiplied, new churches were established, prejudices were eradicated, and Bible principles inculcated.

Thus the work was carried forward for several years, Elder Thompson being always in the van.

But about the year 1836 he was compelled to greatly circumscribe the area of his operations. The demands of his large and increasing family could no longer be supplied by however diligent a use of a small portion of his time. Therefore he ceased in a great measure to preach the gospel in the regions beyond his own county. But there, without money and without price, he has continued until this day to warn the unruly, comfort the feeble-minded, edify the faithful, and point the children and grand-childern of his old pioneer friends to "the Lamb of God that taketh away the sin of the world."

In April, 1849, his wife, who had faithfully shared all his toils and privations, departed this life. She died in faith, leaving with her husband a large family of children.

In 1851 he was married to Mrs. Mary Allen of Connersville; and the year following he removed to his little farm near Fayetteville, in Fayette county, where he expects to pass the remainder of his days. Already tremulous with age; the work given him by the Master well-nigh finished; a large portion of his family beyond "death's cold flood," and all the survivors, save one, heirs of the kingdom; he is only waiting for the welcome moment that shall pierce the vail of mortality and reveal to him what "eye hath not seen."

He has reserved for his burial place a spot in the old church-yard at Flat Rock, desiring that his dust may repose beneath the old vine, which, planted by his own hand over thirty years ago, now shoots forth its branches over the wall.

Elder Thompson is a man of medium height, and slender frame. He was once remarkably stout and active; but heart and flesh are fast failing. His complexion is light. His hair, now white as wool, was once quite dark. His eyes are blue—their expression intelligent, cheerful, benignant.

He is a man of warm and generous emotions; ardently attached to his friends; sincere in his supplications for the whole human family.

Though a man of good natural abilities, yet it is for his goodness rather than his intellectual power that he is so highly esteemed by all who know him.

He is a good speaker and an excellent exhorter. His delivery is fluent and forcible; his manner, grave, very earnest, unostentatious. He pretends to be no more than he is—a plain, humble preacher of the olden time.

Though he has walked for half a century in the midst of a very crooked and perverse nation; yet his Christian character is without spot or blemish.

His whole Christian life has been characterized by supreme devotion to the interests of the Redeemer's kingdom.

At one time especially when sorely pressed for the means of a comfortable subsistence, his friend, Dr. Jefferson Helm, made the most tempting proposals to induce him to exchange the ministerial for the medical profession. But he replied, "*I am engaged in a great work, and cannot come down.*"

Having thus steadfastly suffered affliction with the people of God, well may he look forward to the recompense of the reward. Having sown, in tears, the incorruptible seed, he is soon to return, with rejoicing, to the Husbandman, taking his sheaves with him.

Yours in Christianity,
A. Camp.

MICHAEL COMBS.

Prominent among the early Reformers in Indiana was Elder Michael Combs. He was born in East Tennessee, February 17th, 1800. His father, Job Combs, was of Scotch descent, and of the Presbyterian faith. The Combses were generally an intelligent, high-toned people, though they moved in the humbler walks of life, and were not blessed with liberal education. As a general thing their predilections were not so much for the ministry as for the worldly professions—especially law.

His mother's maiden name was Abigail Coons. She was of German descent. The Coonses were mostly Baptists, noted for their piety and zeal for God. Among them were many preachers, one of whom, John Coons, was imprisoned, in the days of the Revolution, by the English or Episcopal church.

The mother of Elder Combs died when he was quite young; whereupon he and his brother Job were placed in the family of a maternal uncle who was a strict Baptist of the Calvinistic dye. By him the orphan boys were taken exclusively to the Baptist church, where they received a strong bias in favor of that faith.

Being brought up under such circumstances their education was, of course, greatly neglected. They were simply taught to read and write—no more. In early youth, however, they were both very fond of good books; and they read with great avidity every volume upon which they could lay hands. Michael especially became much interested in the historical portions of the Old Testament;

and the account of the creation, the translation of Enoch, the destruction of Sodom, and other important events did not fail to make a deep impression on his mind and heart. The earnest appeals of the Baptist preacher also affected him seriously; and so did the earthquakes that occurred about the year 1811.

On account of these various causes, his soul was greatly cast down and disquieted; and had the preachers of that day spoken according to the oracles of God, he would, no doubt, have been a disciple before he reached his fourteenth year. As it was, however, his religious impressions soon wore away; and he walked in the way of his heart and in the sight of his eyes, unmindful of Solomon's admonition, that "for all these things God would bring him into judgment." Being of a very mirthful and mischievous disposition, he was easily turned altogether out of the way.

About this time, his father, who had married again, determined to remove to Ohio, which was then regarded by the East Tennesseeans as a land flowing with more than milk and honey. Finding no location to suit him, he proceeded as far west as Wayne county, Indiana, where for a short time he pitched his tent. His neighbors were nearly all Quakers, whose quiet worship and solemn demeanor had but few attractions for his two sons, who had accompanied him from the land of their birth.

At length their father settled in Preble county, Ohio, near the line separating it from Indiana. Here Michael fell among a class of Christians called Newlights—a people as different from the Quakers as the Quakers were from the Baptists. It was commonly reported that they denied the divinity of Christ, and the doctrine of the atonement; that they were Arminians; that they held faith to be merely an act of the creature; that they had no creed but the Bible; and that as to their origin they were a people only of yesterday.

By far the most prominent preacher among them at that time and place was David Purviance. One day, when he was to preach near by, young Combs felt like the Jews of Rome when they said "we desire to hear of thee what thou thinkest; for as concerning this sect, we know that everywhere it is spoken against." Accordingly he went to the meeting, and was favorably impressed by the fine personal appearance and the mild, affectionate bearing of the speaker. The text was, "Come unto me, *all* ye that labor and are heavy laden; and I will give you rest." The sermon was the plainest, the most consistent, the most affecting he had ever heard —altogether different from the discourses of the Calvinistic Baptists to whom he had been wont to listen. With them clearness or simplicity was no desideratum. Indeed, the more incomprehensible the subject could be made to appear to sinners, the more indubitable was the evidence that the preacher was "sent from God:" for they reasoned thus:

1. The natural man (sinner) receiveth not the things of the Spirit of God; they are foolishness to him.
2. The preaching we hear is all foolishness to us, (sinners.)
3. Therefore the preaching we hear is "of the Spirit of God."

After hearing Elder Purviance that day, Elder Combs frequently attended the meetings of the Christians. He became convinced of the propriety of their plea for a union of all the saints; and was favorably impressed by the fact that they themselves loved one another fervently, and endeavored to keep the unity of the Spirit in the bond of peace. Therefore, though he did not unite with them, he became a zealous defender of their *characters*, if not of all their views.

On the first of January, 1818, he was married to Mary Edwards, who had been brought up among the Quakers of North Carolina. She of course inclined to that faith, although, to her, it was very far from being "full of comfort." On the contrary, she was a victim of despondency, having been forced to the conclusion that she was one of the "vessels of wrath fitted to destruction." Her husband, though yet a great sinner, became a preacher of righteousness so far as to dispel all her fears of reprobation, and induce her to attend the meetings of the Christians. With them she soon united, being received without baptism, out of deference to her Quaker views. This error also she subsequently corrected; and although forty-two years have since elapsed, she still lives "in hope of the glory of God."

She is the mother of thirteen children, eleven of whom are living; and all of whom, save one, have become obedient to the faith.

Soon after her conversion, Elder James Hughes, "an eloquent man and mighty in the Scriptures," but "*knowing only the baptism of John*," came to a camp-meeting held in that vicinity. Among his hearers on Monday morning was Job Combs, jr., who had, perhaps, spent the previous day in the society of his sinful associates; and who had come there "to see that Newlight cut up" —as he expressed it on leaving home. In a sad, earnest tone the speaker announced his text: "Hear, O heavens, and give ear, O earth; for the Lord hath spoken; I have nourished and brought up children, and they have rebelled against me. The ox knoweth his owner, and the ass his master's crib; but Israel doth not know; my people doth not consider."

The passage touched the heart of young Combs, to

whom it was so beautifully applicable; and for once he resolved to listen respectfully to the preaching of the word. Of its effect he himself could not better tell than in the touching words of the melancholy poet:

> "With many an arrow deep infix'd
> My panting side was charg'd when I withdrew
> To seek a healing balm* in distant shades.
> There was I found by One who had himself
> Been hurt by th' archers. In his side he bore,
> And in his hands and feet, the cruel scars.
> With gentle force soliciting the darts,
> He drew them forth, and healed, and bade me live."

The conversion of Job led his brother to consider his ways, and determine to reform his life. But he was not equally fortunate in obtaining speedily a satisfactory evidence of the remission of his sins. He did indeed forsake his wicked ways and his unrighteous thoughts, and he did experience a great change in his feelings; but he could not give a reason for the trembling hope that was in him. In short, he was converted in *heart* and *life;* but in *state* or *relation* he was unconverted.

After remaining long in this doubtful state of mind, he finally resolved to attempt the cleansing of his way by "taking heed thereto according to God's word." In pursuance of this resolution, he became a diligent student of the Holy Scriptures, which were not long in making him wise unto salvation. Through the whole course of his long and eventful life, that word has been a "lamp to his feet and a light to his path."

He was about twenty-one years of age when he thus took the Bible as the man of his counsel, and *relying mainly upon the purity of his motives and the sincerity of his desires*, ventured to join the church, and regard himself as a Christian. Unable to designate the time

* "To seek a tranquil death in distant shades."—*Original.*

and place at which "the Lord spoke peace to his soul," (a thing which believers generally professed to do,) he was very far from having strong consolation; yet, clinging to his faint hope, he groped his way, relying upon the divine assurance that "the path of the just is as the shining light that shineth more and more unto the perfect day."

About the year 1822 he and his brother Job both commenced exhorting and preaching. A short time afterwards there occurred in their neighborhood a great "revival," many of the fruits of which were of that substantial kind which is "unto holiness, and the end everlasting life." Several young men that were brought into the church at that meeting subsequently became useful and somewhat distinguished preachers of the gospel.

During that meeting many also came in who had been trained up in the Quaker faith. Under the lenient rule which that church (Newlight) still retains, without the authority of one single apostolic precept or example, all these were received into full fellowship without submitting to the initiatory ordinance. Even Elder Combs himself, though a preacher of the gospel, had never yet obeyed it! Though his boyhood had been passed among Baptists, whose views he sincerely received, and for awhile firmly held, yet he had associated so long with Quakers that their traditions had made the word of God of none effect. So true is it that "evil communications corrupt good manners."

Elder David Purviance, who was a man of great independence of thought, seems not to have been among those who (with the good intent of removing what they regarded as a great obstacle in the way of Christian union) were willing to concede that obedience to a positive commandment was a "non-essential." Certain it is that he assumed the responsibility of preaching to the converts above named, and also to Elder Combs, a most convincing sermon relative to the duty of being immersed. So clearly and so powerfully did he develop the subject, that Elder Combs and many others tarried no longer, but arose and were baptized. Such was the singular and circuitous manner in which the subject of this sketch entered into the kingdom.

After his immersion, he began to enlarge the field of his ministerial operations; and it therefore became necessary for him to be licensed. Duly recommended by the congregation of which he was a member, he appeared before the Conference as an applicant for license. For some cause he was not regarded with much favor by that body; and it was by only a small majority that he was commissioned as a preacher of the gospel. This hesitation on the part of the Conference troubled him but little; for feeling that he had received a special call from God, it made no difference whether his preaching was acceptable to that body or not.

At first it was "in weakness, in fear, and in much trembling" that he waited on his ministering. Being very poor, his family were dependent on his labors for their daily bread; and his reputation as a preacher was not such as to command any considerable remuneration. Thus during the greater part of the time he was compelled to labor with his hands for the maintenance of his household. Yet "forgetting those things which were behind, and reaching forward to those things which were before, he pressed toward the mark for the prize of the high calling of God in Christ Jesus."

Acting upon the suggestion of Paul to Timothy, he determined to "*study* to show himself approved unto God, a workman that needeth not to be ashamed." Accordingly he addressed himself energetically to an investigation of the principal doctrines that agitated the minds of those within the church, and blinded the eyes of those without. By a faithful prosecution of this course he rapidly multiplied his intellectual resources, and qualified himself to act successfully the important part subsequently assigned him in the Reformation.

About the year 1826 he removed to Montgomery county, Indiana, having entered eighty acres of land near Crawfordsville. There he found no organized church; but there were a few brethren and sisters, whose religion was bitterly opposed and grossly misrepresented.

He at once volunteered his services as a preacher; but being a stranger there it was feared by the brethren that he might not be able to resist the attacks which, it was certain, any demonstration on their part would provoke. Finally, however, they agreed to let him preach one sermon. At the same time it was privily agreed that a certain old brother, the "wise man" among them, should sit in the "judgment seat" on the occasion. If in his opinion the discourse should indicate present ability and future usefulness on the part of the preacher, they were to commit their precarious cause to his hands. If, on the contrary, the effort should be feeble and unsatisfactory, they were to give him neither encouragement nor a second trial.

The day came. With anxious hearts came also the persecuted few who held fast the Lord's name; while those of the world and of the orthodox churches took their places in the assembly, thinking, "What will this babbler say?" Inspired by the circumstances surrounding his critical position, he made a most happy effort, which won for him, not only the favorable decision of the judge, but also the love and confidence of the entire little brotherhood.

That day was the beginning of active operations in a new and extensive field. It was the early dawn of the

Reformation in that section of Indiana. Many false and injurious impressions were soon removed; the views he advocated found favor in the eyes of a few of his neighbors; and the materials were soon ready out of which to organize a new church.

But before this object could be accomplished it was necessary that he should be ordained. For that purpose he went to the Conference, which convened that year at Old Union, in Owen county. Having passed his examination, he was required to give his examiners a specimen of his sermonizing. For this, the second time, he was successful in running the gauntlet; and it was therefore ordered that he should be ordained to the ministry by Jesse Hughes and Jesse Frasier.

This being done he immediately organized a small church near or upon his farm in Montgomery county. The organization was subsequently removed to Crawfordsville; and thus the present flourishing church at that place had its origin.

From Crawfordsville he visited many points in the White River Valley; at the most, if not all of which points, he was the first to oppose human creeds, and plead for a union of all Christians on the *Bible alone*.

About this time he began to hear startling rumors concerning a certain Alexander Campbell that was said to have appeared, as a great fault-finder, at Bethany, Va. To the most of Mr. Campbell's views as currently reported, he was heartily opposed; but he rejoiced to hear that the confessedly able editor of the Christian Baptist was an uncompromising opposer of all creeds and confessions of faith not given by inspiration of God. But penury and prejudice prevented him from subscribing for the Christian Baptist; and for two or three years he continued his ministerial labors in the manner peculiar to the Old Christian Body.

In the mean time Mr. Campbell made a tour to the West, and Elder Combs improved the opportunity thus afforded of hearing the remarkable man that was causing such commotion among the numerous "branches" of the church. The preacher, who was then in the prime of life, did not fail to bring certain strange things to the ears of Elder Combs, who found but little fault with the views presented. But then it was whispered about that "the half had not been told"—that the speaker with characteristic shrewdness had concealed his objectionable sentiments. Therefore while "some said, He is a good man," others said, "Nay; but he deceiveth the people."

These sly insinuations greatly diminished the effect which the great truths to which he had listened would otherwise have produced on the mind of Elder Combs. As it was, however, his attention was directed to certain passages of Scripture, which in due season convinced him of the error of his way.

Soon after hearing Elder Campbell preach, he became a reader of his magazine. In that the distinction between Christianity and the traditions of men was so clearly pointed out that he could not fail to be convinced of the necessity of reform. Yet, fearing the people, he, for a long while, kept these things in his heart. Gradually adding courage to his faith, he ventured to advocate the ancient gospel in the *corner* though he did not yet dare to proclaim it upon the *housetops*. In this private manner he made a few converts; and thus prepared the way for the change which was soon to follow.

Finally, the few brethren that had gladly, though privately, received the word, prevailed upon him to teach the people, publicly, that they were required to "repent and be baptized every one of them [you] in the name of Jesus Christ for the remission of sins." *This he did for the first time at a protracted meeting held in Edgar county, Ill., in the year* 1833.

This departure from the orthodox track—made with great hesitation and only at the urgent and repeated requests of his brethren—was, as he anticipated, equivalent to a declaration of war. Brethren that had stood by him in many an hour of need, suddenly arrayed themselves against him; sects that had bitterly opposed one another entered tacitly into an alliance to destroy the common foe; and, in Western Indiana, the great conflict between truth and error had begun. Public debates and private disputations were of frequent occurrence; the precepts of the apostles and the example of the first Christians were the all-absorbing topics of the day; and almost every professor of religion, from the least even to the greatest, was converted into a Berean, searching for himself the Scriptures to see if certain things were so.

Into this unequal warfare Michael Combs entered with great zeal, and at a great personal sacrifice. Having preached several years for almost nothing he had just reached a position in which his labors were beginning to be appreciated and rewarded; and in abandoning that position he voluntarily deprived himself of that which afforded a comfortable livelihood, and subjected himself to the necessity of again preaching the gospel without money and without price.

But while there were noble men to make these sacrifices for truth, there were noble women also whose industry replaced much of that which was lost—women who laid their hands to the spindle and whose hands held the disstaff—women who rose while it was yet night and gave meat to their households—women who considered fields and bought them, who with the fruit of their hands planted vineyards—women who looked well to the ways of their households, and ate not the bread of idleness.—(Prov.

xxxi.) The efforts of these busy-fingered Christian mothers must not be overlooked in searching out the causes of the rapid extension of the Reformation in the great West.

About the time the battle began to wax hot, Job Combs, J. Secrets, and Lewis Comer, all valiant soldiers from Ohio, appeared on the field. Secrets was a man of strong mind, mighty in word and doctrine. Comer, of less ability, but of a more excellent spirit, "adorned the doctrine of God our Saviour in all things." Job's gift was exhortation; and in the exercise of that gift he had no superior in that day.

Encouraged by the arrival of these timely reinforcements, Elder Combs continued the good fight of faith. For a period of twelve years he was one of the very foremost in the strife. He and his coadjutors went everywhere in Western and Central Indiana, preaching the word. "And so were the churches established in the faith, and increased in number daily." These results followed because the truth was mighty; the preachers were zealous; the brethren were exemplary; and many of the people were tired of the prevailing systems, and eager to be shown a more excellent way.

In the year 1833 he went into Bartholomew county on some business of a secular character. Conversing, one day, with an old lady and gentleman, on the subject of religion, the parties differed widely and were drawn into quite a spirited discussion. Finally, the old lady observed to her husband, "This stranger talks just like Jo. Fassett." On inquiry he learned that there was a Newlight church near by (at New Hope) and that "Jo. Fassett" was a leading preacher of that order. On Lord's day he went to that place of worship; and there made the acquaintance of Elder Fassett, and of many brethren whose religious views did indeed coincide with his own. He found in Elder Fassett an earnest advocate of the union of all

Christians on the Bible alone; and they immediately set about concerting measures to unite the disciples of Montgomery and the adjacent counties with the Newlights of Bartholomew and other counties to the north and west of that.

For this purpose a union meeting was appointed at the Bluffs of White River, in Morgan county. On the appointed day hundreds of people and a great number of preachers of both parties, met together. It was agreed that the preachers who had been Calvinistic Baptists and those who were called "Aminian Newlights," should preach a few times alternately in order that the differences between the parties might be made manifest. Elder Fassett, being the senior preacher on his side, led off on Friday morning; and the meeting was conducted as agreed upon until the next Monday evening. Both parties having renounced all human creeds, and both preaching for doctrine the Scripture given by inspiration of God, there appeared no material difference between them. All the speakers seemed to be of the same judgment, and to all speak the same thing. As early as Lord's day, it was evident that there were to be no more divisions between those two bodies of Christians. Hundreds sat down together that day at the table of their common Lord; and their communion was "as the dew that descended upon the mountains of Zion—for there the Lord commanded the blessing." The middle wall of partition was completely broken down; and so far as those represented in that assembly were concerned, there were henceforth but one fold and one Shepherd.

This meeting added greatly to the strength of the Reformation. One more subborn *fact* was opposed to those who affected to regard the union of all Christians as a thing by no means feasible.

About the same time Elder Combs was invited to attend a great camp-meeting to be held by the Newlights near Bloomington in Monroe county. Elders Frank Palmer, John Smith, and other distinguished preachers of Kentucky were expected to be present. He was loth to accept this invitation; because the State University was located at that point; and he feared he could not preach acceptably in a region in which he supposed learning did greatly abound. But he finally concluded with Paul when he said, "I am debtor both to the Greeks and to the Barbarians; both to the wise and to the unwise. So as much as in me is I am ready to preach the gospel to you that are at Rome also."

It so happened that the preachers from Kentucky did not come; and but for his presence there would have been a great disappointment. This circumstance inclined the people to listen more patiently to the strange views he presented. He soon secured the attention of the vast assembly—of the learned as well as the unlearned. A general and unprecedented interest was awakened in the community; and during the progress of the meeting more professors than non-professors were converted to the religion of the Lord Jesus. This was the beginning of the Reformation in Monroe county, where the Newlights were very numerous. So well was the work commenced, and so successfully has it been prosecuted, that now there is not a single congregation—perhaps not a single member—of the old Christian body in Monroe county.

Among those who gladly received the word at that meeting was David Batterton, who had been for some time an unbaptized member of the old Christian church, and who has been for many years an elder and a strong pillar in the house of the Lord at Bloomington. His wife also, who had fallen into the Slough of Despond, was rescued through obedience, and made an heir of the heavenly inheritance into the possession of which she soon entered.

At another time he held a meeting in a strong Methodist community in Henry county. Among his hearers at that time was Benjamin Franklin, who had then made no profession of religion. To him the views of Elder Combs seemed both reasonable and scriptural; and he defended them when attacked by those who resisted the truth. At that time and place may have been partially bent the twig, which subsequently took such deep root and shot forth so vigorously.

These meetings are here mentioned merely as indices of the manner in which the truth was propagated in the former days. To mention all—to record the many remarkable conversions of that day—to enumerate the preachers old and young that were taught the way of God more perfectly—to describe the many happy scenes that were enacted at the firesides of those humble people who often spent the greater part of the night in talking of the law of the Lord—would require far more space than can be given in a sketch like this.

For twelve or fifteen years Elder Combs gave himself almost entirely to the word, leaving to his wife the care of his family. During all this time he stood in the front rank of Reformers, and exerted a strong influence in many parts of the State.

But finally the cares of this world choked the word, and he became *comparatively* barren and unfruitful. Though he did not err from the faith; yet, in seeking to increase his earthly possessions, he "pierced himself through with many sorrows."

It was not for his own sake, or because of an innate love of money that, to the partial neglect of the word, he turned his attention to the affairs of this life. But his children were growing up, and he longed for means to educate them and give them a "start" in the world. Impelled by this motive, he plunged into business of a secular kind; and entered upon the dangerous experiment of serving God and Mammon. At first he turned his attention to farming. Afterwards he became a heavy contractor in the construction of railroads; and finally became involved in politics. He was elected to the State Senate about the year 1851, which marked the close of his political career.

The result of all his struggles for gain was by no means satisfactory. What he had made at other employments he lost in his railroad operations; and it is now a source of deep and lasting regret that he did not "flee those things and follow after righteousness, godliness, faith, love, meekness, temperance."

That he made this sad mistake is owing partly to his own erring judgment, and partly to the illiberality of the disciples, who "having this world's goods and seeing their brethren have need, shut up their heart of compassion from him." The blame will be justly distributed by Him who shall "judge the world in righteousness."

About the year 1853 he collected the remnant of his means, and removed to Illinois, still in hope of securing some land for his children. At a subsequent period he moved to Iowa, in which State he still resides, near Bellair, Appanoose county. He continues to preach and do good as he has opportunity; but he is no longer the shining light that he was in former years.

On account of his limited education, Elder Combs has written but little for the press. But he is now preparing for publication a work on a subject to which his attention was attracted in the following manner:

When at the height of his usefulness in Indiana, there fell into his hands a small work on Prophecy, by S. M. McCorkle, who advocated a literal interpretation, and was therefore called a Literalist. After reading the book he sought an interview with its author, who lived at that time in an adjoining county. During the few days which they passed together, each converted the other; and since that period Elder Combs has devoted much time to the study of the prophets. The result of his investigations, as well as the conclusions to which he has come, will, no do ıbt, be fully revealed in his forthcoming book, should he live to complete it. It is sufficient to say, in this place, that his views of the prophecies and of the end of the world, were not generally received by the disciples; and that it was by his advocacy of Second-Adventism, as well as by his becoming entangled in the affairs of this life, that he, to a great extent, destroyed his influence as a minister of the ancient gospel. Let his example deeply impress upon the mind and heart of every Christian preacher the solemn admonition of the great apostle: "*Take heed to thyself and to the doctrine.*"

But it must not be supposed that Elder Combs, having so successfully preached to others, is himself in danger of becoming a castaway. Though his influence may have been injured through philosophy and vain deceit, yet he and thousands of others have been sanctified through the truth which he has preached. Though he may have erred in "believing (as he supposed) all things which are written in the law and in the *prophets;* yet he has ever exercised himself in a hope both sure and steadfast, endeavoring to preserve "a conscience void of offence toward God and toward men." If he has been mistaken in crying, "Behold, the Bridegroom cometh," he is on that account the better prepared to meet Him at His coming.

Elder Combs is a medium-sized, rather heavy set man, being about five feet eight inches high, and weighing about one hundred and sixty pounds. Though now enfeebled by age, he was once a man of much sprightliness and great physical power. In early life he contributed a liberal share of the labor that cleared away the western forest and prepared the way before the plow—hence his fine physical development. He has very pale blue eyes, light or sandy hair, and a ruddy complexion.

He is a man of very fair natural ability. Though his mind is less powerful than some, it is more active than many. Through lack of mental discipline, he is not a clear, safe, sober-minded thinker; but he is strongly inclined to be visionary—prone to embrace new and strange theories. In the domain of thought, he can hardly be styled a "prudent man that looketh well to his going."

As a speaker he used to rank high; and nothing but age has detracted from his merit in this respect. His oratorical or excitable temperament always supplies him with intensity of feeling, which is said to be "the leading element of good speaking, for this excites feeling in others and moves the masses." It was not his habit to carefully prepare his sermons; hence near the commencement of his discourses he was slow—frequently *tedious;* but toward the close his delivery was very rapid, highly animated, and sometimes truly eloquent. At such times it behooved the "preaching brethren" who chanced to sit behind him in the stand, to look well to their toes; for he not only gesticulated earnestly with his hands, but he also wore heavy boots, which frequently and incautiously shifted their position. His discourses were usually of a doctrinal or controversial character; and whatever some of them may have lacked in *depth*, was more than made up in *length;* for he has been known to preach for *more than three hours.* As a general thing, however, his discourses were deep as well as long; and, in the aggregate, they made a deep and lasting impression on the public mind.

As a husband and father he is indulgent, provident, kind, and affectionate. It is doubtful whether David loved his wayward son Absalom more fervently than he loves his eleven sons and daughters.

Next after his family, his brethren share largely in his heart's best affections. For their sakes and to increase their number he has freely given, though he has not freely received. He once owned a valuable little farm and other property in Indiana, but it has all been sold, and the money, little by little, laid at the apostles' feet—cheerfully contributed for the support of the gospel and the extension of the Redeemer's kingdom.

Nor has his generosity been exercised only toward the children of God. Like the "perfect and upright man" of Uz, he has "delivered the poor that cried, the fatherless, and him that had none to help him." "The blessing of him that was ready to perish came upon him; and he caused the widow's heart to sing for joy." In a word, benevolence is the leading trait of his character; and if there is a man on earth who, as he has had opportunity, has "done good unto all men, and especially unto those who are of the household of faith," that man is Elder Michael Combs.

In so doing he has never been weary; and far more desirable than all earthly riches, is his interest in the promise, "With what measure ye mete it shall be measused to you again." Well may he go down to the grave rejoicing in view of that day when "the dead, small and great, shall stand before God—when the books shall be opened, and the dead judged out of those things written in the books, *according to their works.*"

ELIJAH GOODWIN.

Elder Elijah Goodwin was born in Champaign county, Ohio, January 16th, 1807. When three years old his father, Aaron Goodwin, and his gradfather, Elijah Chapman, together with several other families, emigrated to Illinois Territory and settled in the American Bottom, about twelve miles from St. Louis. This locality proving very unhealthful, they resolved to return to Ohio in the Fall of 1813.

Matters being arranged for this purpose, they set out in wagons on their return, but by the time they reached Indiana Territory the winter set in with such severity that they could proceed no farther. They therefore pitched their tents in what is now Gibson county, some five miles north of the present town of Princeton, and there awaited the coming of Spring.

In the mean time his father and others of the company made several excursions into the surrounding wilderness to ascertain the quality of the land, which, it was found, promised a rich reward to the future husbandman. Therefore their purpose of journeying farther eastward, passed away with the winter, and they chose for themselves dwelling places between the forks of White River, in Daviess county, and about twenty miles east of Vincennes, or Old Post Vincent, as it was then called.

At that time there were but few settlements of whites in that part of the Territory, and the stillness of the forest was seldom disturbed save by the red man shouting in the chase. They were therefore subjected to all the dan-

LIBRARY
OF THE
UNIVERSITY OF ILLINOIS

gers and inconveniences incident to frontier life. Not the least of these inconveniences was the absence of the school-master. True, each neighborhood had a nominal teacher, but he was usually a blind leader of the blind, neither "gentle, patient, nor apt to teach." Yet so weak was the element of civilization that even such a teacher could be sustained for only three months each year. Moreover Elijah's parents were poor, and he was often required to be absent from the school that he might be present in the field or in the "clearing." His father usually signed one scholar for the term, and the time was made up by several of the family in such fractions as it often puzzled the "master" himself to reckon.

Under such circumstances, however, he learned to read, and, to him, this was equivalent to an education: for he possessed a mind delighting "to search out the causes of things," and, having acquired the ability to read, he became his own instructor. Among his first acquisitions was a respectable knowledge of the English language. This gave him a power in the pulpit which, in that day, was extraordinary, and elevated him at once to a somewhat conspicuous rank in the ministry. He has been through life an inquisitive and indefatigable student—ever seeking to increase his stock of knowledge, whether in the school-room, behind the counter, at home with his family, or in the houses of his brethren as he has journeyed, preaching. To this studious habit, mainly, he owes, under God, his present honorable position, and to it society is indebted for his usefulness.

Having by such means obtained a tolerable English education, he learned, with the assistance of some friend, the Greek alphabet. With this key he unlocked that classic store-house, in which, to the mere English scholar, are *hid* all the treasures of revealed wisdom and knowledge. He is not, to be sure, a thorough Greek scholar, but by means of his Lexicon he is able to arrive at the meaning of the Scripture, as conveyed in the original words which the Holy Spirit taught. To conclude this topic, Elder Goodwin may be set down as an educated man, who is worthy of double honor in that he is *self-educated*.

His religious training was more carefully attended to, though circumstances were unfavorable. His parents and grand-parents were members of the Methodist Episcopal church, and, until he was thirteen years old, he never heard any but Methodist preachers. The "circuits" in those days being very large, the bishop usually placed, on each, two itinerants, who, by making their appointments eight weeks apart, supplied the "societies" with preaching every four weeks. As the appointment usually fell on one of the "six days," it was very common—indeed customary—for the men who attended to take their guns and dogs with them to church. Arriving at the house of worship, which was usually a squatter's cabin, they would "stack arms" in the outside corner of the chimney, go in, and seat themselves with powder horns and shot-pouches hanging by their sides. The benediction pronounced, they whistled up the errant dogs, and set out in hope of killing a deer on their way home— a hope which was frequently realized.

But it was perhaps not unfortunate that such circumstances existed. As there were then no deified preachers, the believer could worship God even in their absence. There being no magnificent temples in which devotion could parade itself on Sundays, it took up its abode in the *hearts* of those simple people, and manifested itself to the Creator around the family altar. Such worshippers were the ancestors of Elder Goodwin. In his mother Mary and his grandmother Achsah, especially, dwelt the unfeigned faith.

He himself was piously inclined even from a child. He received the religious instructions of his parents with great readiness of mind, and, at a very tender age, was anxious to experience the joys of salvation. Nor did he think of becoming a Christian only—even then, in his childhood, he cherished the hope of being, one day, a preacher of the ever-blessed gospel. Long before he made a profession of religion, he used to steal away to the groves and deliver extempore sermons to the trees. Indeed, like the holy child Samuel, he seems to have been born for the obedience and service of the Lord.

Looking forward to the ministerial profession, he did all in his power to qualify himself to discharge its solemn duties. His father's library contained only a Bible and a Methodist hymn book, but these he made his frequent study until he became very familiar with their contents.

With such a disposition, it is not surprising that he was always delighted when the circuit-riders came round, and greatly interested in their singing and preaching.

Those preachers taught that people could never "get religion" until they should be brought to see themselves as the vilest of sinners. They endeavored first of all to convince them of their *total depravity*, and, in the second place, to afford them a magnified conception of

   ——"What eternal horrors hang
  Around the second death."

Having thus brought them through the darkness of despair to the very verge of the awful pit, they suddenly admitted a flood of light from the Lord's blessed promises of forgiveness and mercy. By this artful manœuvre they transported their hearers from the confines of "outer darkness" to the bright regions of hope; and this rapid transition, this sudden elevation of greatly depressed spirits, the mourners regarded as their conversion, and glorified God! In this plan of pardon there is at least some sound *philosophy*, and for this reason, possibly, it is still followed by many *without the shadow of divine authority*. To young Goodwin's conversion under this system, one thing stood opposed—on a faithful comparison of himself with his profane associates, he could not conclude that he was the chief of sinners. Therefore he remained in the kingdom of Satan, though most anxious to be translated into the kingdom of God's dear Son.

About the year 1819 there came into Daviess county several preachers who called themselves Christians, but were called by various names, such as Newlights, Schismatics, Heretics, etc. The love, rather than "the terror of the Lord," was their favorite theme, and they appealed to sinners with great earnestness and with many tears. Young Goodwin soon became much attached to those despised people, and began to defend their views when opposed by the several orthodox sects.

At one of their meetings held in May, 1821, near Washington, he made a profession of religion, and was soon afterward received into the church. Under the lenient rule of the Old Christian Body, he enjoyed the fellowship of his brethren for several months without obeying from the heart "the form of doctrine." This he did through fear of wounding the feelings of his parents *upon whose faith* he had been sprinkled in infancy. This obstacle was entirely removed as soon as they were apprised of his heart's desire, and, in October following, he was immersed in Prairie Creek by Elder Cummins Brown.

In 1823 his father moved into the southern part of the county to a point several miles from the nearest Christian church. Finding in that settlement a few persons of his faith, the young disciple, then in his sixteenth year, prevailed upon them to hold evening prayer meetings from house to house. At such meetings he at once became a leader, and from that he soon began to exhort and to preach. From the first he was very successful in bringing sinners to the anxious seat to call on the name of the Lord. But to those unfortunate ones who asked and received not, he could only say "pray on." He was at that time, like many preachers of the present day, in the condition of those so forcibly described by Paul, "Desiring to be teachers of the law; understanding neither what they say nor whereof they affirm."

It was in May, 1824, that he first attempted to deliver a regular sermon. His text was 1 Peter, iv. 18. "If the righteous scarcely be saved, where shall the ungodly and the sinner appear?" The following were the divisions of his subject in their order.

I. Define the character of the righteous.

II. Describe the character of the ungodly and the sinner.

III. Answer the question,—"Where shall the ungodly and the sinner appear."

By observing this order he made a most favorable impression upon the minds of his hearers.

He was followed by another preacher, by the name of Abner Davis, who took for his text, "The Lord hath done great things for us whereof we are glad." He made a direct application of the passage to the young speaker that had just taken his seat. He attempted to show that preaching was all-important; that the Lord called and qualified all true preachers; that in the present case he had done a *great thing*, and they were all very glad of it!

From this time Elder Goodwin kept up regular appointments in different parts of the county. As there were no railways and as he was too poor to buy a horse, he travelled at first on foot. In the beginning of his ministry he exhibited greater boldness than most young preachers, nor was he to be discouraged by any ordinary difficulty, as the following incident will show.

He once sent an appointment to preach at a certain point in a distant part of the county. The day came, and after an early breakfast the youthful evangelist set out on foot. Arriving at the place, he found a few persons in the house, and a few others at a preacher's stand in a grove near by. Perceiving that the house would easily accommodate all present, and supposing that all would come in when the exercises commenced, he took out his Testament and hymn book, and began to look for a suitable hymn. Upon this, those in the house arose and marched out to the stand two and two, male and female. Nothing daunted, the deserted preacher followed them, ascended the out-door pulpit, and, without giving them time to retire, began to read the introductory hymn. This attracted the attention of the company, which had by this time become quite large.

After singing and prayer, he proceeded to follow out in regular order the several divisions of his discourse, all the while thinking it wondrous strange that none of his brethren were present to aid and encourage him. When on the last division of his subject, a funeral procession came up, and then, for the first time, he discovered an open grave near him. The hearse was driven up near the stand, where the whole company took seats and listened respectfully to the remainder of the sermon.

An explanation followed, from which it appeared that his appointment had never been published, and that he had preached to people who had come out with no other purpose than to attend the funeral!

Up to this time he had obtained no authority to preach the gospel. But in September, 1825, he applied for license to the Indiana Christian Conference, which convened that year at Blue Spring, Monroe county. Agreeably to their custom they appointed a committee to examine the candidates as to their soundness in the faith and aptness to teach.

On this occasion, as usual, the committee was composed of gray-haired preachers who had been many years in the service. The chairman was Lewis Byram, a man of great gravity, extensive biblical knowledge, and excellent Christian character.

Before this venerable body the youthful candidate, then in his nineteenth year, presented himself with fear and trembling. But to his great surprise only two important questions were propounded to him. 1st, "What think you of Christ, whose Son is he?" 2nd, "What do you understand to be the design of the death of Christ?" To the first he answered promptly, "I believe that Jesus Christ is the Son of God." Thus, having been four years in the church and two years in the ministry, he made the Scriptural confession of faith in Jesus Christ.

To the other question he replied, "I believe that Christ died to reconcile sinners to God, and not God to sinners." A few more inquiries with reference to his impression that it was his duty to preach, closed the examination, and the license was granted by a unanimous vote. His name was accordingly enrolled as a member of the Conference. It being a camp-meeting as well as a Conference occasion, the older preachers were anxious to hear the new member. They therefore appointed him to preach at the afternoon session. To him this was a greater task than it was for Paul to preach before the Areopagus. Before him, in a beautiful grove, sat an immense assembly; behind him were the Elders of Israel. Nevertheless he delivered one of his systematic discourses, at the close of which he exhorted with so much feeling that quite a number of persons presented themselves at the anxious seat.

Hitherto he had attracted but little attention in the Conference, for in those days he wore an old white hat, whose crown, once cylindrical, had assumed a *conical* shape. His coat, also, was "out" at the elbows, and the length of his pantaloons had evidently been determined upon principles of rigid economy. After this effort, however, they asked him many questions, and spoke, in flattering terms, of his ability.

On returning home he reflected much on what he had seen and heard at Conference. It was held that such an organization was absolutely necessary to depose false teachers and prevent incompetent persons from being licensed. But, thought he, from such an examination as that to which I was subjected, what could they learn as to one's ability to preach the gospel? Such reflections on the doings and uses of that ecclesiastical body, the Conference, begat in his mind a hostility to it, which soon made itself manifest.

In the Summer of 1826, he received a letter from some friends in Illinois, near the mouth of Illinois river, requesting him to come out and hold a few meetings in that region. This he resolved to do, taking the Conference in his route. This body met that year at some point in Owen county. After its adjournment he set out on horseback for his Illinois appointments, having just twenty-five cents in his pocket.

There was at that time a flourishing church on Allison Prairie, some ten miles west of Vincennes. He resolved to proceed by way of this church, to spend a night with the brethren there, and preach for them. He reached *Christian settlement* before night, and called on a brother Daniel Travis, to whom he made known the object of his coming. The brother, who looked upon the outward appearance, asked him several questions as to his age, the length of time he had been preaching, etc., and finally agreed to circulate the appointment. Quite a congregation assembled, to whom he discoursed in a manner that fully met their expectations.

Next morning he started at early dawn in hope of reaching the house of a brother by noon. It was necessary for him to keep within the brotherhood as much as possible, for his purse was light and he received little or nothing for his labor in the Lord. Some preached vehemently against receiving any remuneration, but "he had not so learned Christ." Moreover it seemed to him that, if none were receiving more than he, there was no need of warning the brethren against paying the preachers!

Previous to starting, his friend Travis asked him how far he was going. "Some hundred and fifty miles," was the reply. "How much money have you for the trip?" continued the questioner. "*Twenty-five cents*," said the preacher. The good brother then gave him an additional quarter—a liberal contribution in that day—and he went on his way rejoicing.

He reached the brother's by the way-side after the sun had crossed the meridian. But dinner was soon prepared, which proved to be the last meal he enjoyed until he reached the end of his journey. Remembering that "a righteous man regardeth the life of his beast," he spent his money for food for his horse, while he himself *fasted for two whole days*.

Resuming his journey he resolved to travel all that night. In pursuance of this resolution he came, about one o'clock, A. M., to where some emigrants had encamped for the night, at whose fire he stopped to warm himself. He had not been long by the fire when a coarse voice cried out, with a terrible allusion to Tartarus, "What are you doing here?" "Only warming myself, sir," he innocently replied; and turning round, he saw the man who had so rudely accosted him standing at his horse's head, the bridle over his arm, and a gun aimed directly at him. The holder of the weapon seeing him so unconcerned, came up and offered an apology. He said that the night before some one had stolen a horse in the neighborhood; that the thief was expected to return and purloin other property; that the owner of the stolen horse had requested him to watch; and that he had mistaken the innocent for the guilty. "Had you made the least attempt to run," said he, "I would have shot you down in your tracks." After this narrow escape the evangelist pursued his lonely way, and in two days more reached the place of his destination.

Having preached a week or two for his Illinois friends, he set out on his return, intending to reach a camp-meeting on Barney's Prairie, Wabash county, by Saturday night. But at the close of that day he found himself twenty miles from the camp-ground, the road to which ran through a thinly settled region, and was not much travelled. Nevertheless about nine o'clock, P. M. he left the old Vincennes and St. Louis road and set out afresh for the camp-meeting, resolved once more to travel all night rather than fail in his undertaking. Of him this determination to carry out his purposes is characteristic. To fill his appointments he has often imperiled his life in crossing swollen streams; and in every department of his business he is faithful to perform whatever he promises.

About one o'clock the next morning he halted at a farm-house, called the farmer up and inquired the way and the distance to the place at which the meeting was to be held. "It is about six miles," said the kind man, "but light; we will be going thither in the morning; so tarry with us and take a little repose."

By the time the horse was cared for, the good lady was up preparing a lunch for the weary traveller. After some conversation he observed to her: "You resemble a lady of my acquaintance in Indiana, whose name is Day;

perhaps you are of the same name." "No," said she, "as far from it as you could easily imagine—my name is Knight."

After a refreshing nap, breakfast was taken, and Mr. and Mrs. Knight, together with the preacher, were soon on their way to the camp-ground, where they arrived just before the services commenced. A great number of persons were seated before a rude stand in a delightful grove. There were in attendance several distinguished preachers, among whom was the eccentric and talented William Kinkade. Goodwin was immediately invited into the stand and called upon for a sermon. No excuse would avail, so he arose and addressed the people from Romans i. 16: "I am not ashamed of the gospel of Christ."

The following transcript of the original "skeleton" of his discourse, will give the reader an idea of his method of sermonizing in that day.

I. SHOW WHAT THE GOSPEL IS.
II. OFFER REASONS FOR NOT BEING ASHAMED OF IT.

I. *It means Good News; and so it is.*
1. To the sinner as one blind—it offers spiritual vision.
2. To those who sit in darkness and the shadow of death.
3. To the morally diseased—it points to the great Physician.
4. To the guilty—offering pardon.
5. To the poor—offering "an inheritance incorruptible," etc.
6. To the dead—for it offers life eternal.

II. *We should not be ashamed of it, because*
1. It is the Sword of the Spirit, with which we fight the good fight of faith.
2. It is a Directory in the way to Heaven.
3. It is a Will, in which fullness of joy is bequeathed to them that shall be heirs of salvation.

The effort was highly applauded even by the older preachers; yet, to one well acquainted with the Christian system, it is evident that none could learn, from such a discourse, what the gospel of Christ is, or what is to be done, on the part of man, in order to be saved by it.

At the annual meeting of the Indiana Conference in the Fall of 1827, he was appointed to travel and preach during six months of the ensuing year. The Wabash Conference, which embraced the churches in southwestern Indiana and southeastern Illinois, held its annual meeting about the same time. By it also he was appointed to preach half the year within the bounds of that Conference. These calls he accepted; and for the sake of giving each an equal division of seasons, he threw the two districts into one, which gave him a circuit of about six hundred miles. He has, therefore, been a circuit-rider on a large scale! Vermillion and White counties, Illinois; and Posey, Crawford, Monroe and Vigo counties, Indiana, formed the circumference of his circle. He arranged the appointments so as to make a *revolution* every eight weeks. To do this he was kept busy *every day*, for the roads were in a bad condition, many of the creeks were unbridged, and the swamps at times almost impassable.

No definite amount was promised him for his year's service. The brethren simply said, "Go preach the gospel and we will see that you do not suffer." Under such a contract he of course received but very little compensation. Still he filled out the time, had many happy meetings, and saw his labors crowned with a good degree of success.

On the 6th of August, 1828, in Gibson county, Indiana, he was married to Miss Jane Moore Davis, who still lives to share his sacrifices for the gospel, and to adorn the doctrine of God our Saviour by her meekness and "patient continuance in well doing."

Shortly after his marriage he and his wife made a visit to Tennessee, passing through Kentucky. While she remained with a sister in Wilson county, Tennessee, he made a tour through several counties of that State. His preaching was well received, and greatly revived some old churches that had forgotten their first love.

Up to this time he had operated on the mourning-bench system, under the illusion that the Bible is full of authority for proceeding in that way. While *en route* to Tennessee an aged sister, in Kentucky, at whose house he preached, asked him the following question: " Brother Goodwin," said she, " what is Baptism for?" Having looked at the subject no further than he had been led by his seniors in the ministry, he replied, " Baptism is an emblem of the burial and resurrection of Christ: therefore one is baptised to show his faith in these facts." " Then," continued the old lady, " the Lord's Supper shows our faith in the *death* of Christ, and Baptism shows our faith in his burial and resurrection." " So I understand it," rejoined the preacher. " *Why then,*" said she, " *do we, by the* Supper, *show forth the Lord's* death often, *and, by* Baptism, *show forth his* burial and resurrection *only* once *in our whole lives?*" By this inquiry he was completely nonplussed. The aged sister then observed that she was really anxious to ascertain the true design of the ordinance, for she thought there was something in it that all the preachers had overlooked.

Here the conversation ended, but study and reflection began; nor did he cease to reflect and inquire, until he had learned from the teaching of the apostles that Baptism, with its proper antecedents, is "for the remission of sins."

From this apparently trivial incident is to be dated the beginning of his reformation. Here he reached his aphelion, and began to approach the great Light of the World and his satellites, the apostles. Surely God hath " chosen the foolish things of the world to confound the wise, and God hath chosen the weak things of the world to confound the things that are mighty."

Previous to this, one thing had troubled him, but it had not shaken his faith in the correctness of his practice. He was always most successful in persuading people to the anxious seat; but on almost all occasions he found persons—usually of the more sober and intelligent sort—who called upon the Lord in vain, for He would not answer. After almost every protracted meeting, he left many "unconverted" mourners, some of whom sought the Lord again, but others went their ways to infidelity.

Finally he mentioned to older preachers the difficulty which was to him inexplicable; and many expedients were resorted to in order to account for it without calling in question the correctness of the system. Of course that *could not* be wrong, for had not many souls been joyfully converted in that way!

About this time there arose no small stir among the brethren with reference to the Reformation, especially in its bearings upon church polity. Elder Goodwin had long been opposing the organization of the ministers into an ecclesiastical body, which subject he had freely discussed with the ablest preachers in open Conference. The Indiana Conference was soon decapitated by the sword of the Spirit; and the Wabash Conference was not long in experiencing the same fate—the churches assuming an independent form of government; and the preachers becoming amenable to them.

To assist in bringing about this result, was his first public *act* in the direction of reform. But the examination, to which he had been led by the old lady in Kentucky, soon convinced him that the teaching of Christ and the acts of the apostles stood opposed to his teaching and practice on the important subject of conversion. He plainly saw that the apostles preached Christ crucified as the "only name given under heaven among men whereby they could be saved;" and that when the people believed their word, and were willing to obey the gospel, they commanded them to be baptized every one of them "in the name of Jesus Christ for the remission of sins." He saw that in this way thousands became Christians in a single day without the long agonizing process through which his teaching compelled men to pass. He also discovered that in the beginning no one ever came sincerely to the Lord for salvation, and went away sorrowful, as many did in his day.

But how to carry into practice what he now saw to be according to apostolic precept and example, was a grave question. He feared that if he should attempt to substitute the ancient gospel, which was hated, for the received traditions, which were dearly loved, the people would not obey it, and he would have occasion to say with Esaias, "Lord, who hath believed our report." It was not until the Summer of 1835 that he resolved to declare the apostles' doctrine at all hazards, and exhort the people to obey the gospel as believers did on the day of Pentecost. "If," thought he, "I preach the same facts to be believed and the same commands to be obeyed; and if the people believe and obey, surely all will be well, for the Lord is faithful that promised: but if they are contentious, and will not obey the truth, but persist in unrighteousness, then the consequence shall be upon their own heads— I shall have delivered my soul."

From that hour to the present he has never taught the penitent sinner to seek pardon where God has never promised to bestow it. He has learned too that if persons are truly convinced of their sinfulness and really desirous of obtaining forgiveness—if they have "*unfeigned* faith" in Christ and in his gracious promises—they will gladly receive the word and be baptized, both men and women.

Up to this time, except during the year he was employed by the Conferences, he did not "live of the gospel." To support his family he sometimes taught school, sometimes served as salesman in a store, but always preached as much as circumstances would possibly allow.

In January, 1840, he abandoned all secular business and gave himself wholly to the word. He had organized several new churches in Posey county—one at Mount Vernon. These, with some Old Christian churches that had come into the Reformation, agreed to co-operate in sustaining him as an evangelist, at a salary of three hundred dollars per annum. Under this arrangement he labored for seven years, annually enlarging his field, which eventually embraced portions of Illinois and Kentucky.

According to a report contained in the Christian Record of that date, he travelled, during the year ending October, 1845, three thousand four hundred and seventy-two miles and preached three hundred and eighty-two sermons. In 1846 he lost nearly three months on account of ill health, yet he travelled, during the remainder of the year, about three thousand miles and delivered two hundred and thirty-one public discourses.

This will serve as an index of his zeal for God, and as a measure of the influence he exerted as a speaker only, and not as a writer. He has always acted upon the suggestion of King Solomon, "What thy hand findeth to do, do it with thy might."

In June, 1847, he left his old residence at Mount Vernon, and removed to Bloomington, where he became associated with Elder J. M. Mathes in the publication of the Christian Record.

In this connection he continued two years at a considerable sacrifice. The profits arising from the publication were insufficient to support two families, and they received nothing for preaching, though employed nearly every Lord's day and frequently throughout the week. The brethren, with singular views of justice and Christian obligation, seemed to think that the Record sustained the editors, and that therefore they ought to preach for nothing! Strange that they did not see, with equal clearness, that if one half of their farms supported *their* families, they ought therefore to receive nothing for the products of the other half!

Starved out of the editorial chair, he removed to Madison and became the pastor of the church in that city. During two years from April, 1849, he preached for that congregation with very general acceptance and tolerable success.

At the expiration of the second year he accepted a call from the church at Bloomington. The brethren at Madison remonstrated; but his family was then large and his children were demanding mental culture: therefore, for the sake of a better support, and especially in view of the educational facilities afforded by the State University, he returned to Bloomington in 1851, and assumed the pastoral care of the churches at that place and Clear Creek.

In this position he remained until the Fall of 1854, when he accepted an agency for the N. W. C. University. As an agent he was indefatigable; and he did much toward increasing both the funds and the popularity of the institution. He canvassed a large portion of the State, soliciting stock and contributions, preaching the gospel, and, by public lectures and private conversations, awakening an educational spirit among all the people, and especially among those of the household of faith.

Having become a prey to *bronchitis*, and being much exposed in this work, he suspended operations, as agent, for the Winter of 1855–6. But unwilling to be idle during that time, he wrote and published the Family Companion, "a book of sermons, on various subjects, both doctrinal and practical: intended for the private edification and comfort of the disciples of Christ, and to aid the honest inquirer after truth in finding the true church and the law of induction into the same; etc., etc., etc." It is written in a plain, simple style, in which the rigor of logic and the spirit of Christ are happily blended. The popularity of the work is attested by its having already passed through five editions, and by the fact that some of the sermons have been republished in Europe, and some have been translated into the German language.

In the Spring of 1856 he resumed his agency, but upon the urgent solicitations of the brethren in Indianapolis, he abandoned that work in May; on the 27th of which month he became the pastor of the Christian congregation in that city. The church there was, then, in a deplorable condition. Through the influence of those who were contentious, it had been rent into two parties, each of which had their place of worship, and not a few things were being done "through strife and vain glory." It required much nerve and a firm reliance upon the strong arm of the Lord, to encounter such carnality;* and, having done so, he met with an opposition to his pacific measures that he had not anticipated. Under such trying circumstances many a man would have "withdrawn himself," leaving the wranglers to "eat of the fruit of their own way and be filled with their own devices." But realizing the importance of the church located at the capital of the State, and sympathizing with the righteous members that were partakers of the common shame, he resolved to meet all opposition with meekness and never to "give up the ship."

In this position he remained three years, in the course

* 1 Cor. iii. 3.

of which time the conflicting elements were brought together and their affinity re-established. The two folds became one again under one shepherd, and the congregation resumed a prosperous condition and a commanding influence.

Having accomplished this happy result, he resigned his charge, and purchased of Elder J. M. Mathes the Christian Record, of which he became sole editor and proprietor. This valuable religious magazine he continued to conduct, in Indianapolis, until the close of the year 1861. In addition to his editorial labors he made frequent preaching tours through this and other States of the Union, and rendered important service as Treasurer of the N. W. C. University. He was one of the commissioners to organize this institution, and from the beginning he has served as a member of the Business Committee and also of the Board of Directors, of which he has once been President.

At the commencement of the year 1862, in connection with his eldest son, A. D. Goodwin, he began a new volume of the Monthly, and also commenced the publication of the Weekly Christian Record, a family newspaper devoted to the interests of primitive Christianity. Both the paper and the magazine are ably and judiciously conducted, and they exert a powerful influence upon the disciples in the northwest, whose liberal patronage they assuredly merit.

In the course of his ministerial life he has been engaged in ten public discussions, in all of which, save two held prior to his entrance into the Reformation, he has successfully vindicated the truth as it is in Jesus. The first, which occurred in 1829, was a one-sided little affair, for the reason that his opponent, a Methodist preacher by the name of Richey, could not read the notes or comprehend the arguments prepared for him by another.

The second was with Dr. H. Holland, also a minister in the M. E. Church, and a man of considerable ability. It took place in the court-house at Mount Vernon, in the Spring of 1832. Proposition: "Is Jesus Christ the very and Eternal God?" Affirmative—Holland; negative—Goodwin.

His third debate was held near Mount Vernon, in 1837. His opponent was the same Dr. Holland, and the subject Infant Baptism. The fourth, in which he was opposed by Joel Hume, a Predestinarian Baptist, occurred in 1843 or 4. The proposition was the following: "Is it possible for all men to be saved by complying with conditions within their power." In the affirmative, Mr. Goodwin offered twenty arguments, to ten of which his opponent attempted no reply.

He next discussed the Action, Subject and Design of Baptism, with the Rev. F. Forbes, of the M. E. Church. This transpired at Kent, Jefferson county, in February, 1851, and was followed by the immersion of one of the moderators, his wife, and twelve others. In the Spring of 1853 he debated the same propositions with the Rev. James Scott (Methodist), in the chapel of the State University at Bloomington. At the same place in 1854 or 5 he affirmed the following proposition: "A law embracing the principles of search, seizure, confiscation, and destruction of intoxicating liquors kept for illegal sale, would be in accordance with the Bible and the Constitution of the State of Indiana, and promotive of the well-being of society." His opponent was Rev. Mr. Tabor of the Baptist Church.

He subsequently debated with R. Hargrave (Methodist) on the Action and Design of Baptism; and, at a still later period, with H. Wells (Lutheran) on the Action of Baptism. The former took place at Oxford, Benton county, the latter at Jalapa, Grant county.

Finally, in December 1861, he debated the Action of Baptism at Cadiz, Henry county, with the Rev. M. Mahan of the Methodist Episcopal Church. This discussion lasted four days, and, like those preceding, converted to "sound doctrine" many who, turning away their ears from the truth, had been "turned unto fables."

Thus did the subject of this sketch, by the force of his mind and the candor of his heart, find his way, through gross darkness, to the foundation of apostles and prophets, though born, baptized, and bred in a different.faith.

Thus by his own efforts, in the providence of God, has he elevated himself from obscurity to his present honorable and influential position.

Thus has he lived without reproach and labored for his race almost without reward.

Only a few more years, at farthest, will he write, and speak, and pray for the success of the Reformation, which he verily believes to be the cause of God; then will he leave a bright example on earth, to ascend to a glorious inheritance in heaven.

Elder Goodwin is a man of fine personal appearance. He is about five feet nine inches high—erect, well-proportioned, and weighs about one hundred and sixty pounds. His complexion is fair, his hair light and intermingled with gray. He has a well-balanced head, with a fine broad forehead, clearly indicative of great intellectual power.

His mind is clear, logical, comprehensive. He is a deep, constant thinker; and he reasons forcibly, from cause to effect more than by comparison. As a disputant, he is self-possessed, ready, convincing, and, under all circumstances, courteous toward his opponent. He descends to no chicanery to deceive the simple, employs no vulgar wit for the sake of gaining the applause of the multitude, but, by a clear and respectful " manifestation of the truth," he commends himself " to every man's *conscience* in the sight of God."

He possesses an amiable disposition and strong and lasting attachments. Except the cause of Christ, nothing lies nearer his heart or receives more of his attention than his family; the remainder of which consists of the wife of his youth, two sons and two daughters. The rest have fallen " on sleep," among whom was Friend Chapman, a promising son, who having graduated at the N. W. C. University, soon " finished his course" on earth and passed up into the presence of the Great Teacher.

Though he has experienced many occasions of sadness, yet he is uniformly cheerful, and eminently sociable. Indeed, there is not a little humor in his composition, and he enjoys a good anecdote most heartily. This element he sometimes turns to good account, for, sanctified to the Master's use, he constrains all his powers to work together " for good." The following incident will perhaps illustrate the manner in which he is wont to employ his humorous faculty " unto edifying."

Once while on a preaching tour through Henderson county, Kentucky, he stopped one day at a blacksmith's shop to have his buggy slightly repaired. While the work was being done, he inquired of the smith with regard to the religious views of the people thereabout. " Oh," said the smith, " we have some Methodists, some Baptists, some Presbyterians and a few Campbellites." "*Campbellites!*" said Goodwin, " why what kind of people are they ?"

Smith.—A very singular people, I assure you. They don't believe in repentance, in conversion, or in a change of heart. They also deny the operation of the Holy Spirit.

Goodwin.—They must be a singular people, indeed. They deny repentance?

Smith.—Yes, sir. They would ridicule the idea of a sinner's repenting.

Goodwin.—Is it possible! Do they use the Bible in their meetings?

Smith.—O yes, they talk much about the Bible, and "the Bible alone;" but what I tell you is true.

Goodwin.—Do they ever pray?

Smith.—Yes, they pray, and seem quite religious themselves, but they take a sinner without any repentance, baptize him *right in his sins,* and pronounce him a Christian. It is all *water salvation* with them.

Goodwin.—Did you ever hear one of them preach?

Smith.—Yes, I have heard several of their strong men. They didn't deny repentance when I was there, but "*they say*" they always do.

Goodwin.—Did you ever hear a man by the name of Goodwin?

Smith.—No, but I have heard *of* him. They say he is an able man, but he met with his match once.

Goodwin.—How did that happen?

Smith.—Why, he went out to Madison, in this State, and kept bantering until a little Presbyterian preacher took him up and demolished his system completely.

Goodwin.—They had a regular debate, had they?

Smith.—Yes, sir, and I suppose a fellow never before got such a basting.

Goodwin.—Did you hear the discussion?

Smith.—No; but one of our preachers told me about it.

Goodwin.—Who was he?

Smith.—Brother F——.

Goodwin.—I advise you not to repeat the story until you have better authority. I know something of Mr. F——, and I have no confidence in him whatever.

Smith.—That is strange. We all have great confidence in him.

Goodwin.—Well, my good friend, I am the man he told you about, and I never had a debate in any part of Kentucky. The story is a sheer fabrication.

Smith.—(Much confused.) Ah, well! I confess I never had as much confidence in brother F. as I have in some of our preachers.

Goodwin.—Now, sir, let me give you a word of advice. *Be careful how you make statements on the authority of your preachers. All you have said about the views of those whom you call Campbellites are gross misrepresentations. I have preached among them many years, and I know what I say.*

Here the colloquy ended, and Elder Goodwin pursued his journey, leaving behind him a *wiser* if not a *better* man.

In attempting to describe him in the pulpit, one cannot do better than to adopt Cowper's fine description of

> ———"A preacher such as Paul,
> Were he on earth, would hear, approve, and own."

It expresses him precisely; for, without exaggeration, he is

> ———"Simple, grave, sincere;
> In doctrine uncorrupt; in language plain,
> And plain in manner; decent, solemn, chaste,
> And natural in gesture; much impressed
> Himself, as conscious of his awful charge,—
> And anxious mainly that the flock he feeds
> May feel it too; affectionate in look,
> And tender in address, as well becomes
> A messenger of grace to guilty men."

To this it may be added that he is fluent, partly by nature and partly because he never speaks without preparation. His voice, once strong, clear, and melodious, has been somewhat impaired by disease; and his delivery is slightly monotonous. Yet the people everywhere hear him gladly; for his ideas are good and abundant; his discourses pointed, methodical, edifying.

He possesses yet one other trait, which Cowper should have attributed to his model preacher—namely, *boldness in defence of the truth.* This sometimes exhibits itself to good advantage even out of the pulpit, as the following incident will show:

Once when travelling on a western steamer, he observed a number of passengers collected in the gentlemen's cabin and engaged in earnest conversation. Approaching them, he found that one of the company was enlightening the others in regard to a new kind of professed Christians that had appeared in his part of the country. Said he, "They don't believe in any thing but baptism. They will take a sinner in all his guilt, immerse him in water, and pronounce him fit for heaven."

After listening awhile, Elder Goodwin asked, "Do these people have churches?" "O yes, and preachers too," was the reply. "And they require nothing but baptism. I suppose then they never deal with their members for immoral conduct." "Really, I am not sure as to that, but I rather think they do," said the stranger. "Do you think," continued Goodwin, "that they would retain in their fellowship a thief, a blasphemer, a drunkard, or a false witness against his neighbor?" The gentleman, who by this time had become much confused, replied, "O no. I believe they would promptly exclude all such persons." "I perceive then," said the interrogator, "that those people require more than baptism. From your own lips I prove *you* guilty of bearing false witness; and now let me advise you *to be more careful, in future, when attempting to represent the views and practices of men professing godliness.*" He then proceeded, by request, to give the gospel plan of conversion and salvation: the "false witness" was silent, and the company were both pleased and edified.

His success as a speaker is, perhaps, more than balanced by his influence as a writer. From his connection with the Reformation until the present, he has written more or less for several religious papers and magazines, the most of his contributions being to the Christian Record. Since his instalment in the editorial chair—which, to him, is not an "easy" one—his pen has seldom been idle. Enter his sanctum at almost any hour of the day, and you will find him, pen in hand, surrounded by his exchanges and books of reference. You would like to sit longer and enjoy his agreeable conversation, but you feel that you are encroaching upon his time. He is an indefatigable worker. The cause of Godliness, the cause of Temperance, the cause of Union, the cause of Missions, the cause of Education, the cause of the National Government, the cause of Human Liberty, without respect to races—*all* find, in him, an unwearied and unwavering advocate.

His style is more remarkable for its perspicuity than for its vigor, ornament, or conciseness. He never attempts to write any thing beautiful, and his pen assumes considerable latitude of expression, being careful only to keep within the bounds of truth. Though his literary productions never fall below mediocrity, yet he is a *useful* rather than an elegant writer. Extracts would be inserted in this sketch, but for the fact that his writings are so numerous and so worthy of preservation, that they will no doubt be collected and given to the world in book form as soon as he shall have written the last line and laid aside his pen forever. To that certain event he already begins to look forward with regret, but not with fear; for, having been "diligent in business" as well as "fervent in spirit," the testimony of his conscience assures him that he

   ——" From his Lord
  Will receive the glad word,
 'WELL AND FAITHFULLY DONE,
   Enter into my joy
  And sit down on my throne.'"

JOSEPH WILSON.

Elder Joseph Wilson was born in Camden county, North Carolina, October 3d, 1796. His grandparents were members of the Society of Friends; but his father, at the age of eighteen, joined the Baptists, and commenced preaching. Afterwards he removed to Hawkins county, Tennessee, his son Joseph being then six years old. In such schools as Tennessee afforded half a century ago, Elder Wilson received his education. His course of study comprised only spelling, reading, writing, and arithmetic, and even of these branches he obtained but a very imperfect knowledge. He is therefore one

"Whose soul fair Science never taught to stray
Far as the solar walk or milky way."

Hence his speech and his preaching have not been "with the enticing words of man's wisdom," and his extraordinary success as an evangelist is to be attributed, not to the "wisdom of men," but to the "power of God"—to the truth and native force of the principles for which he has contended.

When not more than fifteen years old, amid the gross spiritual darkness that then reigned, he began to feel after God, if haply he might find him, though he is not far from every one of us. For two or three years he searched the Scriptures diligently, but without being able to discover the way of salvation—not because the way is obscure, but because he knew not how or where to search as he ought. Finally he said to himself, "Why do I con-

tinue to read what God never designed to be understood by one like me? The Bible is, to the sinner, a sealed book, a profound mystery: let it be laid aside." Thus had he been taught—thus were all the people taught in that day. "Great is the mystery of godliness" was a favorite text with the preachers, and often did they neglect to preach Christ crucified, in order to comfort (?) the people with the precious doctrine that "the natural man receiveth not the things of the Spirit." 1 Cor. ii. 14. When it is remembered that such preaching still obtains, it is no longer strange that so many have thrown aside their Bibles, as did Elder Wilson, and turned their attention to the unauthoritative productions of men, who, it would seem, write with more clearness and precision than did the Holy Spirit, since *their* works, for the most part, are intelligible! What else is to be expected than an increase of skepticism, and a corresponding decrease of Bible reading, so long as the unconverted—the great majority of mankind—are taught, from the sacred desk, that they cannot understand the revelation of God?

Having despaired of obtaining information from the Scriptures, the young inquirer next applied to his father and other popular preachers, saying, "What shall I do?" They advised him to *pray and wait,* assuring him that God would, in his own good time, grant him faith and repentance unto life. Though this direction was *slightly* different from that given by Peter on the day of Pentecost, yet it was satisfactory to him; and agreeably to it he "waited" until he reached his twentieth year. Under such teaching, alas! how many have waited, in disobedience, until the summer was past, the harvest was ended, and they were not saved!

While waiting for some mysterious, if not miraculous, visitation from God, he examined the Baptist creed, which the preachers seemed to think he could understand, although they claimed that it—like all other creeds—contained only the doctrines of the *unintelligible* Bible, arranged in a more concise and convenient form! To this creed he determined that he would never subscribe, because it contained the doctrine of eternal and unconditional election, which, in his opinion, represented the just and merciful Father as a God of matchless cruelty and injustice.

Next after the creed he read a work on Universalism, entitled "The Works of Winchester." This book taught that a man dying in sin would descend into hell, and there remain until he paid "the uttermost farthing," after which he would ascend into heaven. This doctrine he received and tremblingly adhered to for about four years; but he continually weighed it in the balance of the Scriptures, until at last it was found wanting and abandoned.

About this time he first heard of B. W. Stone, Dany Travis, and others, who had taken their position on the Bible alone; but they were so misrepresented, so denounced as heretics, that he was afraid to let his soul into their secret.

He next applied to the Methodists for advice. They told him that he must repent, come to the mourner's bench, and pray for faith! This doctrine of repentance before faith was then quite common, though it could not justly claim to be either apostolic or reasonable: for how can a man repent of having sinned against a Being in whose existence he does not believe? How can he obtain faith by prayer, when he cannot pray acceptably without faith? Jas. i. 6, 7. These most obvious absurdities Elder Wilson had not then perceived; so he attended a camp-meeting, and obeyed to the letter all the commandments of men. But it was all in vain; for, although he asked, he received not; though he sought, he found not; though he mourned, he was not comforted.

Being sent empty away, he returned home, through the Slough of Despond, and again resolved to await God's time. Yet he often prayed for a heart of flesh, and for some satisfactory evidence of his pardon; and if pardon had been dispensed simply in answer to prayer, he certainly would have obtained it, for never was a man more sincere, more humble, or more willing to perform whatsoever the Lord might require at his hands.

After some months, he again applied the Methodist machinery. At the close of a season of prayer they asked him *how he felt.* He replied that he had neither seen any "great light," nor experienced any unusual feeling. They then inquired if he loved the Saviour; and being answered affirmatively, they decided that he had religion, and that it was necessary for him only to join the church, and go forward in the discharge of his Christian duties. Thus did they dispose of this rather difficult case. He wondered that his conversion should differ so much from that of many others, but then he was reminded that, "*without controversy, great is the mystery of godliness*"! This being a satisfactory explanation of the anomaly, he attached himself to the M. E. Church, and was immersed on the —— day of March, 1821. The same day he was promoted to the office of *class-leader*—an office not often mentioned or clearly defined in the constitution of the primitive church!

In May, 1821, he was married to Miss Anna Goad, daughter of Steven Goad, of White county, Tennessee; and in Autumn of the same year he removed to Greene county, Indiana, in which no gospel was known to the few inhabitants, save that of *repentance and prayer before faith.*

By this time, through diligent study of the Scriptures, he had arrived at two important conclusions: first, that the Bible is an intelligible book; and, second, that divisions in the church of Christ are contrary to the will of God, and detrimental to the spiritual interests of man. It was not long after he came to these conclusions, from his own reading of the word, until several Newlight preachers moved into Monroe county, and commenced pleading for the Bible alone as a basis on which all Christians should unite. One of these preachers, John Storms, made an appointment to preach in Green county. Elder Wilson attended the meeting; but, as the Newlights were everywhere spoken against, he took a seat in the farthest corner of the house. The great controversy between the adherents to the commonly-received doctrine of the "Trinity" and the advocates of a species of Unitarianism, was then rife in this State. The speaker therefore took for his text the words, "*Whose Son is he?*" upon which he discoursed in such a manner as to make a favorable impression upon the *man in the corner*. The preacher left another appointment; then others came and plead for union among the children of God, until finally Elder Wilson determined to step upon the platform of apostles and prophets, even at the peril of being decried as a Newlight, a Stoneite, a Heretic, or an Apostate.

In March, 1822, he voluntarily withdrew from the M. E. Church; and a new congregation was organized, consisting of himself and nine others. Thus were taken two steps in the right direction—they adopted the right creed, the Bible, and the right name, Christian. Still they retained many errors. They continued to talk of "getting religion," and to teach that it was to be found at the mourner's bench; while the disciplinary power was vested in the Annual Conference instead of the several churches. At one of these Conferences, held in Monroe county, on the 16th of September, 1825, Elder Wilson was licensed to preach the gospel; and in September, 1828, he was formally ordained as an evangelist by John Storms, and

Judge David McDonald, then a travelling preacher, now a distinguished member of the Indianapolis bar.

After his ordination, he began to travel and preach on a more extensive scale—to travel, not in a comfortable car drawn by the iron Pegasus, but on horseback, through mud and dust, through wet and dry, through heat and cold, by night and by day. In all of his journeyings, he at first paid his own expenses, and would accept no remuneration for his services; for he, also, lived in the age in which preachers often expounded the tenth chapter of John, each being unwilling to be the "hireling" spoken of in that connection.

This doctrine — that the gospel should be preached without money and without price—was but too cordially received by their brethren. Hence many of the pioneers have known how to be in want; while but few have, like Paul, known also how to abound. Hence many individuals have been destitute of "fruit that might otherwise have abounded to their account," and many congregations have failed to exhibit that liberality which is "an odor of a sweet smell, a sacrifice acceptable, well pleasing to God." Hence, also, the progress of the gospel has been retarded, because those, whose sole business would have been to preach it, have been compelled to leave the word of God, in order to supply the wants of their families.

The consequences of this false teaching bore heavily upon Elder Wilson. During the first seventeen years of his ministry he received from the churches only about five dollars; and he was often greatly embarrassed for want of money to defray his travelling expenses. When he first began to extend his circuit, he visited once a month a congregation on Black creek, in Daviess county. To reach this he had to cross White river; and not being able, at all times, to command even so small a sum as twenty-five cents, he stipulated with the ferryman to pay him annually, *but not in advance.* At the end of the fourth year he was informed by the ferryman that his account, for that year, was in the hands of an officer for collection. He paid the debt without further legal process; but he was compelled to abandon the work at Black creek, because, as in the vision of Ezekiel, there was a *"river" that he "could not pass over."*

Some years after, he had an appointment in Illinois. Having to cross both the Wabash and White river, going and returning, he required for this purpose four "bits," in the currency of those times; but at the hour of starting the total amount of specie on hand was only three "bits." However, he set out, trusting that the place of meeting would be a "Jehovah-jireh"—"the Lord will provide." The meeting being over, his mind was greatly exercised to discover the means of returning home. There lay the impassable rivers between him and his family, as between the lost souls and the elysian fields lay the fabulous Styx. At last he concluded that his remaining "bit" would secure his passage of the Wabash, and that he would, on reaching White river, prevail upon his old friend, the ferryman, to trust him once more. When he began to put on his leggins, he discovered several knots tied in one of them. He set about untying these, with Christian patience, thinking that the thoughtless children had placed them there; when lo! in the last one a solitary "bit" met his astonished and delighted vision. This secret contribution of some good brother or sister seemed to him a very God-send, and he went on his way rejoicing.

The following anecdote will still further exhibit his straitened circumstances in those days. Once upon a time he and Elder Jos. Wolfe had been on a preaching tour to Illinois. Having crossed the Wabash on their return, they stayed all night with a brother who lived in

Mesopotamia—between the rivers. When about to retire, Elder Wilson said, "Now, brother Wolfe, don't steal my money to-night." "No danger," said he, "that would be breaking a commandment for a very small consideration." "Perhaps not," replied Wilson, "you do not know how much I have." "Yes, I do," said Wolfe, "you have just one 'bit.' You had four, no doubt, when you left home; you paid two for ferriage as we went, one to cross the Wabash on our return; and you have one left to pay your fare across White river to-morrow." He acknowledged the correctness of the reckoning, they enjoyed a hearty laugh, and spent a large portion of the night in talking over their trials, and contrasting their present poverty with the unsearchable riches they hoped to inherit.

The hardships of his family were not less than his own His children were growing up without the means of acquiring an education; and, indeed, they were often but ill protected against the wintry storms. His wife, a most zealous and self-denying Christian, was often in want of suitable clothing to appear even in the plain society of that day. In the absence of her husband she carried on the secular business, and when he was unexpectedly detained, she provided with her own hands, in rain and snow, the wood that warmed her household. At one time he owned a saw-mill on a small stream which would often rise in his absence, and he would thus lose many opportunities for sawing. To prevent this loss, his wife used to run the mill; and, at such times, she has saved thousands of feet of lumber. No wonder that she occasionally felt discouraged. No wonder that, sometimes, when the little ones had retired to their humble couches, the parents sat by the fire, talked of their trials, and applied to themselves the Scripture which saith, "If in this life only we have hope, we are of all men most miserable." But soon they reckoned "that the sufferings of this present time are not worthy to be compared with the glory that shall be revealed in us;" and on the morrow the wife laid hold of the distaff, and the husband went forth to preach the gospel.

But to resume the account of his labors. After abandoning the work at Black creek, he preached with good success in several counties which could be reached without crossing any river.

In May, 1833, he made a visit to Mill Creek, Illinois—preaching by the way at Black Creek, Antioch, Farmer's Prairie, and Little York. At the close of the meeting at Mill Creek several Methodists of that vicinity, being almost persuaded to call themselves Christians, requested him to leave another appointment. He promised to return in August. Arriving at the appointed time he found no small stir among the people. The Methodists were engaged in a revival, and they proposed that Elder Wilson should add his strength to theirs, and that they should have a Union meeting. For this end an extra Methodist preacher had been imported, and a stand erected in a beautiful grove for the joint use of the said preacher and Elder Wilson. They used it jointly for several days, Union being the main subject—and the Baptists and Presbyterians of the neighborhood taking an active part in the meeting. All prayed so fervently for a union of all Christians, that Elder Wilson half suspected, and determined to test, their sincerity. So on the next day he arranged it for the Methodist to speak first and himself to follow. After having spoken about an hour and a half he said, "Well, brethren, we have been together a long time, and no reason seems to have been developed why we should not dwell together in unity. By our hymns, exhortations and prayers, we have professed great faith in the possibility and propriety of a permanent union of all the followers of Jesus; and I now desire to see how many are willing to show their faith by their works." He then placed a Bible on the stand, and requested all who were willing to lay aside their Disciplines and Confessions of Faith and take the Bible as their only creed—to make it known by coming forward and placing their hands on the sacred book. When the congregation arose to sing, there was a general movement toward the pulpit. Sixty were counted—when they came so fast that it was impossible to count them. In the midst of the excitement, search was made for the Methodist preacher. He was found sitting in the pulpit, still faithful, as Casabianca, to his dogmas and his Discipline, all his union sermons to the contrary notwithstanding.

> "From such apostles, O ye mitred heads,
> Preserve the church! and lay not careless hands
> On skulls that cannot teach, and *will not learn.*"

Elder Wilson does not know how many he immersed on that occasion; but in September following he held another meeting, and organized a church, for which he preached quarterly for many years. In his care the church grew so rapidly that it has since been peaceably divided into three flourishing congregations. Is there not reason to believe that churches everywhere would thus increase, if the divine creed were everywhere adopted, and if Christians would all "*stand fast in one spirit, with one mind striving together for the faith of the gospel*"?

About the year 1833 the doctrine of the Reformation began to prevail in Green county to an extent somewhat alarming to those most zealous for the traditions of the fathers. Elder Wilson and his brethren, though they called themselves Christians and professed to take the word of God as the man of their counsel, still held many of these traditions. Hence his brethren were generally in favor of closing the doors of their churches against the so-called Campbellites. But he said, "Not so—these people call themselves Christians and claim to be governed by the word of God. We have long proposed to receive any or all good men on that platform; and although they oppose our views *we must give them a hearing.* It may be that we have not learned as much as we ought, and that they are wise above what is written. Possibly they may prove of service to us, and we to them."

By pursuing this course with his brethren, he perhaps did more to advance the cause of the Reformation than if he had been positively advocating it; for it easily triumphs wherever it obtains a hearing. Stephen might have saved himself from martyrdom, if his enemies had not *stopped their ears* when they ran upon him; and the advocates of the faith once delivered to the saints, can easily silence all opposition to it, if only the ears of the people are not dull of hearing.

Among the most uncompromising advocates of reform, at that time, was Morris R. Trimble. He was making great havoc in the sectarian folds throughout Sullivan, Daviess, Knox, and Greene counties. To preserve the peace and harmony of the churches Elder Wilson and his brother John appointed a union meeting on Prairie creek, in Daviess county. Having preached one night and invited mourners to the altar, a Christian preacher, who happened to be present, remonstrated with him, a Bible man, for preaching doctrine and adhering to a practice for which the Bible furnished neither authority nor precedent. On being thus accosted—to his praise be it written—he did not become angry; he did not say that the brother was "uncharitable," or that he thought there were "good Christians in all churches," or that he "hated controversy." But he replied that he thought the Bible taught as he taught; that he *might* be in error; that he would investigate the matter, and if his doctrine was not contained in the Scriptures, he would never preach it again.

He returns home and begins the search. In Matthew v. 4, he reads, " Blessed are they that *mourn;* and in chapter vii. 7, " Ask and ye shall receive, seek and ye shall find." But by reference to chapter v. 1, he ascertains that Jesus addressed these words to his *disciples*, and not to *aliens*. He comes to Luke iii. 10, where the publicans and soldiers go to John, saying, " What shall we do?" But to his surprise John tells none of them to pray, and by that means to endeavor to get religion. He reads of the young man that ran to Jesus, saying, " What shall I do to inherit eternal life?" Here he hopes to find the authority from Jesus' own lips, but no mention is made of "the anxious seat." When the heart-stricken Jews, on the day of Pentecost, propounded the same question to Peter, he thinks he will surely find it, but it is not there. At last he finds Paul, prostrate upon the ground, crying, "Lord, what wilt thou have me to do?" but Jesus only says, "Go unto Damascus and there it shall be told thee." He follows Paul to Damascus, and almost claims the victory, as he sees him kneel in prayer. As Ananias approaches, he expects to see him bow down beside the blind penitent and wrestle with God for him in prayer; but to his astonishment Ananias only says, " Why tarriest thou? arise and be baptized and wash away thy sins calling on the name of the Lord." Thus he continued his fruitless search until he came to the last of Revelations; and having learned that, in every place, the promise is to "those that do his commandments," he abandoned tradition forever. This reading convinced him that *there are so many divisions among the followers of Christ because there are so many things preached which are not found in the Bible.* He therefore resolved that in the future, he, for one, would teach nothing save what is expressly taught by the Lord and by his apostles. Thus at last he entered fully into the Reformation, where for many years he has remained "steadfast, immovable, always abounding in the work of the Lord."

Not long after this event, distrusting his education and being oppressed by poverty, he determined to quit preaching; to labor henceforth with his hands, and give one-fourth of all the proceeds toward sustaining Elder Trimble in the Lord's vineyard. But he soon became dissatisfied with this species of well-doing; and, concluding that, with his limited education, he could tell the simple story of the cross and repeat the language of the apostles, he again entered the field and preached with his usual success for several years.

About the year 1839 he, at the suggestion of his wife, disposed of the mill property, bought some uncleared land in Daviess county, removed thither, and spent two years in opening a small farm. By means of this farm his four sons were able to maintain the family; therefore, at the close of the two years, he began to give himself wholly to the word. For the next thirteen years he preached constantly in Daviess and the adjacent counties—and wherever a door of utterance was opened to him.

At one time he was invited to attend three protracted meetings in southern Indiana. Having attended the first, he set out for the second in company with two or three other preachers. There was an appointment for night meeting at a private house, or cabin, by the way. When they reached the spot it was raining, yet the house was well filled. Elder Wilson preached, and concluded his discourse with some remarks on Christian union. At the close of the meeting—the rain still falling so that the people could not leave—a large man walked up to him and said, in an excited tone: "A part of your discourse, sir, was uncalled for and entirely out of place." "What part?" inquired the preacher. "That part about union," said the man. "The Lord never intended that we should all believe alike." Ascertaining that his opponent was a Baptist preacher, Elder Wilson proposed that they should seat themselves, talk the matter over, and, if possible, come to the unity of the faith and of the knowledge of the Son of God. The other stoutly objected, declaring that they never could believe alike with respect to Jesus Christ, the operation of the Holy Spirit, Baptism, and many other things. Finally his objections were overruled; the two preachers sat down together; and the following dialogue took place in the hearing of all present:

Wilson.—Do you believe what the Bible says about Jesus Christ?

Baptist.—I do.

Wilson.—Do you believe any thing more concerning Jesus than what the Bible says?

Baptist.—No, sir; I do not.

Wilson.—Very well: now, do you believe there is one living and true God, of whom are all things and we in him?

Baptist.—Most assuredly, I do.

Wilson.—Do you believe there is one Lord, Jesus Christ, by whom are all things and we by him, and that this Jesus is the Son of God?

Baptist.—Yes, I believe he is, and that he is the Eternal Son of God.

Wilson.—Hold, my dear sir; you must take that back. The Bible does not say he is the "Eternal" Son.

Baptist.—Well, I will take it back. But I believe he is *co-equal, co-essential,* and *co-eternal* with the Father.

Wilson.—Hold, my friend; you must take that back also.

Baptist.—No, sir; I will not take back *every thing* I say.

Wilson.—The congregation will bear witness that you said you believe all the Bible says of Christ, *and no more;* and the Bible nowhere says he is co-equal, co-essential, or co-eternal with the Father.

Baptist.—Well, then, I will take it back.

Thus he proceeded until they agreed as to Christ. He then questioned the candid preacher, in the same manner, relative to the operation of the Holy Spirit, and the design of baptism. When they had agreed upon these subjects also, Elder Wilson, having obtained from the preacher his Confession of Faith, turned to the passage which affirms that *none but General Baptists have a right to the Lord's table.* "Here," said he, "is one thing which is not in my book;" and turning on through, he said, "Here is another thing, and here another." The astonished preacher looked at all the passages, and solemnly declared that he would no longer be governed by such a Confession. By this time the clouds, as well as some theological fog, had disappeared; the company separated in perfect good feeling; and in a short time the Baptist preacher and all his flock exchanged their human for the divine creed.

Since 1852 he has preached for various churches in Warrick, Pike, Knox, Sullivan, Vigo, Clay, Owen, Greene, Lawrence, Martin, and Daviess counties, Indiana; and Lawrence and Clarke counties, Illinois. All these counties he has visited annually; his plan having been to hold a protracted meeting each year in every congregation. These meetings are often appointed a year in advance, and are anxiously expected. When the "good time coming" arrives, the brethren flock in from great distances.

They enjoy a pleasant reunion; and have emphatically a "big" meeting, which not unfrequently closes with from twenty-five to fifty additions to "the saved."

Thus he continues to this day; throughout south-western Indiana "witnessing both to small and great, saying none other things than those which Moses and the prophets did say should come."

It is now *thirty-seven years* since he began to turn men to righteousness. During this time he has organized some forty churches, and introduced about two thousand persons into the kingdom of God's dear Son. Nor has he only introduced them—he has also, like "a good minister of Jesus Christ," put the brethren in remembrance of their religious duties, and nourished them up in the words of faith and sound doctrine.

If, in point of that intellectual power which is acquired by education, he has received only one talent, this one he has not "digged in the earth" and hid, like many who employ the most splendid endowments in groveling and covetous pursuits. To him will the Master say, when he comes to reckon, "Well done, good and faithful servant; thou hast been faithful over a few things, I will make thee ruler over many things."

Such, briefly, is the history of Elder Joseph Wilson; the following is, still more briefly, the *man himself*. He is about five feet ten inches high, and weighs about one hundred and sixty pounds. He was blessed by nature with such an excellent constitution that, despite the exposure to which his profession has subjected him, he has enjoyed through life almost uninterrupted health.

His head forces, especially memory, are very good; but the heart forces predominate. It is by his goodness, rather than his greatness, that he influences the people. His example is more potent than his precepts.

At home he is kind, provident, hospitable—ardently

attached to his family and to his friends. To the religious training of his children—of whom he has ten—he was very attentive; and he has lived to see them all become obedient to the gospel.

In the social circle, he is agreeable, but rather disposed to be grave; seldom, if ever, indulging in "foolish jesting, which is not convenient." He knows but little of the requirements of polite society; but his pure heart is deeply imbued with that charity which "doth not behave itself unseemly."

In the pulpit, his manner is direct, unpretending, and somewhat peculiar. When he rises to preach he spreads the open Bible tenderly before him; elevates his open hands, with palms down, until each arm forms a right angle at the elbow, and says, "Let us read a portion of the word of the Lord." He then repeats from memory one, two, or three chapters, as may suit his purpose, and proceeds in a cursory manner to expatiate upon the more important portions of his text. His language is neither elegant nor chaste; his words being often in the wrong mood and tense, but always from the heart. His delivery is slow at first, but toward the close quite animated. In argument he is not weak; in exhortation he is decidedly strong. His favorite theme is Union, and his greatest conquests have been in that direction.

In the church he has always been beloved as a brother. He is now looked upon as a father in Israel, in whom there is no guile; and whenever, in his annual round, he departs from a congregation, there is no little sorrowing lest they may see his face no more.

It will not be long until these fears are realized. Having well nigh completed his sixty-sixth year, the time of his departure cannot be far distant; but he is ready to be offered up, knowing that there is "laid up for him a crown of righteousness which the Lord, the righteous Judge, will give him in that day."

LIBRARY
OF THE
UNIVERSITY OF ILLINOIS

F. W. EMMONS.

Francis Whitefield, the eldest son of Horatio and Abigail Emmons, was born February 24th, 1802, at Clarendon, Vt., which was also the birthplace of his mother. His father was born at Cornwall, Conn. His grandfather, Solomon, was also a native of Connecticut, and a son of Woodruff Emmons, who was born on the Atlantic ocean while his parents were making the passage from England to America, about the year 1720. Woodruff was a son—perhaps the second—of William Emmons, a native of Great Britain, and the eldest son of Carolus Emmons, who, according to tradition and a coat of arms, (a fac-simile of which is now in the possession of Francis W.,) was a general under William and Mary, by whom he was knighted about the year 1690 for "five victorious battles in the field of blood."

Solomon Emmons was an officer in the Revolution of '76; and Horatio served from near the beginning to the close of the war of 1812. From time immemorial the family seem to have been a warlike and long-lived people.

Abigail, the mother of Francis W., was the youngest daughter of Whitefield Foster, who was the son of Benjamin Foster, a native of England. In religion the Fosters were Universalists; in politics they were Federalists.

When his father entered the army, Francis W., then a wild youth of eleven summers, went to reside with an uncle, Daniel Smith, at Sheldon, Vt. There he was measurably *tamed* by being subjected to hard labor on a farm.

His uncle Daniel was a staunch Federalist, and bitterly opposed to the war; so also was *his* father, Elihu Smith. Daniel gave aid and comfort to the enemy by smuggling cattle into Canada, in which business Francis W. assisted most reluctantly; and when the roar of the battle of Plattsburg (in which Francis' father was engaged) was heard at Sheldon, old Elihu, a devout (?) Presbyterian, prayed most fervently for the success of the British. But notwithstanding these evil associations, young Emmons remained a firm Democrat, or Republican, as were his father and grandfather before him.

Returning to Swanton in 1815, he spent a portion of his time in school, and a portion in laboring for the support of his mother and her family, who resided at that place.

On the 7th of April, 1816, he and his mother made a public profession of faith in Christ, were immersed, and united with the Baptist church at Swanton.

The next year he became a clerk in the store of A. & C. Harmon, Burlington, Vt., in which position he remained a year and a half. Feeling that it was his duty to preach the gospel, he, at the expiration of that time, returned to Swanton to make arrangements for qualifying himself for his high calling by a further improvement of his education.

In the prosecution of this design, he had to struggle against strong opposition both at home and in the church. His brethren were free to declare that they did not believe he ever *could* preach; while his mother's advice was, "*Be any thing but a poor Baptist preacher.*" Finally, however, she consented that he might follow his own convictions of duty, and bestowed upon him, departing, her choicest blessing.

His first remove was to Georgia, Vt., where he attended a good school during the Summer of 1819. The ensuing Winter—being then eighteen years of age—he taught school for four months near Plattsburg, N. Y., after which he again returned to Swanton.

In the Spring of 1821, with only twenty-five cents in his pocket, he once more bade adieu to the loved ones at home; and, with a staff in one hand and a little bundle of clothes in the other, started off to go—he knew not whither. His first thought was to direct his steps to Phillips Academy, at Andover, Mass.; but, with the advice of some well-informed friends, he changed his purpose, and entered the Baptist Literary and Theological Seminary, at Hamilton, N. Y.

There he united with the Second Baptist church, by which he was licensed to preach. There he also went through the regular course of studies, requiring three years, defraying his expenses by serving as librarian, or at whatever else his hand could find to do. Among his classmates were Jacob Knapp and Pharcellus Church; the latter of whom was his bosom friend and *chum;* and both of whom have become distinguished Baptist ministers. At the same time Jonathan Wade and Eugenio Kincaid, now missionaries to Burmah, and John Newton Brown, D. D., the compiler of the "Encyclopedia of Religious Knowledge," were also students of that institution.

Having completed the course at Hamilton, which it seems was chiefly theological, he repaired, in 1824, to Columbian College, D. C., and there devoted himself to studies more purely literary in their character. Entering the Preparatory, he passed regularly through the Freshman, Sophomore, and part of the Junior years, paying his way by ringing the bell, acting as college postmaster, and, in a word, by consenting to be a kind of academic factotum.

While a Sophomore, he edited, for a short time, "The

Columbian Star," to which paper he made frequent contributions during his connection with that institution.

During the Summer of 1826 he served as a missionary under the direction of a Female Missionary Society at Richmond, Va. Furnished by them with an old horse, very like Don Quixote's "Rosinante," and also with a letter of commendation from their Secretary, (Mrs. Jane Keeling), he set out to preach the way of life and salvation—first in the vicinity of Richmond, then in the regions beyond the Blue Ridge.

On account of certain financial embarrassments Columbian College was closed in the Spring of 1827; at which time Mr. Emmons entered Brown University, at Providence, R. I. He was graduated at this institution in September, 1828.

Soon after his graduation he accepted a pressing call to supply, for a few weeks, the pulpit of the first Baptist church at Eastport, Maine. Before the period of his first engagement expired he was again employed for six months; and before the expiration of this time, he was permanently settled as their pastor, being ordained as such in the first Baptist church at Providence, R. I., in May, 1829.

On the 31st of August following he was married to Mary Ann H., eldest daughter of Rev. Zenas L. Leonard, of Sturbridge, Mass.

A year or two prior to this event, he became a reader of the "Christian Baptist." Its searching expositions, enforced by the unsatisfactory fruits of his own ministry, greatly weakened his faith in the gospel he was then preaching. On this account he became much dejected. He fasted, prayed, and spent much of his time in solitude. His health finally failing, he resigned his pastoral charge on the 31st of December, 1829, and soon after returned with his wife to her paternal home in Massachusetts.

In the Spring of 1830, having partially recovered his health, he opened a school in the old Academy at Killingworth, Conn. On Lord's days a little congregation of Baptists met together in the Academy, for whom he preached gratuitously as long as they were disposed to hear. This, however, was not very long; for as he received and read the Millennial Harbinger, it was soon whispered about that he was a "Campbellite," and that his influence in both the pulpit and the school-room was extremely dangerous. Therefore the ears of the Baptists grew "dull of hearing;" and both they and the Congregationalists withdrew their support from his school. By this means the number of his pupils was reduced to four or five, and these were the children of Universalists or Infidels.

In the Summer of this year, leaving his school in charge of Mrs. Emmons, he made a tour to Bethany, Va., where he formed the personal acquaintance of Alexander Campbell, with whom he spent several days most pleasantly and profitably.

Leaving Bethany, he returned by way of New Lisbon, Ohio; to which place he removed with his family in the Spring of 1831. Here he opened a school, which was well patronized—the doctrine of the Reformation being more popular than at Killingworth. Indeed, the Baptist church at this place claimed to be reformed; but it was still so far from the ancient order that neither he nor any of his family united with it.

While residing at New Lisbon, and at the request of Elder A. Campbell, he carefully examined his (Campbell's) second edition of the New Testament, comparing it with the common version and with the original Greek; and communicated to him many valuable notes, emendations, and suggestions for an improved version. His services in this particular were acknowledged by Mr. Campbell in the preface to the fourth edition, and also in the preface to the Family Testament.

In the Spring of 1832 he removed to Wellsburg, Va., where he took charge of Brooke Academy. There he found a genuine Christian church, with which he united, and in which he became a shining light, holding forth the word of life. There too his health again failed, and it was feared that Consumption had marked him for his victim. But it pleased God that he should not then die; and after a brief season of rest he was again ready for the Master's service.

In December 1833 he and his family came to Madison, Indiana, on a visit to Mr. George Leonard, an uncle of Mrs. Emmons. Soon after their arrival Mrs. Leonard died; and Mrs. Emmons, at the request of her uncle, entered into the mother's place, and for nearly a year took the oversight of his children with her own. During this period Mr. Emmons visited many portions of Indiana, having then no other occupation than the preaching of the word.

In the Spring of 1834 his brother William A. came also to Madison, and they two went off together into the interior of the State, in search of a suitable place to which to remove their families. They finally fixed upon Noblesville, in Hamilton county, twenty miles north of Indianapolis. Thither they removed in the Fall of that year, arriving there on the 30th of November.

Elder Emmons immediately secured a District school, which he taught during the winter of 1834-5, in the old log school-house at Noblesville. He labored also "in word and doctrine;" and through his influence two little churches, a Baptist and a Christian, became one, being united on the *Bible alone*.

In ministering to this church while it remained weak and persecuted, he passed some of the happiest days of his life. But in process of time false brethren were brought in unawares; roots of bitterness sprang up among them; and the spirit of strife and contention supplanted the spirit of love and forbearance. There was "that woman Jezebel;" and there too were "Hymeneus and Alexander." On account of these "debates, envyings, wraths, strifes, backbitings," etc., all of which grew out of some difference of opinion relative to the organization, order, and discipline of the churches, Elder Emmons asked and obtained a letter of dismission from that congregation, which action placed him, religiously, precisely where he stood on coming West.

"After this amicable separation from the church at Noblesville," writes one who knew him in that day, "he remained several years a resident there, travelling pretty extensively through the State and the northwest, including Kentucky. Though a member of no particular congregation he still ranked and passed as a brother and preacher among us: attended all our State and most of our District and County Co-operation meetings, of which he was frequently secretary."

During all this period his mind remained uncorrupted "from the simplicity that is in Christ." He discarded all human appliances for the conversion of sinners; and taught the people to observe *all* and *only* those things which the Lord has commanded.

In the Winter of 1836 he was appointed by the Senate of the Indiana Legislature to report the proceedings of that body, for publication in the newspapers. By his pen the public were kept thoroughly posted with regard to the great system of internal improvements, which was, that Winter, discussed and adopted.

At Cincinnati, in the Winter of 1837, he was associated with E. P. Cranch, Esq., in taking down and writing out for publication the Debate between Campbell and Purcell, on the Roman Catholic Religion.

In the same year he published "The Voice, or An Essay to Extend the Reformation"—a little 18mo volume of 252 pages.

In the Winter of 1838 he had a spirited little controversy with a young Methodist itinerant, by the name of Berry—subsequently the "Rev. Lucien W. Berry, D. D., President of the Indiana Asbury University." Some letters passed between them, which were published by Mr. Emmons in a pamphlet of thirty-six pages, with "Marks and Remarks." This elicited from Mr. Berry a pamphlet of forty pages, titled, "The Deformer Reformed, or Corruption Exposed." This was responded to in another little pamphlet of sixty pages, titled, "The Afterclap—Showing the Origin of the Corruption," etc., etc. No reply was elicited; so here the warfare ended.

In the Fall of 1842, Elder Emmons returned to New England; and in the absence of a Christian congregation, and at the urgent solicitation of some of his early friends, he soon after united with the First Baptist church in Boston, which church was then under the pastoral charge of Dr. R. H. Neale, his old friend and fellow-student at Columbian College.

On account of this return to the Baptists, after "having tasted the good word of God," he has been regarded by many as vacillating—as a double-minded man, unstable in all his religious ways. But the facts, when properly understood, hardly justify such a conclusion. It is perhaps nearer the truth to say that his unfortunate difficulties with the brethren at Noblesville; his strong attachment to those Baptists who were the friends and companions of his youth; and the fact that on his return to the East, he found no congregation of Disciples with whom he could conveniently worship;—induced him to renew his connection with a church to which (though containing many pious and devoted people) the Lord cannot say, as to the church at Pergamos, "Thou holdest fast my *name*, and hast not denied *my* faith."

The last fact—that there was no congregation of Disciples convenient—will have little weight with those who remember the words of the indomitable Roman who said, *Viam aut veniam aut faciam*—" I will either *find* a way, or *make* a way." These will think that Elder Emmons ought to have *found* a Christian church or *built up one;* but they must not charge him too hastily with unfaithfulness. His fault seems to have been, chiefly, lack of energy—" the very head and front of his offending hath this extent, no more." That he has not denied the faith is clearly established by indubitable testimony.

In a letter to J. M. Mathes, he himself says, "In uniting as I did with the First Baptist church in Boston, in 1843, *I renounced no Reformation principle that I ever held.*" The pastor of that church, Dr. Neale, says of him : " His reception into my church was owing to my knowledge of his character as a Christian, and not to any sympathy with the peculiar speculative notions in which it was somewhat natural for him to indulge." " For these ' peculiar notions,' and ' theological speculations' "—says Elder E. in his letter to Elder Mathes—" or for the *faith* and *teaching* contained in them, has my name been cast out as evil. I have been looked upon as a speckled bird, having had no *call*, and no *pastoral charge* in any Baptist church since 1830. * * * So, for my Reformation principles—nicknamed ' Campbellism'—for their *avowal* and *advocacy*, I have been, still am, and expect to be a *living martyr.*"

He acknowledges no creed but the Bible ; preaches no baptism but that "for the remission of sins ;" employs his pen in support of no faith but that " once delivered to the saints;" and wherever in his travels he meets with a congregation of Disciples, with them he fraternizes, advocating their cause. He is still to be regarded, therefore, as a Reformation preacher; and as such his history is continued.

For a short time after his return to New England, he supplied the pulpit of the Baptist church at Sturbridge, Massachusetts; preaching also elsewhere as he had opportunity. He sought a permanent location as pastor of some Baptist congregation; but, (as already intimated,) owing to his connection with the Disciples out West, he sought in vain—for no call was given him.

Having, while residing at Noblesville, indorsed for his brothers to a considerable amount, he found himself much involved in their debts. To extricate himself from these financial difficulties, he made several visits to Indiana, where he again preached the "ancient gospel," as in former years.

The Winter of 1845–6 he spent in Washington city, letter writing, office seeking, etc. In the following Spring he purchased a small farm near Globe Village, Mass., to which he removed with his wife and four daughters, and upon which he has resided ever since.

Having studied medicine more or less, and practiced it in his family since 1832, he, in the Winter of 1846–7, attended a course of lectures at the Worcester Medical College, at Worcester, Mass. In 1856 the Metropolitan Medical College of New York city bestowed upon him a diploma and the honorary degree of M. D.

In the Fall of 1847, he was brought out on the morning of election day, in opposition to the two regular nominees, and elected as the Representative of the town of Sturbridge in the next General Court. He was elected as a Democrat; and so far as he had taken any part in politics, hitherto, he had acted with the Democratic party.

But soon after taking his seat in the Legislature, some resolutions relative to the Mexican war were brought before the House. Before casting his vote he defined his position on the war and on slavery, in a speech which was published and mainly endorsed in the Boston "True Whig." Since that time (1848) he has been identified with the Free Soil party.

In the Legislature he distinguished himself by his zealous and able advocacy of a more stringent liquor law. He was chairman of a committee of fourteen members— one from each county in the State—which committee reported a bill corresponding in its main features with the Maine Liquor Law. In the discussion on this bill, Mr. Emmons advocated its passage in two telling speeches, which were printed in pamphlet form.

The measure was at that time defeated; but at a subsequent session it was revived and finally passed. Though at the time of its passage Mr. E. was not a member of the Legislature, yet his printed speeches were freely circulated in the House, and no doubt exerted a strong influence in favor of the proposed law.

In the Summer of this same year he attended the Commencement of his *alma mater*, Brown University; and was then and there declared to be a Master of Arts.

In the Fall of 1849 some forty members of the Emmons family, residents of New York, Connecticut, and Massachusetts, met in Convention at Canaan, Conn., to take into consideration an advertisement of a large Emmons estate in England for heirs in America; which advertisement is said to have appeared in some English paper. By this Convention F. W. Emmons was appointed to go to England to look after the said estate.

Accordingly, on the 1st of January, 1850, he embarked at Boston in a packet ship for Liverpool. The result of his efforts in quest of a fortune has not been made public;

but it is known that he had the pleasure of visiting, at little expense to himself, many of the principal cities and important towns of England—among which were Manchester, Birmingham, the old walled town of Chester, and the great metropolis, London.

From the period of his return from England (May 1850) until 1855, he devoted the most of his time to cultivating and improving his little farm in Massachusetts.

At the date last mentioned he was employed as a recorder in the office of Thomas Spooner, Esq., Clerk of the Courts of Hamilton County, Ohio. During the last few years he has, perhaps, spent more time and performed more labor in that office than in the sacred desk.

Ever since his return to the East he has preached less than in former years; and during the whole of his ministry it has been more by his pen than by his tongue that he has exerted a considerable influence and made himself widely known. In addition to the publications already mentioned, he has been a contributor to the Millennial Harbinger from its commencement until the present. For it he has furnished a great variety of articles— Journals, Essays, Letters, Sermons, Reviews, etc., etc., over the signatures of "F.," "Francis," "Adolphus," "Philologus," "F. W. E.," and his name in full. Articles from his pen have also appeared from time to time in other reformation periodicals—"The Evangelist," "Christian Preacher," "Heretic Detecter," "Journal of Christianity," Christian Record," "American Christian Review"—and in several Baptist and other papers—religious, literary, medical, and phrenological.

For the most part his articles have been of a critical, exegetical, or reformatory character; and, although at times a little speculative, his has been in the main "a most wholesome doctrine and very full of comfort."

His pen still active; his mind yet sound in a sound

body; his treasures of wisdom and knowledge increased rather than diminished by the liberality with which he has given to the world; there is good reason to hope that, for years to come, he will remain "a strong pillar in the house of his God."

Francis W. Emmons is five feet ten inches high. His weight, never over one hundred and forty pounds, is now less than one hundred and thirty. His dark-brown hair is straight and very fine; his eyes light blue, or gray; his complexion rather dark. His teeth—all sound at three-score—testify, by their presence and by their color, that he neither chews nor smokes tobacco; while his keen eye and healthy glow indicate that he is "temperate in all things."·

His mental organism, physical resources, leading traits of character, etc., are thus described by the celebrated phrenologist, L. N. Fowler—with the omission of a few particulars which are unimportant, or known to be incorrect. He says:

"You have a very marked temperament. The nervous system predominates; but you have a high degree of the muscular organization, which gives you an unusual amount of activity, restlessness, and the desire to be constantly employed.

"Your constitution is naturally tough, exceedingly so; and you have endured more than one in thousands. But the ability to manufacture vitality is not so great as the desire to exhaust what you have; so that you will find it necessary to strictly obey the laws of life in order to avoid premature decay. You cannot do half you wish— for your spirit is ahead of your physical ability to perform.

"You are characterized phrenologically for having a very positive and almost eccentric cast of mind. Your head is uneven, and the large organs are very sharply developed, so that the mind acts with more than ordinary intensity.

"You have an unconquerable will, and are very independent and self-relying.

"You are noted for cautiousness, forethought, and for the desire to avoid difficulties and dangers. Whatever you engage in is accomplished, as though there was much at stake; you never do any thing carelessly.

"Love of children constitutes your leading social peculiarity. You are not inclined to seek company as a source of enjoyment.

"You are noted for your intellectual abilities. You can attend to business that requires observation, knowledge of the qualities of things, and the condition of circumstances; or you can think originally and investigate new principles successfully.

"You are remarkably orderly and systematic. You plan out all your work, do it according to rule, and as well as you possibly can, the first time trying.

"You have a very keen appreciation of wit; and enjoy a joke very highly—are much amused by your own mirthful emotions.

"Your intuitive impressions of character are very correct. Few men decide so quickly on results as you; and you seldom have occasion to change your first impression.

"You are kind-hearted and generous in your feelings; are respectful in your general intercourse with society; are sanguine, enthusiastic, cheerful, buoyant, and always encouraged by prospects ahead.

"You are not a marvellous man; but are governed by judgment. You do not imitate others—are a perfect original.

"You are a direct, plain, free-spoken man, and abominate hypocrisy. You can keep things to yourself by saying nothing, but if you begin to talk you are compelled to develop your real sentiments. You are not cruel, and are opposed to capital punishment, or any kind of chastisement for the purpose of gratifying a revengeful feeling.

"You are hungry, mentally and physically; have an eager, unsatisfied mind; and the more knowledge you acquire the more anxious you are to increase your store.

"Although money slips through your fingers easily, and you are not necessarily a good financier, still you have a strong desire to accumulate and do as much business as you can.

"You are particularly fond of the grand and sublime in nature; are quite punctual in your engagements, and have an excellent memory of places.

"You are distinguished, then, for intensity, activity, distinctness, and positiveness; for independence, will-power, humanity of feeling, intuition of mind, originality of thought, power of criticism, and love of order; for mechanical judgment, fondness for children, and love of home. But you need more sociability, more affability of manner and control over your feelings in speech, more executive power in the form of destructiveness, more spirituality and belief in the supernatural, more versatility of manner, freedom of speech, memory of statistics, and general musical ability. *You will wear yourself out and use up your entire machinery before you get through with life.*"

In the above description the main features of his character are presented; but some do not appear with sufficient distinctness. His love of order, for instance, deserves more prominence. On this point the following testimony was borne by A. Campbell, in the Millennial Harbinger: "Our beloved brother Emmons is a great lover of good order, and precise on all points to a scruple; and therefore an effort for a perfect system of order comes as naturally from him as light from the sun." On account of this remark Mr. Emmons wrote for a while over the signature, "A Precise Brother."

Closely allied to this and also too much in the background is his *punctuality*. He is always "in time;" and in filling his preaching appointments, if permitted to follow his own inclinations, he speaks at the appointed hour whether the congregation is present or absent. This disposition he once gratified in a remarkable manner, while on his missionary tour through "the hill country" of the Old Dominion.

The attendance upon his ministrations was *often* very meagre; but one day he arrived at a little dilapidated church in advance of every one else. The appointment was for twelve, M.; and when the hour came—though not a soul was present save himself—he sang a hymn, prayed, and proceeded to preach from Heb. ii. 3: "*How shall we escape if we neglect so great salvation!*" When about half through his discourse two women entered, looked round in amazement, sat down for a few moments, then arose and departed. The preacher continued to the final amen; and having penciled upon the pulpit the day, the month, the year, and *the text*, he and his bony steed,

——"With wandering steps and slow,
Through *Eden* took their solitary way."

"Your language is not sufficient for the fluent expression of your ideas," says the phrenologist; and the remark might be verified by a number of witnesses. Dr. Neale of Boston says of him: "He is not a popular preacher. *He has not the gift of extemporaneous utterance.* The pen is obviously his *forte*. He is fond of essays and theological disquisitions; and his written compositions are usually clear, vigorous, and to the point."

He himself understands that he is, like Moses, "slow of speech and of a slow tongue." Therefore it has been his habit to read his discourses; and when he appears before a strange audience he pleasantly introduces his manuscript as his " brother Aaron."

Take him all in all, he is an amiable Christian gentleman; "tender and well beloved in the sight of all his brethren." His early friend, Dr. Neale, but spoke the sentiments of many in the following words, with which we close this biography. He says:

" I love to think of him—not as a theologian, preacher, or writer, but as ' brother Emmons' of Columbian College days. I see him now, taking his walk with cane and umbrella, in rain or sunshine, his hat over on the back side of his head. He generally preferred to walk alone; but if a friend was with him the conversation would be on some religious or literary topic—the lesson of the day or the meaning of a difficult passage of Scripture. He never indulged in petty scandal.

" I could say much more in praise of my friend Emmons, but he is—I rejoice to know—still living; and I trust the day is far distant when it will be proper to speak with the freedom usually indulged in reference to departed worth."

SAMUEL K. HOSHOUR.

Very many persons are under the impression that the subject of this sketch is a native of Germany. This impression is incorrect. He was born in York county, Pennsylvania, on the 9th of December, 1803; and has never so much as stood upon transatlantic soil. His American ancestors, nearly a century before his birth, came from the vicinity of Strasburg on the Rhine; and *their* ancestry had in them more of the French than of the German element. The immigrants to America, having settled in a community totally German, in time lost the French characteristics, as also the language; and at the time of his birth they spoke only American German.

Samuel K. was the oldest of six children; and in his fourteenth year he lost his kind father, who was in principle a Mennonite, though a member of no church. His mother was a Lutheran after "the straitest sect," conscientious in what she believed to be the will of God. Though a firm believer in Infant Rantism, she did not insist upon the sprinkling of her children, in opposition to the views of her husband, who regarded it as a relic of Popery. The neglect of this rite, however, did not prevent her from imparting to her first-born early religious instruction. On the contrary, whenever she had an opportunity, she would relate to him gospel facts, and teach him short, impressive prayers. On all proper occasions she took him to the house of God, and never failed to put into his pocket a copper for the congregational treasury—

UNIVERSITY OF ILLINOIS

thus teaching him to practice Christian liberality, a lesson he has never forgotten.

At the death of his father, who left considerable property, he was placed under the control of a *guardian*—in this, as in many other instances, a palpable misnomer. By this high-minded (?) guardian he was, for several years, hired out on a farm at very low wages; for, owing to the density of the population, and the consequent slight demand for laborers, he, at the age of sixteen, could obtain only four dollars a month for his services.

His residence among strangers as a hireling was not by any means favorable to the development of either his moral or intellectual endowments. He went to school but little, and as he had greater fondness for extracting the finny tribes from their element and opossums from their retreats, than for extracting ideas from books, he spent the most of his time in the first-named employments; nor did his views of the sanctity of the Sabbath at all interfere with such pursuits even on that day. Under such circumstances, his progress was so slow that at the close of his sixteenth year he had not quite reached the "rule of three," which, in that day, was generally regarded as the *ultima thule*—the last island—in the ocean of scientific truth.

About this time his guardian and relatives concluded that he ought to learn a trade; and he was required to make choice of his pursuit. To him the county in which he lived was the world; so with his limited vision he surveyed hastily the several employments of his neighbors, and decided in favor of the *tanning business!* It was accordingly arranged that he should be indentured to learn the trade of his choice, at the beginning of the year 1820. But what a trifling incident often changes the direction of human life, and conducts to a different destiny the immortal soul!

During the summer of 1819, he was hired to the owner of a large grist mill, in which he was usually employed on such days as were unfavorable for outdoor pursuits. The proprietor of this establishment was a better miller than bookkeeper; and, as his employee could write a legible hand and repeat the table for dry measure, he set him to posting his accounts, which work was satisfactorily performed.

In the Fall of that year the citizens expressed great apprehensions that they should be without a school the ensuing Winter; for the old Swiss gentleman, who, for years, had been wont to teach in the Winter, and in the Summer go into parts unknown, mending old clocks and soldering leaky tinware, had not returned at his usual period—

> "One morn they miss'd him on the accustom'd hill,
> Along the heath and near his favorite tree."

As the mill was the rendezvous of the leading minds of the community, their apprehensions were often expressed in the hearing of the miller, who one day found means to quiet their fears: said he, "Here is Sammy Hoshour, who can write a pretty good hand, can multiply and divide, and reduce pints to bushels: he can control the small ones, and if larger ones will not obey let them be kept at home. This proposition pleased many, but some doubted. However, necessity and the miller's influence invested him with the birch, the symbol of school-room authority in that day. He was then seventeen years old; the community was purely German; and he knew no English save a few sentences gathered from Yankee tin-peddlers. Contrary to his own expectations and those of the doubting ones, his didactic administration was a success, and gave general satisfaction.

It was expected that, at the close of the term, he would

relinquish the birch and enter upon his apprenticeship; but when the time arrived he had forty dollars in his pocket, a spirit of inquiry had been awakened in his mind, and he had caught the scent of something more agreeable than a tannery. He therefore changed his former purpose, with the consent of his guardian, and determined to procure, with the proceeds of his school, some further scholastic attainments.

This resolution, though he knew it not, was an important step in his life—it was the beginning of his literary career. He soon after entered, for the first time, an English school, being then a stalwart, awkward, and verdant rustic. His first recitation was so unique and so *germanic* that it subverted the gravity of both teacher and pupils. Yet, submitting with stoical indifference to these slight discourtesies, he remained in the school until he obtained a fair knowledge of arithmetic, and a slight acquaintance with the *nonsense*, as he supposed, of English grammar. His money being exhausted, he returned for awhile to the plow; and on the approach of winter he entered upon his second administration as teacher.

In his eighteenth year he united with the Lutheran church. Soon after this event, a copy of Pilgrim's Progress fell into his hands, which was the first book he ever read through. Besides the religious influence it exerted upon him, it stimulated his desire of knowledge. Believing that sacred knowledge was best of all, and that the Christian ministry was the repository of it, he greatly desired the requisite qualifications for entering into that vocation.

His guardian, being a Mennonite, and opposed to a learned ministry, refused to furnish him with the means of further educating himself; but a wealthy maternal uncle, who was a staunch Lutheran, consented to supply him with money until he should possess his patrimony.

He then entered an English classical school of high repute at York, Pa. His highest aspiration at that time was to become a good German preacher. The idea of ever addressing English audiences had not yet entered his head.

But English declamations were required in the school, and when his day came all the pupils were eager to hear the "Dutchman." Having determined to make up in *spirit* and *sound* what he lacked in *orthoepy* and *inflection*, his speech was well received; and as he passed out the Professor encouragingly predicted that, by proper effort, he would become a good English speaker. From that moment he sought to become *English*, and with such success that one cannot now detect the slightest German accent in his pronunciation.

In this Institution he completed about an equivalent to the regular college course to the close of the sophomore year. Here, too, by excessive study, he so seriously impaired his health, that his advisers urged him to change his location. Accordingly he repaired to the Theological Institute at New Market, Virginia, then under the control of Prof. S. S. Schmucker. By more temperate study, by frequent exercise in the rugged sections of that country, and by a free use of the mineral waters of that region, he partially recuperated his overtaxed powers, and was enabled to complete the course of study there pursued, which course embraced the collegiate studies of the junior and senior years, in connection with theology—theology, not according to the Bible, but according to the standards of the Lutheran church.

At this time the Principal, Prof. Schmucker, was elected Professor of Theology in the Theological Seminary at Gettysburg, Pa. Besides his duties in the Institute at New Market, the Professor had served three small congregations as their pastor. His flocks were so much attached to him that they refused to let him go, unless he would first provide an acceptable substitute. As it was necessary, in this pastorate, to officiate in both English and German, and as no other of the many students could do this so well as Elder Hoshour, he was nominated and received as the successor of Professor Schmucker.

In the same year, 1826, he was married to Miss Lucinda Savage, daughter of Jacob Savage, Esq., of New Market, Va.

Tenacious of the traditions of his theological fathers, fully impressed with the greatness of the Lutheran church, and not a little inflated by the fact that he had been counted worthy to wear the mantle of his preceptor, he entered upon his clerical duties with great zeal for God, though with very little knowledge of His word. In the pulpit he was not always mindful of Paul's admonition "to speak the things that become sound doctrine." Like too many young preachers he estimated the value of his preaching, not by the number of correct and lasting impressions made on the minds and hearts of his hearers, but rather by the excitement they manifested, and the quantity of tears they shed. Hence, in the preparation of his sermons, he collected all that was terrible in the domain of fear, and all that was touching in the realms of love and suffering. Then, as now, this style of preaching was popular; and, like Ezekiel, he was to the people "as a very lovely song of one that hath a pleasant voice, and can play well on an instrument."

His fame soon extended eastward; and, in 1828, he received and accepted a call from a congregation in Washington county, Maryland In this place, also, he was popular among all sorts and classes. Such, indeed, became his reputation, that in about two years he was invited to follow his old preceptor, and take charge of the congregation at Gettysburg, Pa., the seat of Pennsylvania College, and also of the Theological Seminary of the

General Synod of the Lutheran Church. But his Maryland charge so heartily remonstrated against his removal that he consented to stay with them.

His pastorate was about eight miles from Hagerstown, the county seat, in which there were at that time about five thousand inhabitants, among whom Lutheranism was the predominant religion. Among others was a large and influential congregation which had been for years under the pastoral care of Dr. B. Kurtz. Owing to his proximity to this place, Elder Hoshour frequently occupied the Doctor's splendid pulpit, and so acceptable were his ministrations that, in 1831, he became their pastor, Dr Kurtz having been called to another field of labor.

In his stipulations with the "Council" relative to his pastoral duties, there was one feature that greatly assisted him to become a heretic—if indeed he is one. It was made a part of his duty to lecture each Wednesday evening on the Holy Scriptures; and, in order to fulfill this part of his engagement, he was compelled to study the Scriptures in their proper connection. This he had never done before, though he had been preaching for five years; for, in the theological seminary, he had taken the *regular* course prescribed in such institutions—that is, to study human dissertations upon theology, church history, the art of sermonizing, etc., and to examine the *Bible* only as referred to by the standards of the particular sect! But in performing this new duty, he entered into the school of Apostles and Prophets. He began lecturing alternately on Matthew and the Acts of the Apostles, expounding the doctrine in the light of the context, and giving copious geographical delineations, accompanied by the history of places and events. Proceeding in this way, it was not long till he entertained the opinion that the religion of the Bible was very different from that in popular repute. He perceived that the former was sober, solid, a matter of principle; while the latter was full of excitement, vapory, and not a little unscrupulous. He became daily more enamored of the ancient gospel, and less confident in the popular theology; more desirous of the sincere milk of the word, and less concerned about the tenets of his church. His preaching grew more and more evangelical, and soon the light of the great Luther was almost lost in the brighter effulgence of the Apostle Paul.

In preparing the last class of catechumens for "confirmation," he used the catechism very sparingly, but required them to commit to memory large portions of the New Testament. On the day of confirmation he did not use the liturgical form, but confined the ceremony to the 24th verse of the 16th chapter of Matthew, the import of which he had previously explained to the candidates. This departure from the usages of the Lutheran fathers met no opposition, such confidence had the congregation in the knowledge and integrity of their pastor.

In his further investigations of the Scriptures he began to call in question of the consequences ascribed to the fall of Adam, and especially did he become intolerant of the Calvinistic view of that subject. The ability or inability of the sinner was a subject upon which he bestowed much thought.

While reflecting upon this subject he made a visit to his father-in-law's, at New Market, Va., where there came into his hands, one day, three numbers of the Christian Baptist. Of the editor, Alexander Campbell, he at that time knew but little, nor was he by any means favorable to the views of the Baptists. Yet he glanced at some of the articles, and was better pleased than he anticipated with both the style and the matter. One article especially, on The Natural Man, (I. Cor. 2,) he read with no common interest, for the thoughts therein expressed were very similar to some that had flitted through his own mind.

In a few weeks he returned to Hagerstown, and resumed the regular routine of his pastoral duties, but still that article on the Natural Man, like the ghost of murdered Banquo, continually confronted him.

Thus matters went on till the Spring of 1834, when an event took place which wrought a change in his views of Baptism and in the aspects of his whole future life. About six miles from Hagerstown was a densely populated region called Beaver Creek, rich in things material, but poor in things spiritual. A large school-house was the usual place of preaching, and prior appointments took the lead in its accommodations. Most of the different sects had a few adherents in that region, who occasionally procured the services of their respective ministers. Elder Hoshour frequently preached to them the Lutheran gospel; Methodists, Episcopalians, United Brethren, and Tunkers also visited them; but none were successful in making proselytes.

In the Spring of 1834, an unexpected religious commotion occurred in the Beaver Creek region. A new preacher made his appearance, dauntlessly advocating views that negatived a great amount of the previous preaching at that point. He called himself a disciple of Christ, but as he distributed copies of the Millennial Harbinger, the sects called him a Campbellite. He soon made an impression upon some minds that had hitherto been regarded as impregnable. His very success created great opposition, yet with Peter's boldness he continued to proclaim the ancient gospel without much deference to the religious leaders of the day, whom he hesitated not to challenge to the defense of their tottering systems. "The common people heard him gladly," and he was not long in making proselytes to "the ancient order." Persons of superior standing in the community, who, the clergy supposed, never would consent to be "dipped," did submit to immersion, evincing unmistakable sincerity in their profession of the Christian faith. In a few months over forty persons were immersed, and an active church established at Beaver Creek, on the foundation of the Apostles and Prophets.

The fame of this preacher spread far and wide, but as he was regarded by the orthodox as an arch heretic, Elder Hoshour in his clerical dignity would not honor "such a fellow" with a hearing. But he listened to the accounts given of him by others, and when informed that the preacher taught that all spiritual influence, in order to conversion, is exerted through the word, he would pleasantly observe: "He is for all word, the Methodists for all Spirit—both extremists—but we Lutherans occupy the middle and true ground, contending for both word and Spirit."

There was at this time a Lutheran brother with whom Elder Hoshour had lived in fraternal intimacy for several years. He had been "converted" at a great Lutheran revival, and had spent considerable time in preparing himself for the ministry; but being, like Moses, "slow of speech," he devoted himself to teaching. While the revival was progressing at Beaver Creek he became the teacher in the spacious school-house in which the meeting was held. He therefore almost necessarily became a hearer of the new *heresy*. Having formerly been a boarder in the house of Elder Hoshour, and being much attached to him, he often visited him at his parsonage in Hagerstown. In the course of one of their interviews the pastor asked him how the Campbellites were progressing. He replied that they were still immersing some; "and," said he, "I tell you there is more truth than poetry about those people after all. I have learned more from them about the order in which the Scriptures should be read; more about their proper divisions and the special object of each division, than our ministers of systematic theology ever taught us. I say this," continued he, "with all deference to you. I have enjoyed your ministrations; but the *theory* to which you are wed will not permit you to represent matters as those people do." "Ah!" said the *Reverend* Mr. Hoshour, "I fear you are almost persuaded to be a Campbellite." "No matter," replied the other, "I intend to honor and obey the Saviour as I understand him in his word."

Thus ended their interview, and ere long the pastor heard that his friend had been immersed, and had become an ardent advocate of the ancient gospel. In a short time the *apostate*—for so he was regarded by the orthodox—made a second visit to his friend Hoshour, who asked him his reasons for leaving the Lutheran Church. Among other reasons assigned he said that during his membership in that church he had never been taught the connection between Luke xxiv. 46, 47, and Acts ii. 38—that when anxiously seeking the pardon of his sins he had never been directed to Peter's answer to the question, "What shall we do?"—in a word, that Christian Baptism had a significance, a *design*, which the Lutheran pulpit entirely ignored. This was a startling revelation to the questioner, for, although he had been for nine years a preacher in the oldest Protestant church, the connection between the passages above referred to had never engaged his attention.

We must conclude that very many prominent preachers of the different denominations are equally ignorant to this day, else we cannot charitably regard them; for they *do not teach* this connection, and if they understand it and yet preach it not, they are guilty of "handling the word of God deceitfully."

This statement of reasons naturally led them into a discussion of Baptism. On the design—for the remission of sins—they had no controversy, for that is a cardinal doctrine in Luther's catechism and in other formularies of the church he founded. Though the doctrine was believed by Luther, it was entirely overshadowed by the unwarranted prominence given to faith. This was somewhat pardonable in him, for human nature is prone to extremes, and in avoiding the formalisms and penances of the Pope he overleaped the commandments of Jesus Christ. His errors may be overlooked, but his successors are without excuse.

But, to return. The subject and the "mode" of baptism were not so easily disposed of by the two friends. On these they joined issue, but the discussion closed without any immediate results of importance.

During the interview, however, Elder Hoshour obtained some facts relative to the teachings and practices of the Christians that seemed rather significant. Yet with respect to the "mode" of baptism he regarded them as ultra. The Theological Institute, though it had failed to acquaint him with the Scriptures, had not neglected to furnish him with the stereotyped objections to the universal prevalence of immersion. The varieties of climate; the scarcity of water in certain localities; the inconvenience and *indecency* of the practice; its incompatibility with the easiness of Christ's yoke—all forbade the conclusion that immersion is the only Scriptural baptism! But he was soon to be dispossessed of all this opposition to the truth.

Early in the Summer of 1834 his ministerial duties led him a few miles beyond Beaver Creek, where the troublesome meeting was still in progress. On the way he met a Methodist friend who at once beset him with a representation of the ruinous influence of the "Campbellite" preacher. He stated that the class-leader had encountered the preacher in debate; that he had been vanquished; that he had gone over to the enemy; that their class was about broken up; and that the preacher was more defiant than ever. "Now," continued the speaker, "he must be withstood, and you are the man to oppose him successfully, for I once heard you preach on the conversion of the eunuch, and I think you showed plainly that it is not *certain* that he was immersed." This flattering invitation he did not then accept, but promised to consider the matter.

Having joined two loving hearts in the bonds of matrimony, he set out for home. As he rode along he meditated upon what had been told him until the fire of controversy burned within him. But prudence whispered to him that, before he consented to meet this Goliath of the "Campbellites," he had better examine his *sling* and be assured that he had a sufficient number of missiles to prostrate the giant. In obedience to this timely suggestion he resolved to examine the whole subject of Baptism, and to supply himself with all the arguments pro and con. O that every preacher in Christendom would do likewise, with regard to that and every other point of material difference! Then would the truth have free course and run and be glorified! Then would God also be glorified in the salvation of souls! Then would the followers of Jesus be joined together in one mind, speaking the same thing! Then would infidelity perish and the world would believe that God had sent his Son to be their Saviour! But alas! "this people's heart has waxed gross, their ears are dull of hearing, and their eyes have they closed."

In his investigation, he resolved to begin with the fathers and standard authors of his own church. He first consulted the voluminous works of Luther, in the original German; and, on the two thousand five hundred and ninety-third page of the tenth volume, he found Luther's sermon on Baptism, preached in June 1520. The very first page of this sermon put him in possession of a fact hitherto unknown to him, viz., the meaning which Luther attached to the German word "taufe." The following is a literal translation of the passage:

"In the first place, Baptism in the Greek language is called Baptismos (βαπτισμος) and, in the Latin, Mersio—that is, as when a person *dips something entirely into* the water, the water will *cover it;* and although in many places, it is *no more the custom* to push the children into the font and dip them, but only to bepour them with the hand out of the font, yet it ought to be—and would be right—that a person should, *according to the signification of the word 'taufe,'* WHOLLY SINK the child or candidate into the water, and baptize and draw it out again; as the word "taufe" comes from *tiefen,* as when a person *sinks one* DEEP *into the water and dips.*"

After reading this passage, penned by no other hand than the great and authoritative Luther's, he wisely concluded that if it should happen to be in the possession of his opponent it would prove a formidable weapon.

The next standard author consulted was Dr. Mosheim, a Lutheran also, and a historian of high repute. On the 108th page of his Church History he found the following vexatious passage:

"The sacrament of Baptism was administered, in this (the first) century, *without the public assemblies,* in places appointed and prepared for that purpose, and was performed by an IMMERSION of the *whole person* in the baptismal font."

The next author was Michaelis, one of the most learned men of the Lutheran church, who, on the 506th page of his "Dogmatic" expresses himself as follows:

"The external act of Baptism is *dipping under water.* This the Greek word βαπτιζω signifies, as every one acquainted with the Greek language must admit. The baptism of the Jews was performed by immersion; so also was that of John the Baptist, and of the first Christians. Of this we have a proof in the fact that baptism without immersion and only by pouring was allowed *in case of the sick*, in the third century, and it met contradiction as an *innovation*. * * * *Immersion was practiced till the thirteenth century*, and it is desirable that the Latin church had never *allowed a deviation from this*. But it (the deviation) *did occur*, and at the Reformation it was not altered—that is, *changed to its primitive form.*"

Weighed down by these stubborn facts from the writings of the fathers, he abandoned the idea of meeting the defiant Goliath. Like David encumbered by the armor of Saul, he said, "*I cannot go with these.*"

The result of his investigation was a firm conviction that immersion in water is the only Christian Baptism. In the mean time a better understanding of the New Testament and of the Constitution of the Church of which the Saviour said, "I will build it," had exhibited to him the futility of infant membership.

Here he found himself surrounded by circumstances that could not but severely test his piety and his moral courage. The beloved pastor of a large and influential congregation, living in fine style and receiving a good salary, a splendid prospect spread out before him and his children, yet no longer a believer in the doctrines he was expected to preach—dissatisfied with his own baptism, his conscience pleading for adherence to the right and fidelity to the word of God, he was in a condition to be fully realized only by those who have passed through a similar process.

Finally, like Moses, he chose to suffer affliction with the people of God, rather than to enjoy the pleasures of sin for a season. He resigned his charge without, at that time, revealing the special reason; and, in September, 1834, officiated for the last time in the splendid pulpit of his beloved congregation. These were to him dark days, and at times his spirits were greatly depressed; but he leaned on the word of the Great Shepherd—His rod and His staff, they comforted him.

Though he could no longer preach, conscientiously, the Lutheran gospel, yet he did not immediately obey the gospel of Christ. His faith in the former system having been destroyed, his mind was reduced to a kind of chaos, and it required a little while for apostolic *order* to appear. It was not till the last Lord's day in March, 1835, that, without the knowledge of his family, he was immersed in the vicinity of Hagerstown, Md. On reaching home his wife was greatly distressed, both because she was yet much attached to the Lutheran church, and because, with a mother's solicitude, she saw in the future nothing but penury and "the cold world's proud scorn" for herself and her little ones.

In the town he was the principal theme of conversation. Many denounced, some pitied, and a few commended him. As he walked up the street on Monday morning, none of his former brethren appeared to recognize him. Like Cæsar,

"But yesterday he might have stood against the world—
Now, none so poor as to do him reverence."

The Presbyterians passed him coldly, all because he had demonstrated his genuine piety by forsaking all for Christ's sake and the gospel's. None but the Episcopal minister gave him so much as a gentlemanly salutation. Nor were these the only chilling influences that he had to encounter. A pious mother that had taught him the first lessons in religion, maternal uncles who had taken a lively interest in his education, and were proud of his pulpit performances, brothers and sisters who were strongly attached to him as a champion of the Lutheran faith, were all in their turn to be confounded. In his interviews with them he made good use of the word, and expounded matters in such a manner that, although they would not obey the gospel, they could not severely chide him for having obeyed it.

Soon after his immersion, he left Hagerstown, and resided temporarily with his father-in-law at New Market, intending to emigrate to the West the ensuing Fall. During his sojourn at New Market, where he had been installed as pastor nine years before, he often met the sheep of his first flock. To them, also, he had become a stranger, whose voice they were no longer willing to hear. The doors of his old church were closed against him; but the Baptists, out of personal respect, opened to him their house. When he preached on the *action* of baptism they were delighted; but when he pressed upon them the *design*, they manifested a spirit closely akin to that of the Athenians, when Paul declared to them the resurrection of the dead, (Acts xvii. 32.)

During the three months that he remained in that vicinity, he preached every Lord's day, wherever he could obtain a hearing. At the close of the last sermon at New Market, a highly respectable lady — a member of the Lutheran church — came forward and made the required confession. It was announced that she would be immersed on the next morning. Returning home, his father-in-law met him on the pavement, and informed him that his wife, Mrs. Savage, intended to be immersed at the same time. On the banks of the stream, at the appointed hour, she made the confession which is "unto salvation," and, with the other woman, was buried with the Lord in baptism.

Some time before this, as he was returning home from an appointment, his wife met him in the hall, saying, that she had been studying the New Testament, that she was satisfied that he had done right, and that she intended **ere** long to follow his example. Accordingly, on the next day after the baptism of her mother, she and three others, one of whom was also a Lutheran, were immersed in the same stream. Nor were these only immersed—they all arose to walk in newness of life.

Prior to his departure for the West, he spent three weeks preaching in the vicinity of Hagerstown, among his former acquaintances. In this time he immersed eleven persons, of whom five were Lutherans, two Methodists, and four "from the world." At sunrise of the last morning that he remained, he immersed the two Methodists, who both came up out of the water shouting and praising God. Yet this was heresy!

Finally, on the 16th of September, 1835, he set out for the West. While he was on the way, the Synod of Maryland met; and although he had consented, at the request of the Secretary, to withdraw privately, yet that august body formally and solemnly excluded him as a dangerous errorist. The following is a transcript of the original bull of excommunication, taken from the "Minutes of the Evangelical Lutheran Synod of Maryland, held at Woodsborough, Frederick county, in October, 1835:"

"The committee on paper No. 1 now reported, and, after some discussion, it was

"*Resolved*, That the Rev. Mr. Hoshour, having changed his religious creed in some of the essential and fundamental articles of religion, as held and taught among us, has thereby voluntarily separated himself from all connection with the Lutheran Church, and cannot longer be considered a member.

"*Resolved*, also, That the Synod, for the above reason, expunge the name of S. K. Hoshour from the list of its ministers; that it no longer considers him a member of the Lutheran Church, and that he may live to see, feel, and acknowledge his errors, is the prayer of all those to whom he was once ardently attached."

Such was the last step in his final exodus from the "*Evangelical* Lutheran Church."

On the 16th of October, 1835, he arrived, with his little family and less means, at Centreville, the county-seat of Wayne county, Indiana. His object in coming West was to procure a small farm, and, "in the sweat of his face," make an independent though humble living. But he soon found that his literary pursuits and sedentary habits had greatly disqualified him for the business of a farmer. He no longer enjoyed it as he did, when an unlettered swain in Pennsylvania. Therefore he soon abandoned the plough, and commenced teaching a district school near Centreville at twenty dollars per month—an unprecedented salary in that day. Such was his success that, in a short time, he was elected Principal of the Wayne County Seminary, in which he taught four years to the entire satisfaction of the community.

During all this time, he employed his Lord's days in disseminating the simple gospel as he had learned it and most devoutly cherished it. In Centreville, the court-house was his sanctuary, in which he officiated as both preacher and *sexton!* On Saturdays he prepared the wood, and on Sundays made the fires and preached. His audiences were mostly composed of the more intelligent non-professors, and the more liberal adherents to the several sects, who were generally attentive, and disposed to approbate his preaching.

The Reformation was then in its infancy at that place. There was only one family—a man and his wife—that openly adhered to the cause for which Elder Hoshour plead. These, himself and *his* wife, at that time constituted the Church of Christ at Centreville. He acted as bishop, the lone brother as deacon, and the two wives as deaconesses! There was, therefore, little cause of strife and division in that church, *for each member had an office!*

Though there were no contentions within, it was not long until he felt from without the sharp points of sectarian bigotry and intolerance. Low chicanery and tact were resorted to in order to counteract his influence in the pulpit. But he occasionally made a proselyte, and by the help of others succeeded in building up a good and substantial church at that place.

After he had been there one year, the Baptists, many of whom sanctioned his preaching, insisted upon his uniting with them. He consented to do so, *provided* they would allow him to urge upon all "seekers," Peter's answer to the question, "What shall we do?" Acts ii. 37. To this there was some objection, and the union did not take place.

In the process of time, the majority of the Baptists united with the Christians, to whom they delivered over their commodious house of worship.

In 1836, the Legislature of Indiana appointed him a member of the Board of Trustees of the State University, at Bloomington, in which capacity he served very efficiently for three years.

At the Annual Commencement of 1839, the Faculty and Trustees of that Institution conferred on him the honorary degree of A. M.

With Dr. Wylie, the late distinguished President of the State University, he enjoyed an intimate and most agreeable friendship. They communed freely on the subject of religion, and the doctor interposed but few objections to the views of his friend. He afterwards published a small work entitled: "*Sectarianism is Heresy,*" which, *possibly*, was suggested by what occurred in some of their interviews. At any rate he was not a man who closed his ears against the truth, as the following incident will show.

On one occasion, in Commencement week, the chosen

speaker for a certain evening did not arrive. The college chapel being crowded to overflowing, President Wylie invited Elder Hoshour to supply with a sermon the place of the anticipated speech, at the same time giving him liberty to choose his own theme and speak his mind freely. He accepted the invitation; took, as his subject, *Man's Duty*, Ecc. xii. 13, and proceeded to preach the ancient gospel to perhaps the largest and most intelligent audience he ever addressed. There were seated around him, on the rostrum, President, Professors, the Board of Trustees, the Executive of the State, and several *literati* from abroad; while before him were the *elite* of Bloomington and many visitors from various parts of the Commonwealth. He was then in the vigor of his manhood, and the discourse is said to have been one of great power. It was doubtless the masterpiece of his whole life.

In the Fall of 1839 he removed to Cambridge City, where he became the principal of a large and tastefully-constructed seminary. There he taught for seven consecutive years, and always had a large number of pupils, many of whom were from abroad. Several of Indiana's distinguished sons were educated in his school, among whom were Major General Lewis Wallace, and the present efficient Executive, Governor Oliver P. Morton.

During his residence at Cambridge City he preached on Lord's days either in the village, or at points from which he could return in time for school on Monday morning. Himself, his wife, and one brother in Christ then composed the church at that place. Thus it happened a second time that his flock were all officers! But they relied on the promise, "Where two or *three* are met together in my *name*, there am I in the midst of them."

With this weak force he had to combat strong opposition to what was stigmatized as *Campbellism*. As a teacher the several sects esteemed him highly, but upon his preaching they looked with suspicion, if not with contempt. Under all these discouragements he continued to preach plainly, scripturally, and sometimes polemically; but being afraid of building, on the apostolic foundation, "wood, hay, or stubble," he refrained for a long while from any attempt to proselyte. Still he immersed the first year some half-a-dozen substantial members, and the second year about as many. In 1842 he procured the assistance of Elder John B. New, and held a protracted meeting, which resulted in twenty-five additions, most of whom were persons of means, intelligence, and moral worth. Built up in that way, the church at Cambridge City has not yet fallen down; on the contrary, it has been enlarged from time to time, and is at the present writing in a prosperous condition.

During the eleven years that Elder Hoshour taught at Centreville and Cambridge, he preached every Lord's day except ten; often riding long distances after night-fall, through mud, and rain, and cold. During the greater part of this time he preached twice each Sunday; and for all these faithful labors, which shattered his constitution and destroyed his physical comfort for life, he received less than five hundred dollars — not fifty dollars per annum.

About the year 1846 declining health compelled him to abandon the school-room, with limited means and a family of seven children. For the support of his family he afterwards resorted to teaching the German language in the various Institutions and larger towns of the State; but, for the benefit of his race, he continued to preach the gospel almost "without money and without price," as he had done for a score of years. Though but few men gave unto *him*, he desired to share with all men the unsearchable riches of Christ. Though he himself met with few real sympathizers, his own heart swelled with sympathy for all whose errant feet he found in the way of death.

In 1852 he purchased a small farm near Cambridge City, where he expected to pitch his tent for the remainder of his life, and give himself more fully to the work of the ministry. But being strongly importuned to aid in the construction of the Richmond and Indianapolis Railroad, he invested largely in this, to him, unprofitable enterprise. On account of this investment he became involved in debts, to extricate himself from which he was compelled to sacrifice the rural home which he had provided for his old age.

In June, 1858, he was elected President of the North-Western Christian University, located at Indianapolis, Indiana. In this capacity he served three years, at the expiration of which time the Institution was re-organized, and he became Professor of Modern Languages—the position which he desired, because it was far less laborious, and more suitable to his taste and genius. The functions of that office he still discharges to the credit both of himself and of that department of the University. In vacation he goes about proclaiming the word, and during the session he occasionally preaches in the city—sometimes for the congregation with whom he worships, more frequently for the German Methodists, in their own language, and not unfrequently—so amiable a heretic is he—for his first love, the Lutherans.

But, ere long, he must rest from his labors. Already the almond-tree begins to flourish, and the grasshopper to be a burden. Already the strong men begin to bow themselves, and those that look out of the windows to be darkened. Soon shall the silver cord be loosed, the golden bowl be broken. Soon shall he go to his long home, and the mourners go about the streets. No man is more ready to be offered up, for without once having put off the armor of God, he has fought a good fight. Though nearly all else has been sacrificed, he has kept *the faith*, and strong in that faith he will descend to the tomb,

> "Like one who wraps the drapery of his couch
> About him, and lies down to pleasant dreams."

Elder Hoshour is a frail, homely man, of an air decidedly German. His stature is five feet nine or ten inches, and his weight about one hundred and forty-five pounds. He has a sallow complexion, a highly bilious temperament, raven black hair, and dark hazel eyes, full of subdued fire. His is a singularly shaped head, which, upon the whole, is an unfair index of his intellectual ability. His mind is of the reflective caste, active, logical, comprehensive, and still vigorous, though impaired by the infirmities of the flesh. If its power be estimated, philosophically, by the resistance it will overcome, or the height to which it will elevate a given body, it will be found to be greatly above the average. In its escape from theological darkness to biblical light, it overcame early prejudices, clerical pride, family and church affinities, and all sectarian restraints in the form of liturgies and creeds; and despite the force of that gravity which, in this unscrupulous age, drags down the conscientious man, it has elevated its possessor from the obscurity of a German orphan boy to a conspicuous rank among the ministers and educators of the age.

As a scholar he deserves honorable mention. The principal events of the world's history, and a general knowledge of the several sciences, are carefully stowed away in his retentive memory; and one will not easily approach him with any subject on which he may not converse intelligently. He reads five different languages and fluently speaks three—the English, the German, and the

French. He is not fond of speculative theories, but drinks oftenest and deepest at the sacred fountain: hence his knowledge of the Scriptures is deep and extensive.

Since his entrance into the Reformation he has never been a sensation preacher. His *forte* has been to edify the church; to "enlighten the eyes of their understanding," that they might know "what is the hope of his calling and what the riches of the glory of his inheritance in the saints." He has, however, proselyted a goodly number to the faith of the gospel; but very few, if any, of whom have returned to the beggarly elements of the world. Those whose hands he puts to the plow seldom look back.

In the pulpit his style is somewhat peculiar. "Teaching and preaching" is his motto; hence, after singing and prayer, he usually expounds a chapter; after which another hymn is sung and he rises to preach. To the eyes of strangers this habit sometimes presents him in a false light, as the following anecdote will show: On a certain occasion an ex-member of the Indiana Legislature, who was also a disciple, was giving his opinion of President Hoshour. Said he, "I went, one day, to hear him preach, and he made a complete failure. He talked a few minutes—and talked very well too—then suddenly stopped and took his seat. The brethren sang another hymn, at the conclusion of which he took a new text, *tried it over again*, and did pretty well!" The Honorable had really taken the first performance for a failure, though, in fact the programme was carried out to the letter.

In his palmy days he was a good speaker, but his elocution is now much impaired by age and bodily infirmities. Yet he still commands the attention of his audience by the number and quality of his ideas and the copiousness of his diction. But few men can make a more thorough analysis of a passage, draw from it more practical lessons, or discourse upon it in more elegant terms.

Sometimes he has contended earnestly with those " of the contrary part," but, in the main, he is a servant of the Lord that " doth not strive," but is " gentle unto all men, apt to teach, patient, in meekness instructing those that oppose themselves."

> —— " By him, in strains as sweet
> As angels use, the gospel whispers peace.
> He 'stablishes the strong, restores the weak,
> Reclaims the wanderer, binds the broken heart,
> And, armed himself in panoply complete,
> Of heavenly temper, furnishes with arms
> Bright as his own, and trains by every rule
> Of holy discipline, to glorious war,
> The sacramental host of God's elect:
> Are all such teachers? Would to Heaven all were!"

It is but a slight exaggeration to say of him that as a man—a Christian—he is an embodiment of that charity which " suffereth long and is kind, which envieth not, vaunteth not itself, is not puffed up, doth not behave itself unseemly, seeketh not her own, is not easily provoked, thinketh no evil, rejoiceth not in iniquity but rejoiceth in the truth, beareth all things, believeth all things, hopeth all things, endureth all things." Wherever you meet him—at home, in the social circle, or in the house of his God—you meet

> ——" The man whose heart is warm,
> Whose hands are pure, whose doctrine and whose life,
> Coincident, exhibit lucid proof
> That he is honest in the sacred cause."

Possessing but little worldly ambition, he has aspired, through life, to the kingdom of God and His righteousness, taking but little thought of what he should eat, what he should drink, or wherewithal he should be clothed. Hence he is one of the "poor of this world whom God hath chosen heirs of the kingdom." And now, at the age of nearly threescore, with no means of support save his hands and his head, and racked with pains superinduced by exposure and excessive mental labor, he is compelled to toil unremittingly for his daily bread. Having devoted his best days to the interests of Zion, he has reason to feel that his declining years are neglected by the brotherhood whom he loves and has faithfully served. On account of this neglect, present and past, gloom settles down upon his earthly future; but his pathway to the life to come "shineth more and more."

It is said that, to one journeying to the far North, the mysterious Aurora increases in splendor as the sunlight fades away, and that to one arrived at the open sea that surrounds the pole, the hidden sun would appear again, sweep round the horizon, and never set. Such to Elder Hoshour is the journey of life. Having crossed the bright regions within the tropics, and passed through the checkered scenes of the temperate zone, he is now plodding on through the Arctic circle, where the shadows of a long night are falling around him. But as his sun declines, shutting out from his vision the glories of this world, the light from Heaven shines with increasing splendor, revealing the brighter glories of the world to come. Soon will he reach the great Open Sea—Eternity—where his sun of life will re-appear, and run round in a circle of never-ending felicity.

WILLIAM WILSON.

Elder William Wilson, the blind preacher, was born in Fleming county, Kentucky, September 23d, 1808. His father, Thomas Wilson, was a man of more than ordinary intelligence, concerning whose ancestors nothing is known. His mother's maiden name was Jane Hughes. She is of Irish descent, and still survives.

Both his parents were for years zealous members of the Presbyterian Church; but soon after the great revival at Cane Ridge, in 1801, they both embraced the views of B. W. Stone, and took upon themselves the name given first in Antioch.

Elder Wilson has been blind from his birth. In childhood he could, with great difficulty, distinguish bright objects when near him in a clear light; and it was hoped that surgical skill might secure for him a more perfect vision. Accordingly, when in his fourteenth year, he was taken to Lexington to be operated upon by Dr. Dudley, who thought a cure might be effected. While on his way to that city, he was in ecstacy at the prospect of having the veil lifted and the glories of the external world exposed to his view. When asleep bright visions came and went, and in his wakeful hours still brighter day-dreams floated before his mind. But all these pleasing anticipations soon vanished away, and gave place to a gloom deeper than ever before. The operation performed, and the pain, which for several days rendered him delirious, having subsided, the bandages were removed, and he was informed that he was hopelessly blind.

No words can express his deep disappointment on receiving this sad intelligence. His sightless eyes became each a fountain of tears, and his soul shuddered at the presence of the thick darkness which was to encompass it forever.

But haply, in human experience as in nature, the sunshine succeeds the shadow. Hope soon shed its cheerful beams upon his drooping spirit; he resigned himself to his sad fate, and resolved to be through life as happy and agreeable as possible. In this effort he has been strangely successful. The morning of his life has been far from wretched, and the feeling of his old age is well expressed in the following beautiful lines, which are attributed to Milton:

> "I am weak, yet strong;
> I murmur not that I no longer see.
> Poor, old, and helpless, I the more belong,
> Father Supreme, to Thee.
>
> O merciful One,
> When men are farthest then Thou art most near;
> When men pass by my weaknesses to shun,
> Thy chariot I hear.
>
> Thy glorious face
> Is leaning toward me, and its holy light
> Shines in upon my lonely dwelling place,
> *And there is no more night.*
>
> On my bended knee
> I recognize thy purpose clearly shown;
> My vision Thou hast dimm'd, that I may see
> Thyself, Thyself alone.
>
> I have naught to fear;
> This darkness is the shadow of thy wing;
> Beneath it I am almost sacred—here
> Can come no evil thing.
>
> O! I seem to stand,
> Trembling, where foot of mortal ne'er hath been,
> Wrapt in the radiance from that sinless land,
> Which eye hath never seen.

> Visions come and go;
> Shapes of resplendent beauty round me throng;
> From angel lips I seem to hear the flow
> Of soft and holy song.
>
> 'Tis nothing now—
> When heaven is opening on my sightless eyes—
> When airs of Paradise refresh my brow—
> That earth in darkness lies.''

But to return to the facts and incidents connected with his history.

In the year 1826 his father emigrated from Kentucky, and settled in Putnam county, Indiana. To remove the dense forest that covered all their land, required much labor, a portion of which was cheerfully performed by the afflicted son. By means of his other senses he could burn brush, pile logs, and even fell trees, though this was attended with great danger to himself. It was only by putting his hand on the trunk that he could ascertain which way the tree was falling and this procedure left him but little time to make good his retreat. Sometimes, too, the limbs stripped from neighboring trees fell around and near him; but he escaped unharmed from all these "perils of the wilderness."

As soon as his father had built a cabin he converted it into a house of prayer. In it he brought together his few neighbors, as often as he could secure the services of a preacher; and in a short time there was organized therein a small church. Of him, therefore, as of Moses, it may be written, "this is he that was with the church in the wilderness."

Elder Wilson inherited from his father a strong desire of knowledge—so strong that he would at any time forsake his playmates to hear any one read. The Bible was read oftenest; and from it, therefore, he received the most of his instruction. He never went to school—never enjoyed the advantages of the system which has been devised for the education of the blind. To him knowledge, as well as "faith," came "by hearing, and hearing by the word of God."

If others of his day experienced difficulties in entering in at the straight gate, he experienced more; for while they could search the Scriptures for themselves, he was compelled to content himself with such portions as his friends chose to read. Under such circumstances he made but little progress toward the kingdom. For several long years darkness rested upon things eternal as well as upon things temporal; and the spiritual soon proved a greater affliction than the natural blindness, which he had learned to regard as "but for a moment."

Finally in the winter of 1828 his uncle, James Hughes, who had come to the knowledge of the truth, came over from Kentucky to Putnam county, preaching the "ancient gospel," and convincing the churches (Old Christian) that Baptism, in connection with faith and repentance, was divinely appointed for the remission of sins. This doctrine produced no small stir among the people; but was nevertheless very generally received.

In the light of this teaching Elder Wilson saw at once, and clearly, what he must do to be saved; and what had been the difficulty with all the "mourners," whom he had seen vainly seeking the forgiveness of their sins. With joyful haste he fled for refuge to lay hold on the hope set before him; confessed the Saviour before men; and was straightway "buried with him by baptism into death." From that time to the present his peace has been as a river.

Thus it appears that his first religious step was in the right direction—that from the beginning of his new life he has been identified with the current Reformation.

Eighteen persons were added with him to the little

church established at his father's; and, in the Summer following, Elder Hughes returned and baptized about forty others. Among these were several young men, nearly all of whom began at once to pray in public, and some of them to exhort. Indeed, but few of the disciples of that early day were "ashamed of the gospel of Christ." In the absence of preachers, of whom there were but few, they considered "*one another* to provoke unto love and good works, not forsaking the assembling of themselves together, as *the manner of some is.*"

Foremost among the young disciples was William Wilson, who entered upon his public ministry soon after his immersion in 1828. At first his efforts were feeble, owing to his lack of education and his inability to read the word; but his heart's desire and prayer to God was, that he might become an able minister of the New Testament. Stimulated by this desire, he ceased not to teach and to preach according to the grace given him from on high.

For a year or two his labors were confined to his own county; but in the Summer of 1830 he began to travel, and within the next few years he visited various portions of the State, being very successful wherever he went. In 1834 he visited Kentucky. The subject of religion being then greatly agitated in that State, he was everywhere favored with large audiences, and therefore sowed bountifully the "incorruptible seed." He returned home by way of Hamilton, Ohio; from which place he was compelled to complete his journey without the assistance of a guide. In so doing, he experienced many difficulties and escaped many unseen dangers. Not the least of these was the crossing of streams; for it was only by the rippling of the shoal water that he could distinguish the fords, and when this expedient failed, he depended entirely upon the guidance of his horse.

During the two years following he travelled extensively in Western Indiana, occasionally passing over into Illinois. He devoted his whole time to the work of the ministry, receiving for his services what was barely sufficient to defray his travelling expenses.

On the 15th of August, 1837, he was married to Miss Susannah Goff, who, as the mother of four sons and three daughters, still lives to share his toils, and sympathize with him in his affliction.

In 1838 he made another visit to Kentucky, passing through Cincinnati, and preaching almost daily to large congregations along the route. During the interval between April and August, he preached through the upper counties of that State, adding quite a number to the churches of that region.

On his way home the following incident occurred: On the morning of his departure from Cynthiana he had a presentiment that some evil would befall him that day; and the farther he rode the more gloomy became his thoughts, though he strove to turn them into a brighter channel. Late in the evening a rustling was heard in the dry leaves by the road-side, and, turning her eyes in that direction, his wife (who was accompanying him) saw a ruffian-like man raise his gun to his face, and aim it at her husband. On being hastily apprised of the fact, Elder Wilson calmly inquired of the supposed highwayman how far it was to the next inn, adding that he was blind and a stranger in those parts. The man lowered his gun, muttering some unintelligible reply; and the frightened travellers laid whip to their horses until assured that they were entirely out of danger.

The following Spring he again went to Kentucky, and preached several months in company with Elder John G. Ellis, of Covington. They immersed nearly two hundred persons, the majority of them in Kenton and Boone counties.

Returning home, he spent the Fall and Winter, as formerly, in edifying the churches in various parts of Indiana; in introducing the ancient gospel into destitute places; and, especially, in assisting his fellow preachers at protracted meetings, which were his chief delight, and the places, above all others, in which he could render efficient service.

In the Spring of 1840 he once more crossed the Ohio to preach the glad tidings of salvation in the land of his nativity. This tour was confined, mainly, to the counties of Bath, Montgomery, and Fleming, in which he made many proselytes to primitive Christianity. He could have made many more, but for the want of some one to do the immersing—a work which he could not perform. On this account he often left large congregations in tears, without giving an invitation to lay hold of the hope set before them.

In the year 1843 he attended a great meeting held at Louisville by Elder Benjamin Hall. Wishing to continue that meeting, Elder Hall dispatched him to Newcastle, to fill his (Hall's) appointment at that place. The brethren at Newcastle were greatly disappointed on hearing that the expected preacher would not be there. They were not well pleased with the dress and general appearance of the strange substitute; and there was a disposition on the part of the church not to let him preach. None supposed that he was "a workman approved unto God;" and some feared that he would say things of which they would all need to be ashamed.

However, as there was no other preacher present when the people came together on Saturday morning, it was agreed that he should officiate. He therefore took the stand, and delivered a discourse which moved many of his suspicious hearers to tears. At night, and on the next day, other preachers that had arrived discoursed to the people, but with no visible effect. On Sunday evening Elder Wilson again occupied the pulpit; and in response to his invitation, several came forward to make the good confession. From that time he was the chief speaker; and before the close of the meeting, twenty-two persons were received into the heavenly family, and made heirs of the heavenly inheritance.

At that meeting he met with an old friend by the name of Fitzgerald. This kind gentleman, one day, entered the room where he was sitting, saying: "Brother Wilson, take off your coat." The preacher obeyed without asking any questions. Mr. F. then had him to put on a new one, worth thirty dollars, observing, after a moment's inspection: "It fits you nicely; accept it as a present from your unworthy friend, and remember me often in your prayers." In more respects than one, therefore, he was never better rewarded than at Newcastle, Kentucky.

On another occasion, his raiment experienced a change of a less agreeable character. During one of his long preaching tours, his coat faded to such an unsightly color, that it would have made him quite unhappy, had he possessed seeing eyes, or the modishness of some later divines. But, as it was, he knew nothing of his misfortune until his return home. Thus he demonstrated that,

> "When ignorance is bliss,
> 'Tis folly to be wise."

Once more returned to Indiana, he continued to preach wherever there was opened to him a door of utterance. Among the many interesting meetings held by him, was one at Marcellus, in Rush county. It was on a beautiful Sunday; and hundreds of orthodox Christians—many of them from Rushville—came out to hear the Blind Preacher.

Knowing their views and feelings, he determined to make a special effort to present the truth in such a manner as to allay their prejudices, if not to convince them of their errors. In this attempt he was not wholly unsuccessful. Many of those of "the contrary part" declared that he had "said the truth;" and some were ready to say : "Almost thou persuadest me to be a Christian." Indeed at another meeting held near by he did lead some of them, through obedience, into "the glorious liberty of the children of God."

About the same time he preached, on a certain Monday, at Hanover church, near Morristown, in Shelby county. His subject that day was Matt. vii. 21 : " Not every one that saith unto me, Lord, Lord, shall enter into the kingdom of heaven; but he that doeth the will of my Father who is in heaven." The congregation was deeply affected; and at the close of the discourse several persons made the confession which is unto salvation. He preached again in the afternoon with similar results. *Eighteen*, in all, were added that day to the saved. Among the number was an old revolutionary soldier, with all his house.

It has already been seen that Elder Wilson has been "in journeyings often," "in perils in the wilderness," "in perils of waters," and "in perils of robbers." It is equally true that he has been "in perils in the city," and in "perils among false brethren," as the following facts will show.

Being once at Versailles, Ky., and intending to go from there into Clarke county, he was advised to proceed by way of Lexington, and preach to the congregation in that city. Having received a letter of introduction to one brother F., the proprietor of a hotel in that place, he set out for Lexington. He delivered the letter to the godly (?) landlord, who, after glancing at its contents, said, "Brother Wilson, I cannot entertain you." Proceeding to another place to which he was directed, he was again informed that he could not be accommodated. He then returned to the hotel, in front of which he sat a long while before his brother, the landlord, (who had been summoned,) made his appearance. When he *did* appear, it was only to say to him, emphatically, "You can't get to stay here." The poor preacher, who had dismissed his guide, requested that he might be conducted to the residence of Dr. Dudley, who, he hoped, had not forgotten him. This request, also, was gruffly refused. Out of sheer necessity, therefore, he alighted from his horse, and entered, uninvited, into the bar-room, hoping that he might meet with some one who would conduct him out of the inhospitable city. Ever and anon, as he sat waiting, the fearful proprietor came in to assure him that he could not be entertained.

Finally a deliverer came, from whom he learned, as they rode to the country, that the landlord was entertaining a large number of sporting gentry, that had come to the city to attend the races, and seek their fortunes in games of chance. It was for *their* accommodation that the door had been closed against the *unprofitable* servant of the Most High God.

After this experience in a fashionable city, he proceeded to Clarke and Montgomery counties, where his preaching was well received, and crowned with his usual success.

For the last ten or twelve years, his labors have been confined for the most part to Indiana; and, within the limits of the State, there is scarcely a county which he has not visited. He has been most successful in proselyting sinners, many hundreds of whom have, through his instrumentality, been made partakers of the inheritance of the saints in light. He has also accomplished something in the great work of persuading the obedient among the sects to be called only by the name Christian, and be governed only by the word of God. Though himself uneducated, he moreover contributed his portion for the establishment of the N. W. C. University, which is now exerting a powerful influence in favor of primitive Christianity.

For his abundant labors he has received but little "of corruptible things, such as silver and gold;" yet, on reviewing the past, he rejoices and is exceeding glad, knowing that great is his reward in heaven.

Though it has pleased the Lord to afflict him by darkening forever the windows of his earthly tabernacle, and though he has otherwise suffered much for his name's sake, yet, while he *looks not at the things which are seen,* but at the things which are not seen, he feels that his light affliction is but for a moment; and that it worketh for him a far more exceeding and eternal weight of glory.

His days of darkness are now almost ended. Soon the vail shall be lifted, and those things "which God hath prepared for them that love him," be revealed to his enraptured vision.

Elder Wilson is a small, thin man, not exceeding one hundred and thirty-five pounds in weight. Having been enveloped all his days in thick darkness, he has been unable to take that free, out-door exercise so essential to physical development. On this account he looks wan and haggard, like a prisoner in a damp dungeon.

He has a fine head, especially in the frontal region, and one sees at a glance that nature bestowed on him an uncommon endowment of intellect. But the mind, sitting ever in its dark chambers, and often famishing for food, has been dwarfed like his body—a misfortune which seems to distress him more than all other afflictions. He never murmurs, because to him returns not

> "Day, or the sweet approach of ev'n or morn,
> Or sight of vernal bloom, or summer's rose,
> Or flocks, or herds, or human face divine;"

but ever and anon the shadow of despair settles for a moment on his furrowed face, and his conversation is interrupted by the sad exclamation, "Ah! if I hadn't been shut out from *the light of education*."

Like a poor beggar at the gate, his mind sits all the day long at the tympanum of the ear, receiving pittances of knowledge from the passing sounds. In this way he has acquired an amount of information that would seem almost incredible. With the Bible especially, he is remarkably familiar. He quotes it freely and with tolerable accuracy in his preaching, always giving chapter and verse.

In the pulpit he appears pretty much as a blind man appears everywhere. He is a good singer, and while the congregation is assembling he usually sings, by himself, some plaintive air, which softens all hearts, and swells to the very brim the fountains of tears. On rising to preach —if it be in a strange place—he first makes a brief reconnoisance of his position; then repeats a chapter from memory, and addresses a short prayer to the throne of the heavenly grace. After another song, and without resuming his seat, he announces his text and begins his discourse. With a clear, sharp voice, he speaks slowly at first, but becomes more animated as he progresses. He stands quite still, save a slight rocking motion, and makes scarcely a gesture—for he is a stranger to the *grace* that is seen in motions. He is a good natural logician, and is inclined to be argumentative. In adducing the proof of his propositions, he brings together texts widely separated in Holy Writ, weaving them into his discourse with remarkable force, precision, and beauty. In his better days he was a *very* effective speaker, excelled by few in pathetic and stirring exhortation; but latterly his powers, both reasoning and persuasive, are on the wane.

In religion, where all must walk by faith, he keeps pace with the foremost of his brethren. He is noted for godliness, brotherly kindness, and charity—for his disposition to "weep with them that weep," and his readiness to "deliver the poor that cry, the fatherless, and him that hath none to help him."

Revelation lights up every step of his dark way, not only dispelling despondency, but also supplying him with habitual cheerfulness. If you are at leisure, he enters freely into conversation, smiles at the reception of every new idea, and laughs outright at the relation of a good anecdote. When your business calls you away he paces the floor, feeling the way with his ever-present cane; or sits for hours in silent communion with his Maker and his own busy thoughts. Occasionally, at such times, his low plaintive voice is heard, as he sings to himself some consoling stanza like the following:

>"Precious Bible! how I love it,
> How it doth my bosom cheer,
> What hath earth than this to covet?
> O what stores of wealth are here!"

He is himself something of a poet, and many of the songs he sings are of his own composition. The following is one with which he often breaks the "solemn stillness" which pervades the house of God just previous to the commencement of divine service.

>"Take warning, take warning, poor sinners, I pray,
> You now hear the gospel, O come and obey,
> Lest your sun, it should set, and you can't find the way,
> For darkness will hinder—in it you must stay.
>
> Take warning, old people, while it's called to-day;
> While Jesus invites you, O come and obey,

Lest Death it should call and you too have to go,
And alas! like the stubble, have no fruit to show.

Take warning, young people—the youth have to die;
The messenger, Death, it will not pass you by;
In the cold arms of Death you soon may lie low,
And alas! like the chaff, have no fruit then to show.

Here, parents and children—they surely must part,
All ties must be broken that bind heart to heart.
Oh! think of the friends that are called from time,
To the hand of cold death they have had to resign.

Their pains and their groans can ne'er change their state—
Oh! the sorrow of mortals what tongue can relate!
Though *they're* silent in death, *we're* still moving along,
But we'll all have to die, and before very long.

To yonder dark prison, poor man, you must go;
While fettered by Death you must in it lie low.
It is solemn but true, O sinner don't wait,
You had better prepare before it's too late.

Swift hours will pass, which gold cannot restore—
When favors are gone you'll be wishing for more;
But the harvest is past, the summer is gone,
And the poor disobedient forever undone."

One other specimen, in which he has embodied thoughts and hopes that were ever present with him, must terminate this personal description. To fully appreciate it, one must hear him sing it as he sits all alone in an adjoining room:

"There is a kingdom I do view,
And to this place let us pursue:
No poisonous breath shall enter there—
O may I in that kingdom share.

It is a kingdom of delight,
Its subjects all are dressed in white,
Their uniforms shine like the sun—
O let us to that kingdom run.

There parents, children, all shall meet,
Their joys shall ever be complete,
From pain and sickness ever free—
O let us to that kingdom flee.

So let us run that we may gain,
And ever in that kingdom reign,
Where peace and joy forever flow,
And *e'en the blind no darkness know.*

That glorious day is rolling on,
When I shall see the heavenly throng,
And with the blood-washed millions stand,
Rejoicing in that sun-bright land.

Come, angels, strike your loudest strain,
The saints with you forever reign ;
There shall our tears be wiped away,
My night be turned to endless day."

LOVE H. JAMESON.

THIS distinguished pioneer was born May 17th, 1811, in Jefferson county, Indiana Territory. His parents were both natives of Virginia, whence they emigrated to Kentucky—his father in 1795 and his mother in 1803. Soon after their marriage they again turned their faces toward the Northwest, and in the Fall of 1810 settled for life on a creek called Indian Kentucky, in the county and Territory aforesaid.

His father, Thomas Jameson, was born of parents who were members of the Kirk of Scotland, consequently he was sprinkled in infancy and trained up a Calvinist in the strictest sense of that term. His mother's parents held the views of the Church of England, but for some cause she was not christened according to the usages of that church. By some means she had imbibed the doctrine of Arminius, and was, therefore, directly opposed to her husband on the subject of religion.

But united in heart and fortune, they soon came also to "the unity of the faith and of the knowledge of the Son of God." In the year 1816, by the hand of John McClung, a young coadjutor of B. W. Stone, they were immersed into the Lord Jesus and became members of the old Christian Church.

In the Spring of 1818 the father of Love H. chanced to form the acquaintance of Mr. Joseph Bryant, a brother-in-law of Alexander Campbell. From Mr. Bryant he heard for the first time of Mr. Campbell, and of the changes he

recommended in the return to the "ancient order." Soon after he received a pamphlet published by Thomas and Alexander Campbell, in which was presented at length "The Basis of Christian Union." This pamphlet was published in 1809, three years before its authors withdrew from the Presbyterian Church. With its contents Mr. Jameson was well pleased, and would gladly have read more from the same source; but from that time he heard no more of the Campbells, or of the Reformation, until the year 1826.

Among the first religious impressions made upon the mind of Elder Jameson was a profound respect for the Holy Scriptures. Many portions of them he committed to memory at a very tender age, and their declarations he was taught to regard as an end of all controversy. In a word, he was carefully trained up "in the way he should go," and now that he is old he has not departed from it.

His education was attended with all the difficulties incident to frontier life. There were but few schools, and they were conducted by incompetent "masters." His first teacher, especially, still holds a place in his memory as an inexorable tyrant. It was, perhaps, a blessing that the sessions were short and at long intervals; for had he been kept long under such instructors, he might have been characterized in after life by a hatred rather than a love of literary pursuits.

It was a happy necessity that kept him the greater part of his time under the tuition of his kind parents, who used due diligence in the education of their children, especially their first Love. Before he was three years old they purchased for him a primer, and by the help of its pictures he soon became familiar with the names of the letters. This done, the advance to spelling and reading was easy and rapid.

In penmanship he certainly enjoyed the *disadvantages*

of a "new system." With a rude pencil of his own manufacture, he executed the characters on *linden slabs;* nor were these implements displaced by pen, ink, and paper, until he had learned to write a legible hand. This he soon accomplished; and by the time he was seven years old he was so good a scribe, that when his first teacher came round with the "Article," he had the honor of signing his father's name to that instrument.

From 1818 to 1828 he attended school each Winter; and each Summer assisted his father on the farm. His principal study, during that time, was Arithmetic; no attention being paid to English Grammar, because it was the prevailing opinion that *it* was calculated only "to make fools of the children." The teachers readily encouraged the popular prejudice against a subject of which they themselves were grossly ignorant. Geography was then an "untaught question;" and as for Algebra—had its name been mentioned, those simple pioneers might have mistaken it for that of the striped horse (Zebra), or some more terrible "varmint." Still, what little was taught he learned; and, in addition to that, he spent his leisure hours at home in reading every book and paper upon which he could lay hands. "Weems' Lives of Washington and Marion," "The History of the Twelve Cæsars," an old "History of London," and a stray copy of "Morse's Geography," containing numerous historical accounts, were read and re-read until he could repeat many portions of them from memory. The historical portions of the Old Testament, also—especially those relating to the deliverance and subsequent wars of the Israelites, were made as familiar as the tales of the nursery.

Aside from his progress in other matters, he, at an early age, displayed a remarkable talent for music; and, in the former days of his ministry, he was prominent among the sweet singers of the Reformed Israel.

In 1826 his father commenced taking the "Christian Baptist." This opened to him a new field; and, with respect to the whole family, this was the beginning of a new era. He longed for the coming of every number; and when it came, it was his happy privilege to read it through in the hearing of his parents and any friends that might happen to be present.

The information received from this source, together with the knowledge derived from his early reading of the Scriptures, made him quite a formidable disputant in the private discussions of those times. These were of frequent occurrence; for Beverly Vawter was already presenting, with clearness and boldness, the distinctive features of the Reformation, while all his fellow-preachers, and many of the common people, were bitterly opposing him.

Thus things went on until the Fall of 1829. In September of that year a protracted meeting was held on Indian Kentucky, near the residence of Thomas Jameson, at which place it had been customary to hold a meeting each Fall, for the last ten years. There being no houses of worship, the people assembled by day in the groves, and, at night, there was usually preaching at several different cabins in the neighborhood. On Monday of the present meeting it was noised abroad that on the night before several persons had "got religion" at the house of an old brother Eccles. This intelligence threw the whole community into an uproar.

For some time previous to that the Reformers had rather outnumbered those who held fast the traditions of the fathers; but, the event of the preceding night being known, a great many rallied under the orthodox banner, and, for a single day, restored that party to the ascendancy. They controlled the meeting; they preached; they invited mourners to the altar; and had the satisfaction of seeing many "converted." About noon the great assembly repaired to the water, songs being sung all the way. On the bank of the stream Elder Jameson confessed the Saviour, and was straightway immersed by one who understood, as well as himself, the design of the ordinance.

From this time forth there was great religious excitement in that region. But the way which they called heresy, gradually gained ground despite the most obstinate resistance. Elder Jameson took a prominent part in every social meeting; and it was soon insinuated that he had a talent for preaching, and that the command was to "occupy." Especially did Elder Vawter, and an aged brother McMillan, urge him to do the work of an evangelist. Yielding to their importunities, he consented; and on the evening of December 25th, 1829, he preached his first discourse. From that time to the present, a period of thirty years, he has been constantly before the public.

During the greater part of the year 1830 he was engaged in teaching, principally for the benefit of his younger brothers and sisters. While thus employed he prosecuted diligently the work of self-instruction; and having acquired a pretty good knowledge of his mother tongue, he began the study of Greek. In this, his first text-book was Ironside's Grammar, which, in his judgment, was most appropriately named. It was written in Latin, and *to acquire a knowledge of either language he had to first understand the other*. He was, therefore, in much the same predicament as those who are taught that they cannot obtain faith until they pray for it, while at the same time they cannot pray acceptably without faith! Yet by the aid of lexicons and of his teacher, he penetrated, in places, even Ironside;

and was soon able to read the New Testament in the original Greek.

In the mean time he and Elder Vawter continued to hold meetings at various points in Jefferson and the adjacent counties, baptizing not a few.

In the Fall of 1832 he visited New Castle, Georgetown, Clintonville, and other points in Kentucky. On this tour he made the acquaintance of Elders F. R. Palmer, John Smith, John Rogers, J. T. Johnson, and other distinguished pioneers of that State, from whom he received many valuable suggestions relative to the work of the ministry. Returning home, he again engaged in teaching, still preaching regularly, however, and immersing many, among whom were several of his pupils.

In the Spring of 1833 he visited Rising Sun, where he made arrangements with D. D. Pratt, the Principal, to spend the Summer and Fall in the seminary at that place. This he did, studying chiefly English Grammar, Algebra, Rhetoric, and Greek. During his connection with this institution he defrayed his expenses by instructing the preparatory classes. He also preached regularly for a congregation some distance in the country; and under his labors quite a number were added to the little church. From the very first he seems to have cast the net on the right side of the ship.

This was the last school he ever attended; but he has been, through life, a diligent self-instructor, and has worked his way up to an honorable rank among the educated men of the church. In the natural sciences, especially, he is quite proficient; and notwithstanding the difficulties under which he began the study of Greek, he has, by perseverance, acquired a critical knowledge of that language. His literary character was such, in general, that, in 1859, the Board of Directors of the N. W. C. University, on the recommendation of the Faculty, conferred on him the honorary degree of A. M.

Leaving the seminary in November he returned to his father's, and once more engaged to teach during the Winter. This, his last school, closed in March, 1834, and he immediately began to make preparations for devoting himself entirely to the ministry as a life work. His father fully set before him the difficulties and privations he would have to encounter as a preacher of the gospel; but he still adhered to his purpose, while he looked not at the things which are seen and temporal, but at the things which are not seen and eternal.

On the first day of April, 1834, he bade adieu to home and friends, and set out for Ohio. His first appointment was at Rising Sun, from which place he proceeded to Cincinnati by way of Burlington, Ky. Late in the evening he crossed the river at Covington, and found himself alone in the busy throng of the young Queen of the West. He soon found his way to the house of a brother T. Murdock, who extended to him Christian hospitality. Having tarried here a few days, he proceeded to Carthage, where he renewed an acquaintance, previously formed, with Walter Scott. Together they held several interesting meetings, and finally went to Harrison, on the State line, to fill an appointment for John O'Kane. There they met with Elder Carey Smith of Indianapolis, from whom they learned that all the churches of the town were closed against them, and that they would be under the necessity of holding the proposed meeting in a barn some two miles up White Water.

After a hasty meal the trio set out for the said barn, where they found only about thirty persons assembled. Walter Scott was greatly discouraged, and without ceremony rolled himself up in his great cloak, stowed himself away in a hay mow, and went to sleep. The burden of the day, therefore, devolved on the two wakeful preachers.

Smith delivered an able discourse; Jameson followed with a fervent exhortation; and several persons came forward to make the good confession. At this juncture Elder Scott came hurriedly out of his snug retreat, and, without stopping to remove the bits of hay from his raven locks, joined in the exercises with hearty good will.

As the sun was going down they returned to the village, and repaired to the river to attend to the ordinance of baptism. A great concourse of people were present, and among them a local preacher by the name of Lincoln, who fearing an invasion of the Methodist Zion, determined to offer battle at the water. Elder Scott immediately took his position on a large boulder, and commenced replying to Mr. Lincoln's questions. His faithful co-laborers took their positions around him, Testament in hand; and as soon as Mr. Lincoln would put a question they would turn to the passage containing the proper answer, and hand it up to Elder Scott, who would read it aloud, making such comments as he deemed pertinent. This done, all were ready for another question and another reply. Thus, until the enemy was silenced, raged the Battle of White Water, fought with weapons "not carnal but mighty through God to the pulling down of strong holds." By the singular contest an intense religious interest was awakened in the whole community. From that time till the close of the meeting the "barn" was filled to overflowing; and before they left the town a goodly number had been added to the saved.

This was the beginning of the Harrison church, which was organized in July following with over forty members.

In the mean time Elder Jameson had engaged to preach for the churches at Carthage, Cumminsville, and White Oak. His labors at each of these points were attended with great success.

In the month of June he assisted Elders Walter Scott,

J. G. Mitchell, and Guerdon Gates of Kentucky, in a protracted meeting at Dayton, Ohio. This proved to be a kind of city of Samaria; the gospel met with a cordial reception; and many were brought to the knowledge of the truth and the obedience of the faith.

From Dayton, Elder Jameson visited Harrison, Rising Sun, Vevay, and other points in Dearborn, Ohio, and Switzerland counties. At Vevay he engaged in his first and last public discussion. His opponent was the Rev. John Pavy of the Regular Baptist church.

During the Fall and Winter of 1834 he continued to preach at various points in Hamilton county, making occasional visits to Dayton, and one to Wilmington, where he became acquainted with Dr. Matthias Winans, a distinguished correspondent of the Evangelist and Millennial Harbinger.

Early in the Spring of 1835 he revisited Kentucky, in company with Walter Scott. They preached at Georgetown, and at several places in Scott and Woodford counties, including Versailles, Paris, and Lexington. Of course they did not fail to visit Ashland, where they spent several hours with Mr. Clay under his old-fashioned but hospitable roof.

On returning to Ohio he found letters urging him to assume the pastoral care of the church at Dayton. This call he accepted, and in June, 1835, removed to that city. Soon afterward he visited Connersville, Indiana, where he assisted John O'Kane in a protracted meeting. Together they then went to Rushville, and thence to Indianapolis, then an insignificant town of a few hundred inhabitants, having not a single railroad, and consequently as little communication with the rest of the world as Jerusalem had with Samaria. Bespattered with mud, and wet as a drenching rain could make them, they entered the courthouse where a few persons had assembled; and soon forgot the sufferings of this present time in contemplating the glory that shall be revealed hereafter. At this meeting Elder Jameson met, for the first time, John L. Jones, P. M. Blankenship, Butler K. Smith, and other pioneer evangelists.

Returning to Dayton, he continued his pastoral labors with the most encouraging results. The church at that place, thinking themselves unable to sustain weekly preaching, permitted him to spend a portion of his time in the service of congregations abroad. Under this arrangement he visited, during the remainder of that year and the next, the churches at Fairfield, Wilmington, Maysville, Mayslick, Minerva, Carthage, Harrison, Connersville, Rushville, Greensburg, Indianapolis, and other points in Ohio, Indiana, and Kentucky. His principal co-laborers were D. S. Burnett, Walter Scott, John O'Kane, and R. T. Brown. In pairs and trios they journeyed about on horseback, holding here and there what were literally "big meetings," for they usually continued several days, and resulted in the salvation of many.

In the Winter of 1837 he attended the Campbell and Purcell debate, at Cincinnati; and took part in the long series of meetings which followed that exciting discussion.

In April of the same year he resigned his charge at Dayton, and returned to his old, first field at Carthage, where he found a true yoke-fellow in the person of Dr. L. L. Pinkerton. While at this point he also preached regularly for the churches at White Oak, Burlington, Mount Pleasant, and Harrison. He made one tour through Rush and Fayette counties, Indiana, and one through a portion of Kentucky.

In December, 1837, he was married to Miss Elizabeth M. Clark, a woman of such excellent spirit that she was soon counted worthy to appear in the society of the blest.

For the next two or three years he continued to travel and preach as formerly, being present, in the Winter of 1839-40, at the great meeting in Cincinnati, which continued one hundred days.

At this time he was passing—had well nigh passed—the happiest days of his life. Shortly afterward Walter Scott and Dr. Pinkerton removed to Kentucky; some old friends emigrated to the West; others died; and the happy circle in which he had been wont to move, was sadly broken. Under such circumstances he was no longer content with his field of labor. Like the lone Indian who snapped his bow-strings, threw them on the burial-place of his fathers, and departed toward the setting sun, he left with a sad heart the scenes of his joys and griefs in Ohio, and journeyed westward to Indiana.

This general emigration of evangelists was a severe blow upon the cause of reform in Ohio. At that very time, if ever, there was need of united and untiring effort. All that rich and populous region west and north of Cincinnati was stretching out its hands for the ancient gospel, and, by proper exertion, might have been brought under its influence. But the golden opportunity was suffered to pass unimproved, and the field that was ripe for the harvest was never reaped.

In May, 1840, he rested once more with his little family beneath the paternal roof. His first work on returning to Indiana was to revisit the churches for which he had been wont to preach in his youth. This being done, he constantly extended his field of operations, until he had published the ancient gospel in nearly all the cities and villages of the southeastern portion of the State.

In some of these places he received a small pittance for his labors; but, in the majority of them, he received nothing. He therefore knew "how to be in want," though he knew not "how to abound." At no period of his ministry has there been reason to suspect that Elder Jameson was following the Saviour for "the loaves and fishes." During his sojourn in Ohio he never received more than four hundred dollars per annum; and the debts he was compelled to leave unpaid, added not a little to the heaviness with which he left that State. It was only by rigid economy and stern self-denial that he satisfied those old claims, and thus kept the command to "owe no man any thing, but to love one another." Since his return to Indiana his abundant labors in the gospel have afforded him a bare support; and pecuniary embarrassments that were present in his youth, are robbing him of the ease and tranquillity that should accompany old age.

In May, 1841, Elder Jameson located in Madison as pastor of the congregation in that city. The year opened with bright prospects, but it closed in the deepest gloom. At the close of a beautiful day in June, his wife was walking in the garden, apparently in perfect health; and while thus engaged, she was suddenly seized with an apoplectic fit, and almost instantly expired.

After this sad bereavement, he continued his pastoral labors in Madison until the Fall of 1842. In the mean time he made an extensive tour through the Wabash country, including the cities of Terre Haute, Crawfordsville, Lafayette, and Indianapolis.

At the close of the meeting in Indianapolis, he was invited to take charge of the church in that city. This invitation he accepted; and on the 5th of October, 1842, he entered upon the duties of his new pastorate. Before leaving Madison, however, he was again married, to Miss Elizabeth K. Robinson, of that city.

In September, 1843, he accompanied Elder B. W. Stone and others to the Illinois State Meeting, which convened that year at Springfield. After its adjournment, he spent a month in visiting important points in the Prairie State.

In 1845, the State Meeting, which met at Columbus, Indiana, appointed him and Elder John O'Kane to evangelize in the southwestern part of the State. To this mission they devoted the Summer of that year, doing what they could to extend the Redeemer's kingdom, in the midst of the excitement produced by the national difficulties with Mexico.

For several years subsequent to this date he was employed, partly by the church at the capital, and partly by congregations in the vicinity.

Since 1854, he has preached but little in Indianapolis, but he has continued to reside there, laboring incessantly, elsewhere, in word and doctrine. He keeps up his regular monthly appointments at some four different churches; and availing himself of the excellent facilities afforded by the numerous railroads centering at that place, he publishes the glad tidings throughout the entire Commonwealth. Even state lines do not circumscribe his influence; for, in the last few years, he has visited Ohio, Kentucky, Western Missouri, Illinois, New York, and portions of New England.

From first to last he has been successful in his ministry; and the Lamb's book of life will reveal many a name written therein through his instrumentality.

In the personal appearance of Elder Jameson there is but little indicative of the hardy pioneer. Aside from his silvered locks and patriarchal beard, he exhibits but few signs of old age. His cheek is but slightly furrowed; his black, restless eye has lost none of its youthful fire; and he who has known him for a score of years can scarcely detect any loss of grace or elasticity in his step. He weighs about one hundred and forty-five pounds; is about five feet nine inches high, rather slender, and as straight as an Indian.

As he has risen by his own efforts from the humbler to the higher and more refined circles, he has departed from the style of dress, and, somewhat, from the plain and simple manners of the former days; on which account, some, who adhere to the simplicity of the olden time, think him proud. But he is easily approached, uniformly courteous, and always sociable, unless his attention happens to be engrossed with some particular subject

With regard to intellectual ability and scholarship, he is considerably above mediocrity. In the main his researches are extensive rather than deep; yet he is not superficial, and on some subjects he is decidedly original. In biblical criticism, especially, he has evinced greater acumen than many who eclipse him in reputation.

He has not written extensively for the public, but has for many years contributed sparingly to the Christian Record, Millennial Harbinger, and other organs of the brotherhood. It costs him much labor to write for the press; for he composes slowly and with great care; and his manuscript, before it leaves his hand, must be in appearance altogether unexceptionable. It may be on this account that he has not been a more frequent contributor. His prose essays certainly compare most favorably with the productions of many whose names, in full, appear almost weekly in some of the religious papers. Though he does not claim to be a poet, he has written some very respectable hymns, a few of which have recently appeared, over his initials, in "The Weekly Christian Record."

As a pulpit orator he occupies an honorable rank among the preachers of his day. He has an excellent voice; his elocution is earnest and emphatic; in gesture he is free and natural, in language chaste and copious. In speaking he holds his head in a rather elevated position, and turns it about in a peculiar manner, by which alone he would be easily recognized were he, in other respects, completely disguised. Some censorious critics think him somewhat wordy, desultory, and given to repetition. If so, it is not because he lacks ability to be concise and logical; but because he has preached so long and become so familiar with every portion of the Scriptures that he has suffered himself to fall into the habit of speaking without previous preparation. In this particular he is by no means a sinner "above all others"—the fault is as common as it is grievous. He is a bold and uncompromising *defender* of the truth, yet he is not disputatious or dogmatical. His discourse is generally designed to point out the path of duty to saint and sinner, or to expound some difficult passage of Scripture.

As a Christian he is without spot and blameless. In the congregation, in his family, in the round of mirth, in the house of mourning, in every relation of life, his demeanor is "as becometh the gospel of Christ."

Having been from his youth under the influence of that wisdom which has "in her left hand length of days," his willing spirit is not yet fettered by any serious infirmity of the flesh. On the contrary, he is still vigorous and active in the ministry, though

> "The morning of life
> Has vanished away,
> And shadows portend
> The close of the day."

JAMES M. MATHES.

Of all the preachers of Indiana, whether of the past or the present day, none has contributed more to the progress of the current Reformation than the subject of this sketch. He was born on the 8th of July, 1808, in Jefferson county, Kentucky, near the site of the present village of Brownsborough. His progenitors, a few generations past, were inhabitants of the county of Antrim, in the north of Ireland. His grandfather served under General Washington in the war of Independence, as quartermaster of a Virginia regiment. His father, Jeremiah Mathes, was born in Shenandoah county, Virginia, whence, about the close of the last century, he emigrated to Kentucky.

In the year 1804, Jeremiah Mathes was married to Florence Cameron, a descendant of the celebrated Parson Cameron, who is embalmed in Scottish history by the side of the Wallaces and Bruces. Her father, John C. Cameron, an educated Scotchman, also served a long time in the Revolutionary war, and was wounded in the battle of Brandywine.

Elder Mathes is therefore a descendant of two patriotic families, whose spirit he inherits, and whose good name he has never sullied. Though too old to enter, himself, into the great struggle now going on between patriots and rebels, he has sadly but willingly laid his three sons on the altar of his country.

His grandfather, John C. Cameron, after retiring from the service of his adopted land, spent the remainder of his days as a professional teacher—disseminating intelligence,

> "A weapon surer yet
> And mightier than the bayonet;
> A weapon that comes down as still
> As snow-flakes fall upon the sod,
> And executes the freeman's will,
> As lightnings do the will of God."

Religiously he was a Covenanter, as were all the Cameron family in the old country.

On the other side, the Matheses had been Presbyterians almost from the beginning of Protestantism; but early in the present century the father of Jeremiah Mathes, and his whole family, were converted to the views of the Regular Baptists, with whom they all became identified.

About the year 1825, the parents of Elder Mathes became convinced of the errors of the Calvinistic system, and of the folly of all human creeds. In consequence of this conviction they left the Baptist Church and united with the Old Christian body, in Owen county, Indiana, whither they had removed some years before.

James M. was the second of a family of eleven children, six sons and five daughters. Two of his brothers, John C. and J. J. W., are also able ministers of the gospel. The other three, Henry, William, and Franklin, are industrious and well-to-do farmers. All the brothers, together with the five sisters, are still living, and all are faithful members of the Christian Church.

Elder Mathes was strictly brought up in that particular form of Calvinism held by the Regular Baptist Church. His public teachers in these things were John Taylor, Wm. Keller, George Waller, Zacheus Carpenter, and other early preachers of Kentucky, whose names are yet familiar to many aged disciples. In their doctrine were many things hard to be understood, yet he endeavored to believe "every word," because it was believed by his parents, in whose judgment he reposed implicit confidence.

His mother taught him to read when he was very young; and the first act that he can remember is his reading the Holy Scriptures. Thus early was he taught to love the Bible and reverence it as "indeed and in truth the word of the living God." Through this wholesome teaching it is probable that the outline of his character and the course of his future life were marked out before he was eight years old!

Certain it is that at a very early period of his life he manifested a remarkable fondness for public speaking, in which he was promptly aided and encouraged by his parents and grandparents. His grandfather, especially, who was a well-informed man, took great delight in teaching him to make little speeches and take part in simple dialogues. As often as a few of the neighbors would come in, the old gentleman would place the young orator upon a table, where he would pronounce his little orations to an audience far better entertained than many have been by more prosy and more pretending addresses.

At church he watched with a mimic's eye all the movements of the speaker, and, on returning home, he practiced the same attitudes in the delivery of the short and simple speeches which his hopeful grandfather had taught him. Even at that age he had resolved to be a preacher of the gospel; and often would he discourse with great earnestness to his playmates, all seated around according to his directions, and all listening demurely to his admonitions. At a later period he used to write his discourses, one of which is believed to be extant, but in a portion of the country not now accessible. It was written on the following passage in Jeremiah: "O that you had hearkened to my commandments; then had your peace been as a river and your righteousness as the waves of the sea."

Soon after his father's immigration to Indiana, a missionary by the name of Isaac Reed came from Western

New York, and settled in the same neighborhood at a noted Big Spring near Gosport. Being Presbyterians, and having a "zeal for God, but not according to knowledge," they opened a Sunday-school in their own cabin. The establishment of this school was hailed with delight by the juvenile preacher. He attended regularly, applied himself closely, and soon became distinguished for his proficiency in memorizing the Scriptures. "The Shorter Catechism" he also mastered so completely, that he could answer almost every question it contained. Along with these answers, he received into his mind much error; but the inspired texts committed, proved to be as "a little leaven that leaveneth the whole lump." Even the knowledge of the doctrines and commandments of men, thus acquired, has been no disadvantage to him in the conflict of life.

This was the first school of any kind he ever attended. When, in 1816, his father removed with him to Indiana, Owen county was a wilderness from which the savages had not retired before the advancing tide of civilization. It afforded then, and during nine years subsequent to that time, no facilities whatever for education. It was not till the year 1825, that Scott W. Young (who subsequently married the eldest sister of Elder Mathes) came from Kentucky, and taught several schools in Owen county. These schools Elder Mathes attended regularly, and by close application he acquired the rudiments of a common education, including a smattering of English grammar.

From a child he was inclined to wisdom's ways. The simple prayers taught him by his pious parents were seldom neglected until he attained to sufficient age to embody, in words of his own, the grateful emotions of his heart. He often prayed to his Heavenly Father in secret, and inquired of his relatives and friends what he must do to be saved. But they were blind leaders of the blind, anxious, but incompetent, to show him the path of life. He longed to see some great "light from heaven," to "hear the voice of an angel," or, at least, to dream some good, orthodox dream, which would be satisfactory evidence of his acceptance with God. But he could neither see, hear, feel, nor dream any thing that gave him full assurance of his conversion.

He continued in this uncertain state of mind for five long years. He attended the meetings of all denominations, but none of the preaching afforded him any relief, for none was according to the oracles of God—none took away the vail of Calvinism, which was closely drawn over his heart. According to the direction of the Calvinist he endeavored to resign himself to perdition. Following the advice of the preacher of "free grace," he repaired to the anxious seat. All the popular expedients were resorted to in vain. Year after year did the wintry gloom disappear from the face of Nature; but from his brow the dark clouds were not driven. Spring after Spring the vernal sun called forth leaf and blossom; but no mysterious power caused to appear, in his heart, "the tender leaves of hope." On every side of him others glorified God; but he, though equally sincere, had no new song put into his mouth.

Unable to reconcile this fact with the Scripture which affirms that God is no respecter of persons, he presented his difficulty to the ministers, who attributed his ill fortune to his *want of faith*. It may seem strange that under their instruction he had been praying for years without faith. But the fact is they proceeded on the correct assumption that the penitent had faith when he presented himself at the altar of prayer; and when one professed to have obtained pardon they received his testimony as an additional proof that justification is by faith only. But when, as in the case of Elder Mathes, there was a failure in the struggle for remission of sins, they dared not acknowledge the faith of the penitent, for by so doing they would have *disproved at once the " most wholesome doctrine and very full of comfort."* The extremity to which the system was reduced by these failures, gave rise to at least two grievous but popular errors.

1. *The denial of the faith of the unsuccessful penitent, necessarily originated the doctrine of repentance before faith.*

2. The attributing of the failure to lack of faith on the part of the penitent, necessarily originated the idea of *divers kinds of faith.* For since the Scriptures say, "Let him that asketh ask *in faith,*" the preachers were bound to admit that faith is *antecedent* to *prayer.* Now, the praying penitent having *faith,* and the doctrine of "justification by *faith* only" being true, pardon was to be expected, *in every instance,* as a logical, an inevitable sequence. When it did not follow—when the subject did not profess to have "got religion," some objection had to be made to one or the other of the premises. The major premise, that "we are justified by faith only" *could* not be objected to because it was in the *creed.* The minor premise had been *admitted*—namely, that the penitent had faith before he prayed; therefore there remained but one way of escape, and that was by affirming that the faith of the penitent was not of the *right kind.* Hence the origin of such phrases as "faith of assent," "saving faith," etc., etc. The system sought out this invention for the sake of self-preservation—on this ground only is it pardonable.

Sadly perplexed by these absurd teachings, Elder Mathes sought in skepticism the relief he could not find in religion. He doubted, for the first time, the authenticity of the Scriptures; withdrew for nearly a year from the sanctuary; sought to forget God in the company of the gay and thoughtless; devoted his leisure hours to the reading of infidel books; and stopped not in his hopeless career until he reached the very border of atheism.

But in every giddy round of pleasure he saw continually before him the meek and troubled expression of his pious and affectionate mother, who, more watchful than he had anticipated, perceived with pain his every aberration from the path of virtue. Her influence, and that alone, kept him from plunging openly into "many foolish and hurtful lusts that would have drowned him in destruction and perdition."

Finally he resolved to dismiss from his mind, as far as possible, all previous religious teaching; and to read again the New Testament as if he had never read it before. In so doing his doubts were all dispelled, and he again believed with all his heart that "Jesus is the Christ, the Son of God."

The entrance of God's word also gave him light as to the means by which he might obtain pardon. In looking into "the perfect law of liberty," he saw, with some degree of clearness, the plan of salvation; and was made exceedingly happy in believing the truth.

With joyful haste he communicated his convictions to his religious friends, some of whom, to his surprise, expressed serious doubts relative to the safety of his more excellent way, while some confidently pronounced his strange doctrine a delusion of the devil.

Among others he went to see an old brother by the name of John Snoddy, a very candid and pious man, and one of the few that, with B. W. Stone, seceded from the Presbyterian Church in Kentucky. After his youthful visitor had stated his view of the gospel plan of saving sinners, the old brother replied with tearful eyes as follows: "*Brother James,*" said he, "*it is contrary to my experience, but what am I that I should withstand God?*

You are right. It is the Lord's word, and therefore safe. Go on, and the Lord bless you, my son." Italics can not do justice to these "words fitly spoken." They deserve to be inscribed in letters of gold on every sectarian pulpit in the land. They gave great encouragement to the young reformer, who resolved to obey the gospel the very first opportunity.

That opportunity did not present itself for a long time; for in all that section of country there *was not a preacher that would immerse him "for the remission of sins!"*

At that time he had heard of Alexander Campbell, but he knew nothing whatever of his views. He had always heard him spoken of as an arch-heretic; and he had not the remotest idea that Campbell was in advance of him in the very way which he (Mathes) had recently discovered. Elder Mathes is, therefore, another who derived his "*Campbellism*" directly from the Bible. In the absence of other testimony, the fact that so many in that dark era came, each without the knowledge of another, to the same conclusions, from the study of the Scriptures, would be at least strong presumptive evidence that the doctrine they then embraced, and have since maintained, is taught in the book of God.

About the 1st of September, 1827, Mr. Mathes obtained a copy of Campbell's "New Version" and a few numbers of the "Christian Baptist." The former greatly assisted him in arriving at the true meaning of the Scriptures, while his faith was confirmed by the able articles contained in the latter.

In October following he attended a great camp-meeting held by the Newlights at Old Union meeting-house, in Owen county. On Sunday morning he walked out with Elder John Henderson, one of the principal preachers, sat down with him on a log, and actually *taught him "the way of God more perfectly."* At first the good man listened with suspicion; but as the argument progressed he became deeply interested, and, finally, was so overwhelmed with evidence that he exclaimed: "You are right, my son; it is the Lord's plan; and whatever he commands I can cheerfully perform! I am ready to immerse you for the remission of sins." They then returned to the place of meeting, and, at the close of a discourse by Elder Blythe McCorkle, Father Henderson, with a word of *apology* and explanation, invited sinners to come forward, confess the Saviour as he was confessed in primitive times, and be baptized every one of them for the remission of sins. J. M. Mathes and his sister Eliza made the good confession, were immersed straightway by Elder Henderson, and, for the time being, united with the Old Christian or Newlight Church.

Immediately after his immersion he began to take an active part in the public prayer-meetings, exhorting his brethren as often as he was called upon. He also engaged earnestly in teaching from house to house, and by the wayside, the things pertaining to the kingdom of God.

He may be said to have entered upon his ministry when he sat down on the log with Elder Henderson—in fact when he first discovered the divine plan of pardon; for the gray-haired minister that immersed him was really his *third* convert, his sister being the *second*, and old Brother Snoddy the *first*.

On the 5th of March, 1829, he was married to Sophia Glover, a pious young sister in the household of faith. She was born in Virginia, whence her father removed, first to Montgomery county, Kentucky, and subsequently to Owen county, Indiana. Through their long pilgrimage together she has been an exemplary Christian, an amiable and faithful companion. Meek and uncomplaining, she has submitted with cheerfulness to the lot of a minister's wife, and has always encouraged her husband to labor for the salvation of sinners and the extension of the Redeemer's kingdom.

Their union has been blessed with three sons and three daughters, all of whom are still living, and all are members of the Church of Christ except the youngest son.

In June, 1831, he re-organized the church at Old Union, all the members entering heartily into the Reformation except one sister, who joined the Protestant Methodists and became a public teacher of their doctrine. In the absence of more experienced leaders, he was compelled to take a prominent part in the conduct of the new organization, the work of edifying the body devolving almost entirely upon him.

In the Fall of the same year (1831) the first co-operation meeting held in the State took place at Crawfordsville. To that meeting he and Elder T. C. Johnson were appointed messengers. Arriving upon the ground, they found the following preachers in attendance, viz.: Michael Combs, Andrew Prather, Jas. R. Ross, —— Sears, John M. Harris, and Wm. Wilson—only *six*, a number which clearly indicates that the Reformation in Indiana was then in its infancy. At that meeting, and in the house of old brother James McCullough, Elder Mathes made his first attempt at preaching, beyond the bounds of his own congregation.

Returning home, the messengers aforesaid entered with fresh vigor into the evangelical field; yet their sphere of usefulness was necessarily limited. Elder Johnson was clerk of the county; and Elder Mathes was obliged to teach school for a livelihood. Consequently to preach on Sundays, and occasionally to hold a two-days meeting, was the best they could do.

The plan of sustaining an evangelist by contributions from the *people*—for there were no *churches*—had been but slightly discussed, and had met with but little favor

In that quarter of the world, also, the doctrine obtained that a minister of the gospel ought to preach for nothing and board himself. It was generally supposed to be right to feed a preacher's horse, if he was so fortunate as to have one; and also to feed the preacher himself, if he would go from house to house for his meals. There was no law against giving him a pair of socks, especially if, as he sat around the old-fashioned fireplace, his protruding toes invoked a covering; and if he had a river to cross in order to reach his next appointment, it was conceded to be lawful for some rich man to slip into his hand the amount of the ferriage. This last act, however, was perpetrated very stealthily, that the left hand might not know what the right hand did!

Under these circumstances, he did not receive from the churches, during the first ten years of his ministry, an average of one hundred dollars per annum. Even this small pittance was received, for the most part, in articles of food and raiment—country jeans, the broadcloth of those times, being a legal tender.

The perquisites of his office were also few and small. On a certain occasion, he rode some six or eight miles, in very cold weather, to join in happy wedlock a country lad and lass. The ceremony performed, the delighted groom took him to one side and inquired the amount of his claim. He replied that in such cases he usually made no charge; but left the amount to be determined by the liberality of the party benefited. "Well, then," said the new-made husband, "take this, any how," at the same time dropping into his hand three Spanish *bits*, or *thirty-seven and a half cents*.

From 1830 to 1838 he taught school the greater part of his time, but preached on Sundays in the neighborhood, and, occasionally, during his vacations, he held protracted meetings at various points. His labors were mostly confined to the counties of Clay, Owen, Monroe, Morgan, Putnam, and Lawrence. He was very successful in his ministry; many new churches were organized; and hundreds obeyed the gospel and took their stand on the Bible alone.

In the year 1833 he was ordained to the ministry by fasting, prayer, and the imposition of hands.

In the Fall of the same year, while on a tour through Clay county, he met with a violent opposer by the name of Burberage, with whom he first measured swords in public. The conflict was short, but decisive; and hardly deserves to be called a debate.

The following Autumn, however, a regular discussion took place at Pleasant Garden, Putnam county, between him and the Rev. Lorenzo D. Smith, of the M. E. Church. This was a highly exciting contest, which resulted in great good to the cause of reform, and inflicted a blow upon Methodism from which it has not recovered to this day.

In those days he had many little skirmishes with the enemies of the truth; for he was assailed on every hand, and he never declined battle when it was offered.

By this time he had acquired, mainly by his own efforts, a tolerable English education; but his experience in debates led him to desire a wider scope of information, and a more thorough mental discipline—especially did he covet a knowledge of the Greek language. He therefore determined to make an effort to secure these desired objects. Many things stood opposed to the enterprise, not the least of which was poverty. But he rented out his little farm in Owen county, gathered together a small sum of money by selling off his stock, and, in Autumn of 1838, removed to Bloomington, and became a student of the State University.

To maintain his family and defray his expenses in college, he preached regularly for the churches at Bloomington, Clear Creek, Harmony, and Richland. These congregations prospered in his hands, and, despite this extra labor, he made rapid progress in his studies, especially in Greek.

There were with him in the Greek Testament class several young men of Pedobaptist training, and consequently of Pedobaptist views. When the class began, the President, Dr. Wylie, instructed them to translate the original text as if it had never been translated, giving to every word its *primary meaning*, according to their several lexicons. Under this rule they all went on harmoniously until they came to the word βαπτιζειν. This Elder Mathes rendered "to immerse." The Pedoes protested, but he persisted. Unable to silence him by their own arguments, they appealed to Dr. Wylie, who, in hearing their grievances, decided that there was no just cause of complaint—that Mr. Mathes was only *obeying orders*, for such *was without doubt the primary signification of the term*. The decision was final; but the Pedobaptists, wiser than seven men that could render a reason, continued to use the word "baptize."

This was by no means the only concession that the learned Presbyterian Doctor made to his pupil, with whom he condescended to an intimate acquaintance. He frankly admitted the correctness of many tenets of the Reformation, and was, for a long while, almost persuaded to be a Christian.

He remained in the University until April, 1841, and was, at the time of leaving, a member of the senior class. Financial embarrassments prevented him from being graduated.

On leaving college he returned to his little farm in Owen county; and, having made arrangements for its cultivation, he gave himself wholly to the word. Being exceedingly zealous, he labored incessantly night and day; and, in all places, his efforts were crowned with remarkable success. Having learned also to wield the pen, he began to contribute to the Christian periodicals generally; and, by this means, he soon became widely known as an able and earnest advocate of primitive Christianity.

In the month of February, 1842, he met the Rev. James Scott, of the M. E. Church, in a public discussion. This took place at Martinsville, Morgan county, and continued three days. The result of the engagement may be inferred from the fact that, until this day, the Christians have occupied the field in force.

In the Fall of this year he attended the annual meeting at Old Mill Creek, Washington county. John Wright, sr., presided; Absalom Littell, and other preachers, assisted; but Elder Mathes was the chief speaker. The meeting continued only eight days, and closed with *one hundred additions*. Such glorious meetings were frequent in those days, when the disciples had not only knowledge, but *zeal according to knowledge*— when they did not shrink from pointing out the difference between Christianity and various *isms*, through fear of being called "uncharitable." During the year ending May, 1843, Elder Mathes immersed *six hundred and seven persons*. Even a greater number were enlisted under his preaching, but some were immersed by other hands. This was the most successful year of his ministry; but for thirty years past he has proselyted from two to three hundred per annum, making a total of five or six thousand.

In May, 1843, he engaged in another public debate, at Greencastle. His opponent was Rev. Erasmus Manford, the editor of a Universalist paper at Terre Haute, and the great apostle of Universalism in Indiana.

In July of this year he commenced the publication of "The Christian Record," a neat monthly of twenty-four pages. Except the Millennial Harbinger, it is the oldest living advocate of the current Reformation. It was first issued at Bloomington, and it gradually increased in popularity until it reached its maximum circulation of five thousand.

Over these subscribers, their families and friends, he, for years, exerted a controlling influence. Through the columns of his paper he inspired their hearts with zeal and courage; opened the Scriptures to their understanding; showed them how good and pleasant it is for brethren to dwell together in unity; demonstrated the evils—the sin—of sectarianism; and warned them against every delusion, of whatever name or description. Millerism and Universalism, especially, he combated with signal ability, until they were no longer able to offer a respectable resistance.

The cause of education also received special encouragement from his columns. He did much to extend the fame and influence of the State University; and his pen was one of the ablest advocates of the establishment of the N. W. C. University, which is now the pride of the brotherhood. He was one of the original commissioners named in the charter of that institution; and was a member of the Board of Directors from its organization until 1856.

At the beginning of Volume V. the number of pages of the Record was increased to thirty-six, and the amount of reading matter nearly doubled. At the same time the publisher associated Elder Elijah Goodwin with him in the editorial management of the paper. This partnership continued to the middle of Volume VI., first series, when Mr. Goodwin retired from the firm.

In the Fall of 1843 he sold his farm and removed to

Bloomington that he might the better superintend his publishing business.

About the year 1848 he purchased the office, press and stock of the "Bloomington Herald," and commenced the additional publication of "The Indiana Tribune," a weekly family newspaper, neutral in politics.

In the Spring of 1851 he discontinued the Tribune, and removed to Indianapolis, where he continued the publication of the Record. There he also engaged in the book and stationery business; and finally became a stockholder in the Indiana Journal Company.

During his residence in Indianapolis he performed an immense amount of labor. In addition to his editorial employments, he preached a great deal in various parts of the State; was for a while pastor of the congregation in the city; attended to the business of his book concern; and rendered efficient service as a member of the Executive and Building Committees of the N. W. C. University. Under such constant pressure his health gave way; and he found it necessary to undo the heavy burden by changing his locality.

Accordingly, on the 5th of November 1855, he left Indianapolis and removed to a farm which he had purchased, near Bedford, in Lawrence county. He left the city with a sad heart; for he had been unfortunate in his business transactions, and was poorer by several hundred dollars than when he entered into it. He is another of the few who, realizing the truth of the Saviour's aphorism, have chosen to fail in the service of Mammon rather than in the service of God.

For a few years after his removal to Lawrence he continued to publish the Record at Indianapolis; but he finally established a printing office at Bedford, which then became the place of publication. In a few months he again removed the Record to Indianapolis, where he continued to have it issued until June, 1859, when, owing to the inconvenience of editing at so great a distance, he transferred it into the hands of Elder Elijah Goodwin, by whom it is at present controlled.

This excellent periodical Elder Mathes ably conducted through sixteen and a half volumes, which will be invaluable to the future historian, who shall record the Rise and Progress of the Reformation in Indiana.

Improved in health but not in fortune by his residence in Lawrence, he gave up his farm, for which he was unable to pay; removed with his family to New Albany; and became the pastor of the church in that city. This position he occupied from June, 1859, to May, 1861.

While at New Albany he prepared and published a book of four hundred and eight pages, entitled, "Works of B. W. Stone." It is chiefly compiled from the writings of that lamented servant of God, and is a valuable addition to our Christian literature.

He also published, in 1861, a little volume of one hundred and eighty-nine pages, titled, "Letters to Bishop Morris." It contains fifteen letters addressed to Thomas A. Morris, D. D., Senior Bishop of the M. E. Church. The first eleven letters are a review of a small work by the bishop, entitled, "The Polity of the M. E. Church." In the other four the author gives his reasons for not being a Methodist. It is written in popular style; and those who may read it, will be both interested and instructed.

In May, 1861, he removed from New Albany to assume the pastoral oversight of the congregation at Bedford. The estimate placed upon his services at New Albany, may be inferred from the following resolutions, adopted on the eve of his departure:

"*Whereas,* Our beloved brother James M. Mathes has signified his intention to dissolve the relationship which has for some length of time existed between himself as pastor and ourselves as the Christian church in New Albany; therefore,

"*Resolved*, That it is with deep regret that we part with brother Mathes, who, by his Christian deportment, bright example, and able ministry, has won for himself our lasting respect and esteem.

"*Resolved*, That our good wishes, our kind remembrances, and our prayers, will accompany him wherever he may go; and that we can and do cheerfully and cordially commend him to all with whom he may hereafter associate, as a Christian and minister worthy of the love and esteem of the wise and good."

By the church at Bedford he is no less beloved; and his success there has been even greater than in New Albany. Under his able ministry has grown up a large congregation, which is just completing a house of worship second to but few Christian churches in the State. No man living exerts a stronger or more healthful influence over the citizens of Lawrence county.

Both of his married children reside at Bedford, the presence of whom and of a multitude of brethren and friends who fully appreciate him and his labors, greatly lightens the otherwise heavy burden of his long-accumulating cares.

For the last thirty years he has been industriously employed in the evangelical field; during which period his preaching alone has induced thousands to glorify the Father in the confession of the Son. Of these converts over four thousand have been immersed by his own hands. The heirs of salvation have also been greatly multiplied by many evangelists whom he has induced to enter the ministry, having first qualified themselves for its work.

If we add to all this the effect of his public discussions, and the influence of his writings—which will no doubt be re-published and read by thousands after his death—we shall then only approximate the blessed results of his self-sacrificing and well-spent life.

Elder Mathes is a medium-sized man, having weighed until recently about one hundred and forty-five pounds. He is now considerably heavier. He is five feet nine inches high, has a full round chest, and great muscular power. He stoops a very little, as he walks with a quick, stealthy step. As he moves along there is nothing ostentatious about him, his dress, or his gait. He has coarse black hair, and his blue eyes indicate a meek and quiet spirit, a sober, reflecting mind. He has a fine constitution, which is but slightly impaired by the infractions of time and toil. True, his hair is sprinkled with gray, and his beard begins to whiten with the frost of age; but his step is still firm, his vigor of mind and body unabated.

The following are the leading traits of his character. 1. *He is a man of great ingenuousness.* To his brethren and friends he opens his heart without reserve; and even in the presence of strangers there is about him no appearance of stiffness or distrust. He never attempts, by any ambiguity of speech or insincerity of action, to appear on both sides of a question, but he promptly chooses his position and frankly gives expression to his views. This element of character manifests itself, especially in his public discussions. In such engagements, however closely contested, he scorns all alliance with equivocation, sophistry, or deceitful handling of the word of God.

2. Very much of his usefulness as well as happiness, results from his eminent *sociability.* Wherever he goes he soon forms the acquaintance of almost every body; all his acquaintances are his friends; and being such they are the more easily persuaded to become the friends of Jesus by keeping his commandments. Aside from the know-

lege of a graver kind, he has an inexhaustible supply of anecdotes, which but few can relate to better advantage or with more pleasure than himself. Though he has transmitted a rich legacy of wit to each of his children, yet he is still blessed above his fellows with that rare faculty which never fails to make its possessor a favorite in the social circle. His wit never descends to obscenity and foolish jesting:—

> "Religion curbs indeed its wanton play,
> And brings the trifler under rigorous sway:
> But gives it usefulness unknown before,
> And, purifying, makes it shine the more."

3. Of such a nature as his, *hospitality* is a spontaneous growth. He uses it without grudging, though not without detriment to his earthly estate. His house has always been a kind of Disciples' Inn, open, and but too well patronized, on all occasions. He is ardently attached, not only to his family, but also to his brethren and friends; and in the entertainment of his visitors, he spares neither pains nor expense.

4. He is a true philomathean—one who loves the truth and searches for it as the covetous do for hid treasure. In the course of his life he has investigated a great variety of subjects, and, although not particularly noted for his scholarship, his mind is well stored with useful knowledge —especially the knowledge of God and of the great plan of redemption. His whole nature is deeply imbued with that wisdom which cometh down from above—which is "first pure, then peaceable, gentle, easy to be entreated, full of mercy and good fruits, without partiality, and without hypocrisy."

5. As a speaker he is always ready upon any subject within the wide range of his investigations. His mental forces are so well disciplined, that they can be brought

into action at a moment's notice; and his retentive memory is well stored with the munitions of intellectual warfare. He is never eloquent; but he speaks with remarkable fluency, and apparently without effort. His voice is clear, mellow, and of more than ordinary compass; yet he does not startle his hearers with his emphasis, nor does he tickle their ears with a great variety of tones: it is the constant flow of well chosen words, each laden with its portion of some good idea, that at once pleases and instructs. There is nothing theatrical about his delivery. During the whole of his discourse he often stands in the very same spot, his feet close together; and his gestures are usually few and unimpressive. Yet, after all, his manner is earnest; his argument is conclusive; his exhortation is warm, seldom impassioned, often effectual. In the selection of his subjects he makes no effort to find "some new thing;" and his preaching is of that quality which "doeth good like a *medicine*," rather than of that highly-seasoned kind, which is pleasant to the taste, but productive of spiritual debility. He does not hesitate to declare the whole counsel of God, nor to expose any or all dogmas that may retard the progress of the truth; but his delivery is so mild, his representations so fair, and his expositions so clear and convincing, that he seldom gives offence. Especially, where he is known, can he, with impunity, utter sentiments which, if expressed by any one else, would be regarded as highly offensive.

His whole pulpit character is pretty well delineated in the following poetical description of

"A vet'ran warrior in the Christian field,
Who never saw the sword he could not wield:
Grave without dullness, learned without pride,
Exact, yet not precise—though meek, keen-eyed;
A man that would have foiled, at their own play,
A dozen would-be's of the modern day;

> Who, when occasion justified its use,
> *Had wit as bright as ready to produce;*
> *Could fetch from records of an earlier age,*
> Or from philosophy's enlightened page,
> His rich materials, and regale your ear
> With strains it was a privilege to hear:
> Yet, above all, his luxury supreme
> And his chief glory was the GOSPEL THEME;
> There he was copious as old Greece or Rome,
> His happy eloquence seemed there at home—
> *Ambitious, not to shine or to excel,*
> But to treat justly what he loved so well."

6. As a writer he has long occupied a high rank, as the popularity of the Record, and of his other publications, clearly attests. With the pen, as in the pulpit, he imitates no one; but dashes on in a bold, free, independent style. He pays but little attention to rhetorical flourishes, but is prolific of ideas, which he conveys to his readers with great force and clearness, though not always in the fewest words. He is emphatically a ready writer, composing with as much ease as he speaks.

7. As a religious editor he was eminently successful, because of his rare qualifications. He possessed a thorough knowledge of the Scriptures and of the tenets of opposing sects, courage to stem the tide of opposition, prudence to avoid expressions that would have engendered unprofitable strife, a nice discernment in the selection of matter, a quick perception of what ought to be encouraged or opposed, and, above all, the ability to wield a swift, vigorous, and untiring pen. In every department of the Christian field he has been useful; but it is chiefly as a public journalist that he has made his indelible mark upon the age.

As already observed, he has not yet been overtaken by the infirmities of age, and his ancestors being remarkable for their long life, there is reason to hope that the day is far distant when his face shall be seen no more in the sanctuary of God. But should he fall to-morrow, his surviving friends may, without flattery or falsehood, inscribe upon his monument that most beautiful and desirable of all epitaphs:

"HE WAS A BURNING AND SHINING LIGHT."

R. T. BROWN.

RYLAND T. BROWN was born on the 5th of October, 1807, in Lewis county, Kentucky. His ancestors, on both his father's and his mother's side, were originally from Wales. His parents were exemplary members of the Baptist church, his father being noted as a leader in the singing exercises of the congregation. His mother still survives, and both the families from which he has descended, have been remarkable for their longevity.

In the Spring of 1809 his father removed to Ohio, and settled near New Richmond, in Clermont county. Shortly afterward a colony from Maine settled in the same neighborhood.

In the formation of that colony Yankee sagacity did not fail to discover that a schoolmaster would be a principal desideratum in the far West. Therefore, Mr. Mark P. Stenchfield, a teacher by profession, was induced to accompany the expedition; as a member of which he was regarded as not a whit less useful than the blacksmith, the shoemaker, or any other artisan. Simultaneously with the round-log domicile and workshop, the schoolhouse was erected in the same style of architecture; and as the smith's hammer was heard Winter and Summer, so Summer and Winter was heard the busy hum of Mr. Stenchfield's school. Thus Master Brown was furnished with a rare opportunity of acquiring knowledge from a truly competent instructor. He was equally fortunate in another respect. Being a weakly lad, of slender habit and feeble growth, his parents relieved him from labor on

LIBRARY
OF THE
UNIVERSITY OF ILLINOIS

the farm (which was popularly, though foolishly, regarded as fatal in such cases), and did all in their power to give him a good education, which they supposed the only means by which he would ever be able to make a living. For several years, therefore, he was sent regularly to the colonial school, in which he made rapid progress, and acquired a thorough knowledge of the common-school branches.

The teacher was a zealous Baptist, who did not neglect the moral and religious training of those under his charge. He made himself the companion of his scholars; entered into all their feelings and sympathies; and suffered no opportunity to escape by which he might impress his pupils with the paramount importance of a pious and devotional life. These lessons made a deep and lasting impression on the subject of this sketch; and together with the counsel and example of his pious parents, they gave direction to the whole current of his subsequent life.

Early in the year 1821 his father removed to Indiana, and settled in what is now the southeastern part of Rush county. But three years before, that section of country was ceded to the United States by the Delaware Indians; and it was only in a few places that the trees had been removed from what had been their hunting grounds. Here the delicate young student was transferred from the confinement and exhaustive toil of the schoolroom to the invigorating labors, hardships, and privations of a back-woods life.

For the first two or three years after removing to Indiana, he was employed much of his time as guide to land-hunters. In this employment he not only became an expert woodsman and a second Nimrod, or "mighty hunter," but here also he began to form the active habits, and to acquire the fondness for out-door pursuits, for which he has been distinguished through subsequent life. The change of occupation also contributed greatly to his physical development. The open air, the ramblings over hill and dale, and the excitement of the chase, strengthened every bone, invigorated every muscle, quickened the morbid action of every part of his system, and, in short, laid the physical foundation without which the intellectual superstructure could never have been reared.

In the Spring of 1822—being then in his fifteenth year—he made a profession of faith in Christ, was immersed, and united with a Baptist congregation known as "the Clifty church."

At that age he had no further opportunity of attending school; but, being passionately fond of reading, and constantly in search of intellectual food, he finally heard of the county library at Rushville. To his famishing mind this was a "feast of fat things" to which he resorted frequently, though distant ten miles, by a road very primitive and, at times, almost impassable. To his education, under these circumstances, the college or university was not essential: he did not need to be *taught;* all he asked was the means of *learning.*

In the Fall of 1825 he had the misfortune to lose his father by a very sudden and violent attack of congestive fever. It was this sad event that directed his mind to the study of diseases and remedies, and determined his profession for life.

In the year 1826 he chanced to meet with a copy of Campbell and Walker's Debate, from which he learned of the publication of the "Christian Baptist," to which he soon became a subscriber. From this date (1826) he is to be reckoned as a Reformer, though he remained, for a short time, a nominal Baptist.

His first overt act in the direction of reform was on this wise: the Flat Rock Association having arrogated to themselves a little of the authority given to the Messiah, drew up certain articles of faith, and recommended their adoption by all the churches of which the said ecclesiastical body was composed. The matter being laid before the "Clifty church," a motion was made "to rescind the old articles and adopt the new." "Brother Brown," then only nineteen years old, called for a division of the question, the first part of which passed by the aid of no vote more cheerfully given than his own. Having thus freed the church, for a moment, from the bondage of human authority, he immediately moved to adopt the New Testament as an exponent of the faith of that congregation. This being offered as an amendment, and promptly seconded, was fairly before the house; and to dispose of it without voting *directly* against the Bible cost them not a little trouble.

From 1826 to the Spring of 1829, his time and attention were devoted exclusively to the study of medicine. His knowledge of this subject, as well as others, was principally acquired without a master; and but few men that have attained to equal eminence in the profession have qualified themselves for it under greater difficulties. Out of the bones of an Indian that had been exhumed near his father's farm he constructed an imperfect skeleton, to aid him in the study of anatomy and physiology. To the "great swelling words," that he encountered when on that branch of the subject, he gave names without regard to unknown rules of orthoepy, and attached ideas without knowledge of their derivation. No wonder, therefore, if he is sometimes liable to criticism in the pronunciation of enormous derivatives.

During the latter part of the period above mentioned, he attended the "Ohio Medical College," at Cincinnati, at which institution he was graduated in the Spring of 1829.

Returning to his home in Rush county, he spent the remainder of that year in search of a location, and in recruiting his powers of mind and body, then almost exhausted by three years' incessant study.

On his return he found the community greatly excited on the subject of Christianity, which excitement had been occasioned mainly by the introduction of a new religious element. Elder John P. Thompson (whose history is given elsewhere in this volume) had begun to proclaim the ancient gospel with great zeal; and under his labors great numbers were being added to all the Baptist churches in that region. But few understood the cause which had given the preaching of Elder Thompson such extraordinary power; yet not even the most rigidly orthodox thought of asking questions or interposing objections during the excitement of a great revival. On the contrary, Revs. Wm. McPherson and Wm. Thompson, both Baptist preachers of some note, fully co-operated in the glorious work, and materially aided in carrying forward the Reformation. Dr. Brown, the eyes of whose understanding had been enlightened, intelligently gave his heart, hand, and voice to the furtherance of the new movement.

But as soon as the excitement began to subside, the Baptist churches became greatly alarmed; and the cry of "*Campbellism*" went up loud and long. The rulers in the Baptist Israel imagined that they saw tares among the wheat, and that it would be doing God service to "go and gather them up." Therefore the work of immolating heretics was commenced.

Dr. Brown, whose impertinent action on the creed question, three years before, had not been forgotten, was selected as *the first victim in the State* to be sacrificed on this altar of sectarian bigotry. He was arraigned on the very general charge of "being a Campbellite," and, as such, was excluded from the Church. The following account of the affair appeared in the "Christian Baptist" for June, 1830:

ARCADIA, RUSH CO., IA., March 15, 1830.

DEAR BROTHER,—A general conspiracy is forming among the "Orthodox Calvinistic Baptists" in Indiana, the object of which is to put a stop to the alarming spread of those principles contained in the "Christian Baptist," and advocated by all who earnestly pray for a "restoration of the ancient order of things;" which they, however, have seen proper to honor with the name of "damnable heresies." I have had the honor of being ranked among the first victims of this conspiracy. I have been immolated on the altar of party prejudice and sectarian jealousy. I have passed through the furnace of clerical indignation, "heated seven times hotter than it was wont to be heated." But the smell of fire has not passed on my garments. Clothed with the panoply of faith, with the volume of unerring *wisdom* in my hand, I would be ashamed to fear a host of sectarians, who have no stronger armor, either offensive or defensive, than their creed.

Nearly four years ago I had the presumption to oppose the doctrine of creeds, etc., in a public assembly, for which I received repeated rebukes by the dominant clergy, who, however, made no attempt to oppugn the arguments I advanced in favor of my position. The three years immediately succeeding this passed with my saying little or nothing on this or any other of the religious questions which, during that period, were agitated; my time being entirely engrossed by studies of a different nature.

After spending some time at Cincinnati, I returned to my former residence in Rush county, and, being more at leisure, I determined to give the Scriptures a careful, and, if possible, an impartial examination. I did so without favor or affection to any party. The effect was a thorough conviction of the truth of the following propositions, viz.:

1. Faith is nothing more nor less than a conviction of the truth of any position from evidence.

2. That faith in Jesus Christ is nothing more than a belief of the facts recorded of him by the Evangelists, to wit: That Jesus of Nazareth was the promised Messiah, and that he gave impregnable proof of his divine mission by his miraculous birth, by the numerous miracles which he wrought while living, and by his death, resurrection, and ascension.

3. The evangelical writings, containing the facts relative to the mighty works which were done by Christ and his apostles, together with the corroborating testimony of the prophecies, form altogether a phalanx of evidence sufficient to convince any reasonable mind that "Jesus is the Christ."

4. I became convinced that the popular doctrine of a partial atonement, and unconditional election and reprobation, were alike antichristian and unscriptural.

These opinions I at all times expressed freely, not a little to the annoyance of my Calvinistic friends. At length, after considerable threatening, the following resolution was adopted by the church on Clifty for my especial benefit:

"*Resolved*, That we will not fellowship the doctrines propagated by Alexander Campbell, of Bethany, Virginia."

I entered my protest against this resolution, as I conceived it was intended to condemn a man without giving him an opportunity of defense. But I soon learned I was to share the same fate. The heresies of Campbellism (as they pleased to call it) were charged home on me. I claimed the right of defense, but was informed it was a crime which did not admit of a defense. I next denied the charge of being the disciple or follower of any man, and required the proof of it. I was again told that no evidence was necessary. Thus, you see, I was charged without truth, tried without a hearing, and condemned without evidence; and thus, in due form, delivered over to Satan as an incorrigible heretic. Several more of this church are destined shortly to share my fate. Bishop John P. Thompson and about forty members of Little Flat Rock Church have been arrested for denying the traditions of the Fathers, and will no doubt be formally excommunicated.*

Notwithstanding these sorry attempts of the clergy to patch the worn out vail of ignorance, which has long covered the eyes of the people, light is dawning apace. Truth is omnipotent, and must prevail.

I shall make a defense of my principles before a candid public, the subject of which I would send you for publication in the "Harbinger," if it would not be too much of a repetition of what you have already said on those subjects in your essays published in the "Christian Baptist."

The above facts I consider as public property.

Yours, in the bonds of Christian love,

R. T. BROWN.

On the fourth Lord's day in May, 1830, the majority that saved Elder Thompson from expulsion organized "The Church of Christ at Little Flat Rock," which church continues to this day one of the largest and most influential in the State. Into it Dr. Brown entered with characteristic zeal; and in it he made the public defense, alluded to in his letter to A. Campbell. This defense had a great and good effect upon the community, and is to be

* By reference to the sketch of Elder Thompson, it will be seen that the attempt to excommunicate those persons was delayed too long—they in the mean time becoming the *majority*.

regarded as the commencement of his public advocacy of the ancient gospel.

Having in 1829 married Miss Mary Reeder, he, in the Summer of 1832, located at Connersville, Fayette county, there to establish himself in the practice of medicine. Here he had to compete with old and experienced physicians under many disadvantages, not the least of which was his religion. The Reformation of the nineteenth century was then and there known only in the caricatures of a prejudiced pulpit; and to be simply a disciple of the Lord Jesus, without being identified with any orthodox sect, was looked upon as evidence of great ignorance or impiety, and was therefore a great reproach. But Dr. Brown was not the man to deny the faith for the sake of popularity, or filthy lucre. Both publicly and privately he proclaimed "all the words of this life," without regard to his own reputation or pecuniary interests. By close attention to business, and a manly advocacy of the truth, he was soon well respected in both his professions. The people favored him with a liberal patronage; and, what was far more gratifying to him, they gladly received the word and were baptized, both men and women. Shut out of the orthodox churches, he made a sanctuary of the court-house, in which he soon held a protracted meeting, being assisted by John O'Kane, at that time located at Milton, Wayne county. A considerable number being added to the saved at this meeting, Elder O'Kane removed to Connersville; and in January, 1833, the Church of Christ at that place was organized.

From this time until the year 1842, he preached extensively through the White Water country; and his name is identified with the early history of many churches in that region.

By these labors, and his arduous duties as a physician, his health was so impaired as to render a temporary abandonment of one or the other of his professions an absolute necessity. He therefore discontinued his own work, and gave himself exclusively to the Lord's.

At the State Meeting held at Connersville, in June, 1842, he, in conjunction with three others, was appointed to labor, in word and doctrine, "for the churches in Indiana." In various portions of this extensive field he spent about a year, exposing tradition in its several forms, and scattering the incorruptible seed broadcast over the land.

By this service his health was not improved. Suffering frequently from hemorrhage of the lungs, his fellow physicians assured him that, if he persisted in preaching, it would be at the cost of his life. He therefore resigned the commission received from the State Meeting, and spent one year in manual labor of that peculiar kind which is required to run a saw-mill. Under this severe treatment all symptoms of consumption disappeared, although he continued to preach the word on almost every Lord's day.

In the Spring of 1844 he located at Crawfordsville, Montgomery county, and resumed the practice of medicine in connection with the preaching of the word.

For years past he had devoted his leisure hours to the improvement of his education—especially to the study of natural science; and his residence in Crawfordsville he made equivalent to a regular course in college. The "Wabash College" being located at that place, he was kindly admitted to a free use of its extensive library and philosophical apparatus. This golden opportunity he improved so well that, in 1850, he received from that institution the honorary degree of A. M.; this being one of the few instances in which it was justly merited.

In 1854 he acted as State Geologist, by the appointment of Governor Wright, who was of a different school of politics, and therefore not influenced, in the selection, by partisan considerations. In this capacity he traversed almost every nook and corner of the State, finding

> "books in the running brooks,
> Sermons in *stones*, and good in every thing."

In 1858 he was elected to the chair of Natural Science in the N. W. C. University, at Indianapolis; to which place he removed in August of that year. There he still resides—distinguished as an instructor, and indefatigable as a preacher. In all his labors, whether as physician, geologist, or professor, he has almost invariably devoted the first day of the week to the ministry of the word. Having thus performed double duty, he ought to be counted worthy of double honor.

He was also among the first, and has ever been among the most zealous, advocates of the Temperance Reform, both in Indiana and in other States of the Union. In company with General S. F. Carey he has travelled extensively as a public lecturer on that subject; and he now stands at the head of the temperance organization in his own State. He preaches the whole of the apostle's doctrine—"righteousness, *temperance*, and judgment to come."

Though he has never been a candidate for office, yet he has always taken an active part in politics. True to his convictions of right and duty, he acted with the Free Soil party fourteen years ago, when it seemed to be a hopeless minority. He was stigmatized as an Abolitionist even before that term assumed an application so general as to include almost every good and loyal citizen. Justly and legitimately the term cannot be applied to him; for although he is firmly opposed to slavery and to the extension thereof, yet he denies, and has always denied, the right of the General Government to abolish it in the States.

For many years past Dr. Brown has exerted no inconsiderable influence through the medium of the press. Many articles from his pen have appeared in the Indiana School Journal, Ohio Farmer, Christian Record, Christian Luminary, and other periodicals—religious, educational, agricultural, medical, and political. In all these departments he is fully up with the times if not a little in advance of them; hence it is not by any means in religion alone that he is to be recognized as a Reformer.

The personal appearance of Dr. Brown is rather homely, yet such as to fasten upon a stranger the conviction that he is in the presence of no ordinary man. He is of medium stature, fitly joined together, and weighs about one hundred and forty-five pounds. His eyes are pale blue or gray, his complexion fair and slightly flushed. His hair, now white as almond blossoms, was once light or sandy—in early youth almost red. His temperament is nervous-sanguine, the latter element predominating. There is, therefore, nothing sluggish about his movements, either physical or intellectual; and for him to be lazy is impossible.

His mind is of the highest order—clear, logical, comprehensive, and of an eminently practical cast. He is *naturally a naturalist*, possessing superior perceptive faculties, combined with extraordinary powers of analysis and classification. It is not extravagant to say that had he been properly educated and introduced to Nature in early life, he might have rivaled Agassiz or Humboldt in the number and value of his scientific achievements.

His scholarship partakes largely of the qualities of his mind. He is well acquainted with history, especially that of the church, and of humanity in its moral and religious phases. With such branches of mathematics as are of practical utility he is sufficiently familiar; but of the abstract theories of calculus he knows as little as he cares. Of the literature of his own language he has a respectable knowledge; but in Greek and Latin he has but little faith and but few attainments. He is well informed with regard to politics, the science of government, and every thing pertaining to the *rights* of man, whether civil or religious. In short he is *practical* rather than *classical;* and comprehensive at the expense of accuracy in little things. He knows more of the present than of the past, and is more familiar with nature than with books. It is in the department of Natural Science that he seems almost omniscient. There nothing is so minute as to have escaped his attention; nothing fathomable, that he has not sounded to the bottom.

He is emphatically an off-hand man. He writes no sermons and but few addresses of any kind. His college lectures, both before his classes and on Lord's days, are all extemporaneous. When he does write, however, his articles are characterized by clearness, force, and originality.

As a speaker he ranks above mediocrity. He has a pleasant voice of very great compass, which he employs with proper emphasis and unaffected earnestness. His language is fully adequate to the prompt expression of his ideas; and if he repeats, several times, a clause of a sentence, it is not because he is unable to complete the proposition, but because he is indulging a wayside thought with reference to some other matter. If some such obtrusive thought entices him a little way from his line of argument, he comes back to the point with an emphatic "but," which is a fair warning that the main subject is about to be resumed. He indulges no flights of fancy, but deals with plain facts. He dilutes no sentiment in a flood of words, studies no attitudes for the sake of appearing graceful; but he expresses himself as forcibly as possible, and if a gesture is added it is designed to impress rather than to please. He abounds less in pathos than in imagination; has no gift of exhortation; hence has never been very successful in proselyting. His *forte* is to instruct the church and to convince the judgments of "them that are without." Those whom he *does* disciple have such "deepness of earth" that but few if any "wither away."

In society and at home he is "a plain, blunt man," possessing more of the *fortiter in re* than of the *suaviter in modo*. True, he is kind, hospitable, and sufficiently affable; but on meeting a friend, he makes no courtly bows, feigns no unspeakable joy, puts on no hypocritical smiles. Though not remarkably awkward in the drawing-room, yet he is not a "star" in circles that abound in small talk; and sooner than spend his days in such a place, he would choose life in a prison where, undisturbed, he might stroke his long beard as he always does when absorbed in meditation.

He possesses an indomitable will; and is noted for great decision of character. He is of that class of men who suffer—not only reproach, but martyrdom, if need be, for their religion or cherished principles. Had he been the editor of the Knoxville Whig the world would perhaps have heard as much of Parson *Brown*, as it has heard of Parson *Brownlow*—they are at least as much alike in one respect as their names.

He is a man of remarkably active habits. Early in the Spring he *spades* up his large garden, because it could not well be ploughed to suit him; and, while thus engaged, he might easily be mistaken, at first glance, for a genuine son of the Emerald Isle. As the growing season advances, he is to be found out in his grounds, planting, weeding, pruning, training, or otherwise laboring. Though neither poor nor penurious, he saws his own wood; and, while thus employed, he arranges in his mind the materials for his next sermon or lecture. If he preaches on Sunday at a distance of ten miles from the city, and if there is no early train on Monday morning, he regards it as a light matter to perform the journey on foot in time to hear his classes in the University. "In time," be it observed, for with him punctuality is a cardinal virtue. When he takes his class into the field to give them a little *practical*, as well as theoretical geology (a thing seldom done by tender-footed Professors), he astonishes them as much by his indefatigableness as by his familiarity with the names, qualities, and positions of the rocks. He is usually the last to cry "halt."

The burden of years is light upon him; and his present condition and appearance, Cowper has well described in the following lines:—

> "A sparkling eye beneath a wrinkled front
> The vet'ran shows, and, gracing a gray beard
> With youthful smiles, descends towards the grave
> Sprightly, and old almost without decay."

GEORGE CAMPBELL.

ELDER GEORGE CAMPBELL was born at Brewer, Maine, on the 8th of February, 1807. He is a descendant of a somewhat distinguished family in the Highlands of Scotland. His grandfather, when quite young, emigrated to the county of Antrim, near Argyleshire, in the north of Ireland, where he married into a Protestant family by the name of Dunning. In commemoration of this part of the Emerald Isle, Elder Campbell received from his parents the name, *George Argyle*, which he has chosen to abbreviate to *George*. Soon after his marriage, and a few years prior to our Revolution, the grandfather emigrated to the New World and settled at Brunswick, in what was then the province of Maine. About the year 1774, he removed to Bangor, then a small village, on the Penobscot, at the head of tide-water. Here he took command of a company of patriot forces, which protected the friendly Penobscots and guarded the northeastern frontier against the depredations of the hostile Mohawks. In this position he served his country gallantly, and became widely and favorably known as Captain Campbell. Elder Campbell, in his boyhood, often sported with the famous claymore which his grandfather wielded against the Mohawks in the struggle for Independence, little dreaming that he was destined to wield, in his manhood, the mightier "sword of the Spirit," which only can make us "free indeed."

His father, Thomas Campbell, was born at Brunswick,

Maine, and brought up in the Presbyterian faith, which was hereditary with the Campbells, as it is with many good people even now. His mother, whose maiden name was Sabara Knapp, from whom he received his first religious impressions, was a Congregationalist, and a member of a Massachusetts family *originally from Germany*. Thus it happens that the blood of three different races courses his veins, blending in him the wit and eloquence of the Irishman, the vigorous intellect and untiring industry of the German, and the dauntless courage and elastic spirit of the Highlander. No wonder, therefore, that he is considered a *rara avis*—a remarkable character.

He was the sixth of a family of nine children, four of whom still survive. As his star arose in the East, he enjoyed better educational advantages than most of his co-laborers, who were struggling up to manhood in the wilderness of the West. When only five years old he entered the New England free-schools, which he attended regularly for six years. The next five years were devoted to hard labor on his father's farm, where he acquired the splendid physical development which has contributed so much to his intellectual vigor. At the age of sixteen he entered Foxcroft Academy, which was fortunately situated near his father's residence. Afterwards he attended the Maine Wesleyan Seminary, then under the able supervision of W. C. Larrabee, late Superintendent of Public Instruction in Indiana. At a still later period, he became a student of Waterville College, where he completed the regular course to the close of the junior year. His tutor, at this Institution, was Parish Lovejoy, who, a few years ago, died at Alton, Illinois, a martyr to the cause of liberty and free speech. Thus it is seen that Elder Campbell, although not a graduate, has undergone rigid mental discipline, and is therefore to be reckoned among the educated men of the Reformation.

From his twenty-third to his twenty-fifth year he was a clerk in his brother's store at Argyle, Maine. While thus employed he wrote and circulated the petition to the Legislature for the incorporation of the town of Argyle, so named in memory of the land of his forefathers.

In the year 1830 he entered upon the work of the ministry among the Liberal Christians of New England. These societies were congregational, composed of Universalists, Unitarians, and Free-thinkers. For a short time he was a member of the Maine Convention of Universalists, or more properly *Restorationists*, since they advocated the doctrine of a judgment "after death," but believed that all punishment would prove reformatory, and that, as a positive infliction, it would finally cease. During the year 1831 he preached for Unitarian Congregational Societies at Atkinson and Orono, Maine.

In 1832 he renounced all fellowship with the whole fraternity of Universalists, went to Boston, and united with the Bulfinch Street Congregational church, then under the pastoral care of the Rev. Paul Dean, who held to the strict and proper divinity of Christ. During the year 1832, and part of 1833, he studied theology under Dr. Dean, and received from the Association in Boston his license to preach. With this commendation he came to Ohio in the Summer of 1833, arriving in Cincinnati just at the breaking out of the cholera in that city. On the first Lord's day after his arrival he preached in the Unitarian church on Fourth street, and on the next day was seized with the cholera. The attack was severe, but God did not permit the silver cord to be loosed. He designed to open the blind eyes that they might yet behold wondrous things in His law.

Having recovered from this illness, he visited his uncle, D. Campbell, in Fayette county, Indiana. Here he continued preaching theology for the space of three years;

here, too, an event transpired which led to a complete revolution in his theological views. In the providence of God he had now arrived near Damascus, where *the light from Heaven* was to shine round about him; he had come to Ephesus, where "the way of God" was to be expounded to him "more perfectly." As this event was the *pivot* in his religious life, it deserves to be recorded in detail.

At this time the Church of Christ at Connersville, Fayette county, was under the oversight of Elder Jesse Holton and Dr. R. T. Brown, now Professor of Natural Science in the Northwestern Christian University, and then, as now, an efficient laborer in word and doctrine. On the arrival of the brilliant New England preacher in that community, there was no small stir among his brethren, who were almost disposed to say of his preaching, "It is the voice of a god, and not of a man"—so satisfactorily, to them, could he establish their cherished theories. They insisted that the Christians should give him a hearing, and he, in turn, was invited to come out and hear the Christians.

Not long after, when the Church of Christ at that place had assembled, "on the first day of the week to break bread," Elder Campbell entered, and seated himself near Dr. Brown. Being invited to preach, he declined. The invitation was renewed; and, thinking there must be some misunderstanding, he frankly confessed that he was not of that "way." "No matter," said the doctor; "for this very reason, we desire to hear thee—what thou sayest." Consenting to preach, he took for his text, Acts xvi. 31: "Believe in the Lord Jesus Christ, and thou shalt be saved;" from which he delivered an excellent discourse relative to the power of faith to purify the heart, reform the life, and save the soul. At the close of the sermon, Dr. Brown followed with some remarks.

He heartily endorsed all that had been said of faith; "but," said he, "there are two chapters in man's life: the past, and the future. Faith, by purifying the heart now, may regulate the future; but it cannot reform the *past*, or blot out the transgressions that are *already recorded* in the book of God's remembrance." He then proceeded to show that, in the divine economy, Baptism, *with its proper antecedents*, is designed to free us from our "old sins," while Faith, by purifying the heart, is to prevent the occurrence of new offenses, and thus present every man perfect in the sight of God. At the conclusion of these remarks Elder Campbell had described with his chair a quadrant of a circle, and was sitting directly in front of the speaker, regarding him with a look very similar, no doubt, to that of the ancient scribe when he said to the Saviour, *Well, Master, thou hast said the truth.* Like the Scribe, too, he was then "not far from the kingdom of God."

While preparations were being made to break bread, he inquired if he would be permitted to partake with them, and received the prompt answer, "*Let every man examine himself;*" which, he says, made such an impression on his mind that, to this day, he has never ceased to "examine himself."

When the congregation retired he had a long interview with Dr. Brown. The questions they discussed engendered no strife. The one, like Aquila, confined himself to the "way of God;" the other, like Apollos, received with meekness the engrafted word; and between them that day was cemented a friendship which has never been dissolved.

Returning to his uncle's, he entered upon a thorough investigation of the doctrine of the New Testament. This he did, not to find support for any dogma, or former religious hypothesis; but devoutly to ascertain, in the light of the divine oracles, what is the religion of the Lord Jesus Christ. This investigation, which was diligently prosecuted for several months, resulted in his union with the Church of Christ at Connersville, in the year 1835. The inductive ordinance he received at the hands of Elder John Longley, now the oldest Christian preacher in Indiana.

Recommissioned by the church at Connersville, he left Fayette county in August, 1836, and soon after became the pastor of the church at Harrison, near Cincinnati. Here he remained three years; and mainly by his labors more than four hundred converts were, in that time, added to the church.

In September, 1839, he returned to Maine to see once more his aged parents and kinsmen in the flesh. Among the friends and relations who joyfully received the word, he had the pleasure of immersing into Christ his venerable mother, with whom, in former days, he had always coincided in religious views. She was a woman of exemplary piety, who, for years, had endeavored to do the will of God so far as she had been able to ascertain it. It was hers to realize the promise: "To the upright there ariseth light in the darkness." To her he was indebted for the moral and religious direction given to his young life; and her letters to him are fine models of a mother's counsel to her son.

In June, 1840, he set out on his return; passed through the Federal capital and other Eastern cities; visited the sacred spot where reposes the dust of Washington — then undisturbed by the shock of fratricidal war; and paused awhile at Charlottesville to see Monticello and the University of Virginia. The State Meeting of the Disciples happening to be in session, he made the acquaintance of many of the chief brethren of that State and Maryland; among whom were Elders Henshall,

Goss, Coleman, and the venerable Father Ferguson. Here, too, he met his distant Scotch relative, Alexander Campbell, then in the prime and vigor of life, whose preaching on that occasion he represents as superlatively eloquent, evangelical, and edifying.

From Charlottesville he returned to Harrison, and continued to labor there and in the adjacent counties in Ohio and Kentucky, until the Spring of 1842. In April, 1841, he was married to Miss Sarah Ann Wile, a worthy sister in the Harrison church. She has been a faithful and self-sacrificing helpmate in all his toils and trials in the gospel and in the cause of education. She is now the mother of six children, five sons and a daughter, who constitute almost the whole of their earthly treasures.

In 1842 he removed with his family to a small farm near Oxford, Ohio; and became the pastor of the church at that place. Here he continued to preach, with great success, for the next three years, making occasional tours through Indiana, Kentucky, and other portions of Ohio.

In the Spring of 1845, the Rush County Evangelizing Association, in Indiana, of which the Hon. J. Helm was then President, and Hon. John L. Robinson, Secretary, called him to the work of an evangelist, and to aid in founding and building up an institution of learning in that county. Responding to this call he removed to Fairview, and in March, 1845, entered the field in Rush county, The great battle between orthodoxy and that which they *called* heresy was then going on in that county, in which conflict he engaged with all boldness and bent his bow valiantly for the truth.

In the Fall of that year he resigned his position as evangelist of the Association and took charge of the Farmington Academy, which maintained a good reputation during his administration. It was subsequently transferred to Fairview, where it continues to flourish,

Elder Campbell being the President of the Board of Directors.

At the State Meeting of the Brotherhood of Indiana, held at Greensburg, Decatur county, in 1847, he introduced a resolution in favor of building up in the State an Institution of learning of the highest grade. This, so far as is known to the writer, was the first movement toward the founding of the Northwestern Christian University, an institution already second to none in the State, and which, if completed on the scale of the projectors, will be second to but few on the continent. The discussion of the said resolution led to the appointment of the University Committee, which was composed of James M. Mathes, Elijah Goodwin, L. H. Jameson, Ovid Butler, and John O'Kane; all of whom were from that time active co-workers in behalf of the enterprise. At the next Annual Meeting they reported in favor of establishing the University, which was subsequently located at Indianapolis, according to a vote of the churches throughout the State. The following year, the State Meeting appointed as their agent, Elder John O'Kane, who obtained the subscription requisite for the organization of the Institution. Elder Campbell was one of the original commissioners appointed by the Legislature, and at the organization he was chosen one of the members of the Board of Directors, which position he still occupies, having been twice re-elected.

In April, 1848, he removed to Cincinnati and became pastor of the Church of Christ in Fulton, dividing his time between that church and his old charge at Harrison. This year he assisted Elder Walter Scott in the removal of the "Protestant Unionist" from Pittsburg to Cincinnati; and ably conducted the paper in the absence of the editor. He also rendered important service to Dr. Horatio P. Gatchel in bringing out the republication of "*McLane on the Com-*

mission," a work that has greatly contributed to the progress of the Reformation.

Near the close of 1848, he, with others, purchased the "Protestant Unionist," which, on the 1st of January, 1849, was superceded by the "Christian Age," of which Dr. Gatchel and T. J. Melish were editors. In a short time Dr. Gatchel sold his interest in the paper, and the name of George Campbell appeared as one of its editors. During the absence of Elder Melish, and during the prevalence of the cholera in the Summer and Autumn of 1849, Elder Campbell had the sole charge and management of the paper. Aided by Elder James Challen, he conducted, in its columns, a discussion relative to the propriety of calling a convention for the purpose of organizing a general Missionary Society. He and Elder Challen successfully plead the affirmative of the proposition until the convention was called and the American Christian Missionary Society was formed. Probably this enterprise was first suggested by Elder Challen; but once suggested it found an earnest, able, and persevering advocate in the person of Elder Campbell. Of the Executive Board of this Society he has always been an efficient member, and much of the time one of its general traveling agents.

In the fall of 1849 Elder Melish transferred his share of the "Christian Age" to Elder D. S. Burnett, who then became the principal editor. Elder Campbell then bade adieu to the sanctum and the city; returned to Rush county, and entered again upon the work of an evangelist. He also assisted Prof. A. R. Benton (now President of the N. W. C. University) in the Fairview Academy; and regularly contributed to the "Christian Age," of which he continued joint proprietor and associate editor.

In 1851 he sold his share of the paper to Elder Benjamin Franklin, but still contributed to its columns, until, after so many changes, it finally fell entirely into the hands of Elder Franklin. Not long after this it died, but by a happy transmigration of soul it soon re-appeared in the present well-known weekly, "The American Christian Review." Of this paper Elder Campbell has been an occasional correspondent. Indeed, he has contributed more to our periodical literature than is generally known. Aside from his editorials, he has furnished occasional articles for the Millennial Harbinger, Western Reformer, Ohio Preacher, Christian Family Library, Western Evangelist, Christian Record, and Christian Luminary. He writes forcibly in very plain style. As when one sees him, it is the *man*, and not the *dress*, that attracts the eye; so when one reads him, it is the *idea*, and not the *language*, that fixes the attention. He employs no grievous words that stir up strife; but his articles are deeply imbued with that charity that "thinketh no evil." His pen addresses itself *ad rem*, and not *ad hominem*.

Being employed by the State Meeting as a home missionary in Northern Indiana, he spent the Winter of 1853 in that field, which embraced the counties of Porter, La Porte, and St. Joseph. Here, in co-operation with brethren R. Wilson and D. Miller, he reconstructed the prostrate church at Mishawaka. This had been a powerful church, but political commotions and various other wranglings had destroyed its influence and laid it in ruins. Its successful reconstruction gave a new impulse to the cause of primitive Christianity in Northern Indiana, which is now a great field "ripe for the harvest."

He finally removed to the northwestern part of the State, and fixed his residence at Oxford, the county seat of Benton county. Soon after this removal, assisted by Elders John Longley, H. R. Pritchard, and J. C. Johnson, under a great oak tree on his own premises, he organized the Church of Christ at Oxford. This was the first church planted at that place; and it was the first house of worship erected in Benton county. It has continued to increase by the edifying of itself in love, until it now numbers nearly eighty members, and is in a prosperous condition.

These missionary labors were to him "the heat and burden of the day." Under their pressure his constitution so far gave way that, from 1854 to 1859, he was never in perfect health even for a single day. Still he remained at his post; often preaching during the paroxysm of either chill or fever; organizing churches in Benton, Warren, Tippecanoe, La Porte, and Montgomery counties; and introducing the ancient gospel into various places in Illinois, Ohio, and Kentucky.

In December, 1858, he removed to Burnettsville, in White county, for the sake of the educational advantages afforded to his children by the Indiana Normal Institute located at that place. Here he was made the general agent of the Institute; and, besides extensive evangelizing operations, he raised by subscription over three thousand dollars for the erection of a new building. This excellent high school is now in successful operation in the new edifice, which is another beautiful monument erected by Elder Campbell in the cause of education.

During his two years' residence at Burnettsville he added sixty-nine to the assembly of the saints; and through the instrumentality of that church several promising students of the Institute have been sent forth into the harvest. These two years, however, he mainly spent abroad; the first as evangelist, the second as agent of the American Christian Missionary Society. In both these departments his labors produced abundantly the peaceable fruits of righteousness.

In December, 1860, he moved back to his old home at Fairview, Rush county, whence he causes the light of truth to radiate. There he happily resides, surrounded by confiding, warm-hearted brethren, very many of whom are his own sons in the gospel. There we leave him, and close the record of his deeds.

The exact number that have been redeemed through his instrumentality cannot be given. Of these he has kept no record, trusting that their names will all be found written in the Lamb's book of life. But, wherever he has preached the word, the disciples have been multiplied greatly; and in the counties of Rush and Fayette, where, with Elders Reeve and Thompson, he has labored so long, multitudes have obeyed the ancient gospel, and its claims are so generally acknowledged that an angel from heaven would perhaps meet with very little success were he to declare in those counties "any other gospel."

He has unbounded confidence in the ultimate triumph of the cause for which he has plead, and to which he has devoted the affections of his heart, the energies of his life, and the most of his earthly substance.

In the providence of God his health has been completely restored, so that he rejoices not only in view of the triumph of Truth, but also in the prospect of long life. He yet possesses a vigorous mind, a stout heart, and a firm purpose to devote his earthly future as he has his past, assured that for all his sacrifices in the life that now is, God will restore him a hundred fold in the life that is to come.

Elder Campbell is about five feet seven inches in height, and not quite so much in *circumference.* He is *heavy* set, weighing about two hundred pounds; and although his heart may sometimes falter, his *flesh* never fails him. His head is very large, and in such close proximity to his shoulders that an observer once said of him, "*That man has no neck.*" It is overgrown with a heavy crop of short, coarse, bristly hair, which, as often as he beholds his natural face in a glass, affords him an example of *uprightness.* He walks like every other fat man, and sits down, when duty permits, with evident satisfaction. The portrayal of his features must be left to the engraver.

His dress is eminently in keeping with his person—rough and serviceable. In its selection he consults comfort, not fashion. His cravat is never of ministerial white, and it very often fronts to one side. He leans upon no *staff* save that which supported David; and displays no *golden chain* but love. In a word, he takes no thought for the outward adorning "of wearing of gold and putting on of apparel."

His *habits*—those immaterial garments that envelop the inner man, the soul, and form the *character* as material garments do the dress—are equally becoming. There is no studied concealment of defects—no egotistical display of virtues. His character, like his body, stands before you in bold, distinct outline. Its principal traits are thus given in an article from the pen of Elder James Challen, than whom, perhaps, no one knows them better:

"He is possessed of a sound judgment, a vigorous understanding, a quick perception, considerable compass of thought, and a power of keeping his mind in abeyance until he has fairly reached his conclusions; and, when reached, he holds on to them with singular tenacity. He is not satisfied with looking at a subject simply in one direction, but seeks to examine it in all its bearings and relations.

"He is a lover of the truth, and is never weary in its pursuit. His thirst for knowledge is at times a passion—an appetite—and his application unwearied and constant. * * * * * He is possessed of great simplicity of character: kind, confiding, and full of warm and strong attachments, which make him a most agreeable companion. He is utterly devoid of all envy and jealousy, and free from every ungenerous suspicion. A constant and devoted friend, a cheerful, pleasant, and profitable companion. * * * * *

"His skill lies chiefly as an evangelist over large fields. He easily adapts himself to every situation in life and class of society; chiefly to the more humble and hard-working. With these he is a special favorite, and is held in high estimation for his plainness and simplicity."

He is a friend in deed to the missionary cause. Operating much of his time in large fields, he realizes that the harvest is great; he therefore prays the Lord to send forth laborers into his harvest, and exerts himself to obtain means for their support. Believing of a truth that faith comes by hearing the word of God, and that salvation is through faith, he does all in his power to send that word to those who sit in darkness and the shadow of death.

The cause of education also finds in him a zealous advocate and a liberal contributor. While others have endeavored to accumulate silver and gold, and houses and lands for their *children*, he has beneficently applied the most of his goods, that, by so doing, he might lay up for *himself* a good foundation against the time to come. "Let the light enter," is his motto; and his heart's desire is to see the sons of our country grow up as fruitful plants, and her daughters be polished after the similitude of a palace.

As a preacher he is plain, pointed, didactic. His sermons are not pleasure parks with their flowery walks, refreshing shades, and fountains spanned by rainbows; but rugged mountains rather, full of useful materials, based on the Rock of ages, their sun-lit tops pointing to Heaven. His subject is often a most familiar passage, and the instruction drawn from it is generally of a practical character. If he employs a figure, it is more for strength than for beauty. If he makes a quotation, it is oftener from the apostles than from the poets—an assertion which is not true of all preachers. There is no effort to gratify itching ears, but an earnest purpose to reach the candid heart; no bombastic flights of fancy, no superfluity of feigned pathos; but in their stead there is depth, solidity, originality, genuine earnestness, and, above all, the *truth* as it is in Jesus. One is not apt, therefore, to become a weary listener; more probably his heart will burn within him while the Scriptures, in their ancient simplicity, are being opened to his understanding.

He has a strong, deep voice, and his loud, rapid, and sometimes vociferous utterance has won for him the sobriquet, *Boanerges*. When excited he gesticulates violently in every direction, and according to no prescribed rules. He apparently loses all knowledge of himself in his subject, and feeling the importance of his theme himself, he easily makes others feel it. He closes every discourse with a powerful exhortation, in which his voice sometimes rises to the highest pitch, and his vehemence kindles into the most impassioned eloquence.

He is not generally regarded as a formidable controversialist; yet in his hands the weapons that are not carnal are mighty to the pulling down of strongholds, and every thing that exalts itself against the knowledge of God. He has never hesitated to assault error, and his attacks have been more successful than those of many who are flattered as champions of truth. But while others have used harsh epithets in public discussions with those whose prejudices were so excited that they were unable to discover the right, he has in meekness instructed those that oppose themselves; and, by a quiet victory, brought them to the acknowledgment of the truth.

There is another trait in his character as an evangelist that deserves to be presented, that it may be imitated. He is a *peace-maker*. Perhaps no man in the Reformation has been more successful in reconciling brethren at variance, and in reconstructing churches destroyed by schism. He is a most zealous advocate of union among all the followers of Jesus, and an ardent opposer of whatever tends to sow discord among brethren. Though he resembles Peter in his elocution, and Paul in his reasoning, he is most like the beloved John, the burden of whose doctrine was, *Little children, see that you love one another.* May the children of the kingdom among whom he has gone preaching, hearken to his wholesome admonitions—may they "do all things without murmurings and disputings, that *they* may be blameless and harmless, the sons of God without rebuke in the midst of a crooked and perverse nation; and that *he* may rejoice in the day of Christ that he has not run in vain, neither labored in vain.

JOHN O'KANE.

THIS distinguished pioneer was born in Culpepper county, Virginia, in 1802. His ancestors were originally from Ireland, and many traits of the Irish character are yet traceable in his own. His parents seem to have been quite poor, and to have had no claim whatever to a place among "the first families" of his native State. Therefore his distinction is due to his own genius, and not to any extraordinary privileges obtained either by purchase or by inheritance.

In his youth he was sent for a short time to an academy, where he received a tolerable English education. In after life, while contending earnestly for the faith, against a host of opposers, he acquired, by his own efforts, a respectable knowledge of the Greek language. This, with the general information acquired by reading, is the extent of his education. It is not, therefore, on account of what he *knows*, but on account of what he *is* and what he *does*, that he is remarkable.

He embraced Christianity at an early age, and at first united with the Old Christian body, or Newlights, in Virginia. Among them he commenced preaching when quite young; but of his ministry east of the Alleghanies little is known.

Sometime between 1825 and 1830 he left Virginia, and made his way—on foot it is said—to Lebanon, Warren county, Ohio. There he prosecuted for some time the work of the ministry; and there, in the year 1830, he was married to Miss Martha Verbryke.

It appears that his conversion to the ancient gospel was effected in the following manner: when zealously opposing what he supposed to be heresy, he saw, in the "Christian Messenger," some articles on "The Plan of Salvation," written by Elder James E. Mathes of Alabama, and ably advocating the claims of the Reformation. There being no opposition to these articles from any other quarter, he determined to reply to them himself. Accordingly he wrote his "No. 1," which was published in the Messenger, accompanied by some editorial remarks, in which he found, to his surprise, that Elder Stone had taken sides against him, and in defense of the views of Elder Mathes. These editorial comments on his "No. 1" were so pointed and convincing that his "No. 2," though written, was never published; and in a short time both he and Elder Stone were preaching the faith which both had once sought to destroy.

In the Spring of 1832 he came to Indiana, locating at Milton, in Wayne county. For the support of his family he engaged in teaching a common-school; but for the good of his race he continued to preach the gospel on Lord's days, and at such other times as he had opportunity. Being charged with "Campbellism," the few meeting-houses were closed against him; but John O'Kane was not the man either to conceal his own light under a bushel, or to suffer it to be extinguished by the proscriptive efforts of those who "loved darkness rather than light, because their deeds were evil." Such pressure only made him the more luminous, and in a little while he became a burning and shining light—almost the only one at that time in Eastern Indiana. Commencing in his own little schoolhouse, he rapidly extended his appointments to others; and when no house could be obtained, he preached to multitudes of people in the open air.

Within the same year, 1832, he crossed over into Rush county, where he was employed for one year to co-operate with Elder John P. Thompson in doing the work of an evangelist. In this service he traversed the counties of Rush, Fayette, and Decatur; and his name is identified with many churches and reformatory movements which originated at that time in that portion of the State.

In January, 1833, he journeyed as far west as Indianapolis. On his arrival there he found the court-house occupied by the Legislature then in session; the "evangelical" churches closed their doors against him; and there was no place for holding a meeting, save in an old log-house on Market street, which the few persecuted saints had rented as a place of prayer. In this he began and preached on three evenings in succession, the house not accommodating one half the people who were anxious to hear the word. In the meantime the Legislature tendered him the use of the court-house on Saturday evening and on Lord's day. There he had an opportunity of speaking before judges and legislators, as well as many of the "common people;" and faithfully did he witness to both small and great, speaking none other things than those which the Lord and his apostles appointed for them to do. "The preaching," says one who heard it, "was so different from any that had ever been heard in Indianapolis before—so bold, so pointed, so convincing, so strongly enforced by the commanding voice, expressive eye, and fine oratory of brother O'Kane—that it seemed to carry every thing before it. All seemed spell-bound, and many were seen to tremble under his mighty appeals." This was a kind of Pentecostal occasion; for not only was a deep and lasting impression made in the city—or rather town—but the representatives and strangers from the several counties, like the "devout men out of every nation" at Jerusalem, carried with them, on their return to their homes, some knowledge of the faith as it was once delivered to the saints.

Elder O'Kane made two or three other visits to the capital prior to the following June, at which time the Church of Christ at that place was organized with some twenty members.

In January, 1833, he and Dr. R. T. Brown organized the Church of Christ at Connersville, Fayette county, to which place he soon after removed, and commenced the publication of a monthly religious paper called "The Christian Casket." While engaged in this enterprise he continued to preach the gospel throughout all Central and Eastern Indiana, occasionally making tours through portions of Ohio and Kentucky.

In 1837 he removed to Crawfordsville, Montgomery county, where he resided for several years, having the pastoral care of the church in that place, and preaching extensively in the western and southwestern portions of the State.

In 1848 he returned to Connersville, and for a twelve-month labored efficiently in fields with which he had made himself familiar in former years.

In 1849 he located at Indianapolis and engaged in the book and stationery business; still proclaiming the gospel, however, both in that city and in many distant parts of the State. Everywhere his labors were attended with the most encouraging results, and to all the disciples of Indiana his name was as familiar as household words.

About this time was conceived the project of establishing the Northwestern Christian University, to meet the educational wants of a great and rapidly increasing brotherhood. Into this enterprise Elder O'Kane entered heart and soul, and to him more than to any other individual its success is to be attributed; for he, more than any other, raised the money with which the magnificent building was erected, and with which the corps of instructors are sustained. In the Spring of 1851 he was appointed by the Board of Directors as a general agent and stock solicitor; in which capacity he visited almost every nook and corner of the State, gathering, for the institution, a rich pecuniary harvest, and at the same time disseminating the good seed of the kingdom to meet the demands of other great and good enterprises in future times.

In 1859 he removed to Independence, Missouri, where he has since resided, and where he is now separated from his friends and brethren in Indiana by a wall of fire. Consequently they have but little knowledge of his ministerial operations in the Southwest; yet they occasionally hear of his affairs—that he is a true patriot, and that he remains "steadfast, immovable," in the work of the Lord.

It is to be regretted that, owing to the unhappy condition of the country, more ample materials for this sketch cannot be obtained. Unquestionably the subject of it was one of the most noted reformers of Indiana; and his history, if given in full, would be replete with good works, remarkable incidents, and anecdotes of the choicest kind. As for himself, he needs no historian to perpetuate his memory. He has made his mark upon the age; his name is familiar to many a devout father, who will transmit it, in connection with fact and anecdote, to his children; and thus he will be held in remembrance even to the third and fourth generations, though not a stone should be raised or a line written.

Elder O'Kane is physically, as well as mentally and morally, a fine specimen of the *genus homo*. He is six feet and one inch high, very straight and slender. His fine head, covered with raven locks, sits with an air of majesty on his square shoulders; and beneath his high, over-arching forehead, sparkle eyes remarkably black and piercing. He walks with an easy, don't-care gait, seemingly criticising, and inwardly laughing at every thing around him. He is certainly more like Democritus than Heraclitus—a laughing rather than a weeping philosopher.

If his personal appearance is singular and upon the whole prepossessing, his character is eccentric and, take it all in all, worthy of imitation. A Phillips would find in it almost as many antitheses and yet as much consistency as he found in the character of Napoleon.

Perhaps the most striking trait is his wit, and the anecdotes of John O'Kane, alone, would fill a volume. His witticisms are usually mixed with the severest sarcasm, or pointed with the bitterest irony. The following are a few inferior specimens:

With a swaggering air an orthodox preacher once refused to debate with him, at the same time observing that he would gladly discuss the doctrinal issues with Alexander Campbell or some of the great leaders of the Reformation. Fixing his keen eyes upon him, and pointing his long finger at him in the style of Randolph, O'Kane replied: "You—*you* debate with Alexander Campbell! Why if one of his ideas should get into your head, it would explode like a bomb shell."

On a certain occasion he was to preach in one of the many ill-constructed meeting houses with dark walls and very small windows. As he walked up the aisle, surveying every thing with a critical eye, he observed in an undertone to a brother that was with him: "Tell them to sing

'Tis darkness here, but Jesus smiles."

At another time when preaching in an old rickety church, from the walls of which the plastering had fallen off in places, he solemnly exhorted his brethren not to neglect the Lord's house, at least while it was so low with *erysipelas.*

A certain adherent of one of the sects once met him, and, extending his hand, said, "Well, Brother John, I used to think you were an unprofitable servant, but I think differently now." "Indeed," replied O'Kane, shaking his hand warmly, "that is precisely what I used to think of you, brother, *but I have never changed my mind.*"

Just before he removed to Missouri, he fell in with one of those young preachers who, in the wisdom of their own conceits, urge the necessity of reforming the Reformation. "Brother O'Kane," said he, "the world will not stand still after A. Campbell dies. Luther performed a great work, but he left something for others to do. So did Wesley; so we think will Campbell; and if the Lord shall see proper to commit the direction of this Reformation to younger heads, be it so." "You young fellows lead this Reformation!" said O'Kane. "As well might one think of harnessing a lot of Shanghai chickens to a train of cars."

Another young preacher was once complaining of the too small remuneration received for his services. "If the brethren do not support me," said he, "I will go where I can be supported." "*When did you take the sop,* brother," inquired O'Kane, slyly alluding to the Scripture which says that after Judas had dipped the sop, Satan entered into him.

With all his wit and sarcasm an element of tenderness is strangely mingled, and the effect of the combination cannot be better described than in the words of a pious old brother who affirms that he has seen him "*laughing out of one eye and the tears coming out of the other.*"

With a dignified and apparently proud bearing he walks humbly before God, having never manifested a disposition to be greatest otherwise than by faithfully performing his duties as a servant.

Ordinarily approachable, and unreserved in conversation, he has the power to assume a stoical indifference to every thing around him, whenever it seems good in his sight.

It is in the pulpit that he exerts his principal influence in behalf of the gospel. His commanding person, his expressive eye, his clear, strong voice, and his free earnest gestures—all contribute to make him a most interesting and impressive speaker. He is well versed in the Scriptures, and familiar with all the dogmas incorporated into the several creeds, upon which instruments he sometimes lays a heavy hand. Yet after all, the effect is produced not so much by what he says as by the admirable manner in which he says it.

As already intimated he does not occupy a high rank as a scholar; and he is strongly disinclined to write for the benefit of the public. Hence his own editorial career was short, and his articles in other periodicals are but few.

In the course of his ministry he has been engaged in many public discussions, in all of which he has triumphantly vindicated the principles of the current Reformation. As a disputant he has but few superiors.

Next after his achievements as a public speaker he has accomplished most as an agent, or solicitor of funds for benevolent purposes; for which office his pleasing address and above all his nice and ready discernment of character eminently fit him. Where almost any other man could not have obtained a cent, he obtained dollars and even hundreds of dollars.

The tact which made him so successsful in this employment, secured for himself also a more liberal support than that which fell to the lot of most pioneer preachers. Yet being a poor economist, and very careless in the management of pecuniary matters, he is in his old age one of the poor whom God hath chosen to be heirs of the kingdom.

Having remembered his Creator in the days of his youth, he has spent the Springtime and the Summer of his existence in the service of the Lord. Now that the Autumn of his days has come, and that his ,

> "way of life
> Is fallen in the sere and yellow leaf,"

the peaceable fruits of righteousness appear in rich profusion; and he has abundant reason to expect an exceeding great reward from Him whose "eyes are open upon all the ways of the children of men, to give to every one according to his ways and according to the *fruit of* his doings."

THOMAS LOCKHART.

This venerable and indefatigable servant of God was born in Patrick county, Virginia, A. D. 1793. His father was brought up in the Presbyterian Church, where he vainly sought religion from early youth until he reached his *seventieth* year! At that advanced age he united with the Dependent Baptists in Washington county, Indiana; was immersed by Elder Peter Wright; and about three years afterward went down to the grave in peace. Through the influence of false religious teaching, a shadow rested upon almost his whole life.

The mother of Elder Lockhart was for many years a Baptist. From her he received his first religious impressions; and as he grew up, the articles of her faith were zealously inculcated in his mind.

When thirteen years of age his parents removed with him to North Carolina, where he remained until he reached his majority. During his residence there the most of his associates were members of the Society of Friends, among whom he imbibed many of the views of that peculiar people.

In the Summer of 1814, while on a visit to Ohio, he volunteered his services in the war of 1812; and during the following Winter was stationed at Detroit. When his services were no longer required by his country he returned to Ohio, and subsequently to North Carolina.

Previous to his visit to the West he had been sent to a common school about one year; and on his return to North Carolina, after the war, he again went to school for

a term of three months. In this short period he acquired the little mental discipline which he has turned to such excellent account. He might have become a much better scholar but for the fact that he expected to pass his life as an humble tiller of the soil, and entertained the foolish notion that, as such, he would never need much education.

This being his view of life, he threw aside his books; and, in the Fall of 1817, was married to Polly Jessup, a most zealous member of the Society of Friends.

Soon after his marriage he removed to the West, and settled in Washington county, Indiana. There he found himself in the midst of Dependent Baptists, Friends, and a few adherents of some of the other sects. Being much concerned as to the subject of religion, he attended the various religious meetings held in his neighborhood, especially those of the Friends and Baptists. Indeed, from his early youth, he had been most earnest in his efforts to "get religion;" but it seemed that God only "laughed at his calamity, and mocked when his fear came." As it had been in his youth, so it continued to be in his riper years. The teachings of neither Friends nor Baptists afforded him any satisfactory knowledge of the plan of salvation; and when he appealed directly to the Lord in prayer, it seemed that He would not answer. After a long, unsuccessful conflict, he sank into the conviction that he was a "vessel of wrath fitted to destruction;" and from this, he easily relapsed into absolute scepticism

At length, when his feet were almost gone, he chanced to hear some Newlight preacher, who, though still blind in part, understood the way of God more perfectly than did his former religious instructors. Though their views of conversion were much like the views of other denominations the Newlights differed from those others in that they attached great importance to the Scriptures, and earnestly exhorted the people to search them diligently, and take them for the only man of their counsel.

Agreeably to their instructions he became, for the first time in his life, a *Bible reader*, and from that book he soon derived more knowledge of Christianity than he had ever been able to acquire from the preachers of those days. With David he could say, "I have more understanding than all my teachers, for thy testimonies are my meditation."

In his case the law of the Lord proved to be "perfect, converting the soul." He soon learned from the Scriptures what he must do to be saved; and in the year 1832 he publicly confessed the Saviour, and was buried with him in baptism by Elder Lewis Comer. His conversion, yea, his whole life, is a verification of that declaration of James, "Whoso looketh into the perfect law of liberty, and continueth therein, the same being not a forgetful hearer, but a doer of the work, this man shall be blessed in his deed." Nor can one well contemplate the long period during which he was striving to enter in at the straight gate, without calling to mind that other scripture which saith, "If thou criest after knowledge, and liftest up thy voice for understanding; if thou seekest her as silver, and searchest for her as for hid treasures; then shalt thou understand the fear of the Lord, and find the knowledge of God."

The meeting at which he acknowledged the Saviour was held near the present town of Plainfield, in Hendricks county, whither he had removed from the county of Washington. This neat little Quaker village was not then laid out, and the great national thoroughfare on which it stands was but recently opened for emigrants to the West.

On returning home from the meeting he found his wife in great distress on account of what he had done. They agreed to refer the whole matter to the law and the testimony, it being solemnly covenanted that the one unable to sustain his or her position, should at once embrace the views of the other. Never, perhaps, did woman strive more earnestly to accomplish any object, than did Mrs. L. to convince her husband of what she verily believed a fatal error. Often, when he unexpectedly entered the house, she hastily slipped the Holy Bible under her apron that he might not know that she had been preparing, in his absence, for the next discussion. She was finally brought to the knowledge of the truth; was baptized; and continued a faithful member of the Church of Christ until her death, which occurred in 1859.

Other strenuous efforts were made to convert him to the Quaker faith, but he remained "steadfast, unmovable."

On the next Lord's day after his union with the church he took part with his brethren in prayer and exhortation. This he continued to do on all proper occasions for several months, at the end of which time he began to accompany Elder John Hadley on his preaching tours.

As there were then but very few churches, they usually preached in private cabins or in leafy groves. Wherever they went the people gave heed to the things which they spake, and by their united efforts many were brought to the obedience of the faith. In their preaching they earnestly opposed all human creeds, and constantly advocated a union of all obedient believers on the Bible alone.

In a short time he began to make appointments for himself; and as early as the year 1833 he had fairly entered into the work of the ministry. Since that time he has ceased not to preach Jesus, and to do what he could to bring the religious world to the *unity* of the faith and of the knowledge of the Son of God.

About the year 1834 he was appointed by a co-operative meeting to travel as an evangelist, with John L. Jones. Together they proclaimed the ancient gospel throughout the counties of Marion, Hamilton, Hendricks, and Morgan. Their views were strongly opposed, but their labors were attended with the most gratifying results.

The witnessing of their success was their chief reward; for Elder Lockhart, at least, did not receive over fifty dollars per annum for his services. For one congregation he preached once a month for three years, receiving no remuneration save a twenty-five cent Testament, presented to him by one who, it may have been, had no disposition to read it himself.

To support his family under such circumstances he carried on a farm, much of the labor upon which he performed by the light of the moon and stars, that he might find leisure to preach the gospel. Five times in the course of his life he has settled in the woods; and each time added another to the fertile fields of Indiana.

During the years 1837 and 1838 he extended his travels into Boone and Clinton counties. There were then in that section but few disciples and but very few churches. Opposition was strong, yet he sowed bountifully the incorruptible seed, some of which fell upon good ground, and contributed to the rich harvest that has since been gathered in those counties.

A peculiar feature of his ministry was the holding of what were called "Investigation Meetings," at which inquiries were freely made and religious views freely discussed. Through these meetings public attention was directed to the word of God; and wherever that is directly studied, there the Reformation makes easy and rapid progress.

From 1838 to 1850 he kept out regular monthly appointments, and went hither and thither wherever there was a demand for his services, or wherever there appeared an opportunity of doing good. Hendricks county was, however, the centre and chief field of his operations, and his influence was scarcely felt beyond the confines of central Indiana. Within those limits he was one of the shining lights, not brilliant but constant.

At Brownsburg, in the northern part of Hendricks county, he has labored most, and with the best results. When he first visited that point, about the year 1838, he found there only about seventeen disciples, who were bitterly opposed by the Regular Baptists, of whom there was a large congregation at that place. This little church he set in apostolic order, and for it he has preached regularly until the present date. Through his labors some three hundred have been added to its number; and from it three other flourishing congregations have derived their origin, namely those at Clermont, Fayette, and Pittsboro.

For the church at Bellville, also, he has been the principal preacher for nearly a quarter of a century, and yet there are few religious teachers whose voice the people of that vicinity will follow more readily than his. In that congregation he has had his membership for twenty-four years; and in that house of worship he has enjoyed the satisfaction of hearing every one of his children—seven sons and two daughters—confess the name of the Lord Jesus.

Since 1850 he has greatly extended the area of his usefulness, having made frequent visits to northern Indiana, and occasional tours through Illinois, Missouri, and Iowa.

During the whole course of his ministry he has held frequent protracted meetings, which have uniformly resulted in many additions to the saved.

There is no earthly record of those whom he has turned from darkness to light; but the number of them is about *four thousand*, among whom are many that are now proclaiming the truth which has made them free.

Thus, directly and indirectly, he has done much, especially in an early day, to further the cause of the Reformation, and to entitle him, when he leaves the world, to the grateful remembrance of his surviving brethren.

Elder Lockhart is a large, heavy-set man, of great physical power and endurance. His height is about five feet eight or nine inches, and his weight not far from one hundred and seventy-five pounds. He has dark, but not black hair, small, keen, blue eyes, a ruddy complexion, and a temperament highly excitable. There is an air of majesty about his fine, large forehead, and a look of thoughtfulness with a shade of sadness on his face; yet his general expression is one of cheerfulness, affability, and pleasant humor. His "earthly house of this tabernacle" has nobly resisted the encroachments of time, so that he is still stout and hearty, and but for the loss of his hair he would be, in appearance, but little beyond the meridian of life.

Nor was nature less kind in the bestowment of his intellectual than of his physical powers; but while the latter were fully developed by the hard labor incident to his western life, the former received but little discipline from the few and inferior schools of earlier days. Having been compelled, also, to eat his bread in the sweat of his face, while preaching the gospel without money and without price, he has had but little time to cultivate his own mind, or store it with many facts save those which are connected with the great scheme of man's redemption. Still he has a sound, well-balanced mind, and a thorough knowledge of the Scriptures, of which an almost incredible number of passages are stored away in his capacious and retentive memory.

He is simple and industrious in his habits; plain and

old-fashioned in dress and manners. Ready in conversation, and equally at home in the humblest cabin or in the society of the more wealthy and refined, he is very highly esteemed by all that know him, while in the eyes of many there has not risen a greater than " Uncle Tommy."

Upon his Christian character there is no serious stain. In the beautiful words of Job, he has put on righteousness and it has clothed him; his judgment is as a robe and a diadem. On this account his words have great weight, and unto him—as they did to the man of Uz—men give ear, and wait and keep silence at his counsel. With respect to his special admirers it may be further said, that " after his words they speak not again, and his speech drops upon them. They wait for him as for the rain, and open their mouth wide as for the latter rain." Job xxix.

As a public speaker he occupies no mean rank among the men of his day. His ideas present themselves promptly; and his language is copious, though frequently inelegant and in rebellion against the laws of syntax. He is not a calm, logical reasoner, but an earnest and desultory declaimer. He has a powerful voice of extraordinary compass, and the words come sounding from his great, heaving chest, like the hollow utterances that escape from a volcano. The chief source of his oratorical power is his excitable nature—his ability to throw his whole soul into his delivery and electrify his hearers. This he frequently does; and, except at the beginning of his discourse, his manner is vehement throughout. He superabounds in quotations from Scripture, both *relevant* and *irrelevant*, and on this single account he is placed, by many, high above other workmen who better divide the word of truth. Nor is he satisfied with the written statements of the inspired witnesses. He authoritatively summons Paul and Peter into the presence of the congregation, and has them repeat their own words, which—he proceeds, in like manner, to show—precisely agree with the testimony of James and John. As he proceeds with the examination of his witnesses he becomes more and more excited, his voice ascends to a higher pitch, his feet become restless, his arms, even to his fingers' ends, twitch convulsively, the blood seems starting from the great veins upon his forehead, and, before he sits down exhausted, it is strange if some are not saying in their hearts, *Men and brethren what shall we do?*

Though himself untutored, he has ever been a fast friend of education. He has done much by way of encouraging young men to qualify themselves for useful and honorable positions in life; and he has done what he could to provide for the mental culture of his own sons. All are qualified for the pursuits of agriculture and commerce; some have gained admission to the legal and medical professions; and one graduated at the N. W. C. University, and now holds a position to which he was appointed by the President of the United States.

Though he has passed through many dark seasons, he is now realizing the promise, "at evening it shall be light." His children, once a burden, now a support to his declining years; his physical wants, once neglected, now well supplied by faithful brethren; and the cause of God, once persecuted in the hands of a few uneducated defenders, now triumphing gloriously in the hands of a well-disciplined host; he is able to say, with the aged Simeon, "*Now lettest Thou thy servant depart in peace, for mine eyes have seen thy salvation.*"

Yours, in Christian love
Jacob Wright

JACOB WRIGHT.

Although the son of one of the pioneers sketched in this volume, Elder Jacob Wright is entitled to a place among the first advocates of the Reformation in Indiana. He was born October the 9th, 1809, near Charlestown, Clarke's Grant, Indiana Territory.

Early in the Spring of 1810, his father, John Wright, removed to a point on Blue River four miles south of Salem, in the present county of Washington, though then within the limits of Harrison. He recollects distinctly when Salem was laid out by his father and the other county commissioners. Probably it received its name—city of peace—from Elder John Wright, the great advocate of peace among all the children of God. Among his earliest recollections are the thrilling incidents that occurred while his parents and their neighbors were shut up in forts to escape the tomahawks of the savages.

Owing, therefore, to the circumstances surrounding him, in early life, his education was only on a par with that of other pioneers who grew up in the Western wilds. His father, realizing in his ministry the want of mental culture, did all in his power to improve the minds of his sons; but Jacob, with the rest, acquired only a superficial knowledge of the lower branches of an English education.

His spiritual training was carefully superintended, especially by his pious mother, whose holy life was a potent argument in favor of Christianity. But being of a lively and rather froward disposition, no deep impressions of a religious character seem to have been made on his mind in childhood or youth.

At a very early age he was married to Miss Sarah Sheets, after which event he put away many youthful follies and became more sober-minded. From this state of mind the transition was easy and rapid to a state of religious anxiety which induced him to attend the meetings and listen to the teachings of the several denominations. In so doing he well nigh made shipwreck of his faith on the fatal rock of doctrinal diversity.

He had been taught that it was the part of charity to believe all men sincere in their religious views and candid in the statement of their respective experiences. Therefore his confidence in religion was severely shaken when he heard men earnestly endeavoring to inculcate doctrines as opposite as the poles, and all, at the same time, claiming to be *directly called and specially qualified by the Holy Spirit.* He could not believe that the Spirit of God inspired such contradictory doctrines; therefore he concluded that those who honestly professed to have been specially called and qualified, were the victims of a delusion; and if *they* were, so, perhaps, were all believers.

When witnesses in earthly courts have already contradicted each other times without number, their testimony is good for nothing when they chance to agree upon a single point. So when these opposing sectaries agreed in witnessing the blessing to be obtained at the "anxious seat," Elder Wright believed them not, and consequently resisted all the tearful entreaties of his friends, who would fain have seen him at that place of prayer. The religious leaders in those days did not seem to think that the sinner's path of duty *terminated* at the "mourner's bench;" but at that point it became so *obscure* that it could scarcely be discerned even by the spiritualized eye of the called-and-sent preacher. In allusion to this fact Elder Wright is wont to say, in his plain style: "The preachers wanted us sinners to do *something* in order to be saved; but neither they nor we could ever clearly understand what that 'something' was." But for these difficulties he would, no doubt, have obeyed the gospel long before he did; and it is probable that he never would have obeyed it had not those dark places been illuminated by the dawning light of the Reformation.

Finally, however, he heard some enlightened preacher observe that "man's duty is simple and may be narrowed down to two points, *faith* and *obedience*. This remark directed his mind to something tangible; and it was not long until both he and his wife were immersed, in humble submission to the will of the Lord.

They united at once with the congregation of Free-will Baptists at Blue River, which church had been organized by his father on the apostolic foundation, and which, with all the surrounding Baptist churches, came into the Reformation at the time of the great union effected soon after between them and the Reformed Silver Creek Association.

He immediately began to take part in the meetings for public worship; and in a short time it was whispered about that he ought to preach the gospel. But to this he was firmly opposed; for his father's experience had taught him that the minister's life is one of severe trial.

While this matter was pending, he met with a severe affliction in the loss of his wife. She died of consumption in the Summer of 1832.

Humbled by this sad dispensation of Providence, and seeing the fields on every hand "ripe for the harvest," he yielded to the importunities of his friends, and resolved to devote his life to the service of the Lord. On the third Sunday in August, 1832, he was ordained to the work of the ministry.

He was at that time in feeble health, and was thought

to be in the first stage of consumption; but he continued to preach the word with all the energy he could command, his labors being crowned with some success, and his health being finally restored.

On the last day of March, 1833, he was married the second time, to Rachel Denny, who has been, and still is, a faithful helpmeet in the gospel.

In May, 1834, he removed to Martinsburg, where he entered into the cabinet business. His cabinet shop was also, per necessity, his *theological seminary*. He used to keep a Bible on his work-bench; and while resting he would read a few verses on which to reflect while he plied his tools. In this way he acquired much of that thorough knowledge of the Scriptures, for which he is now noted.

While prosecuting his worldly business he did not neglect the "great salvation." From the very first, his Sundays were regularly employed in the Master's service; and each succeeding year the area of his operations was enlarged, his influence increasing in a direct ratio.

During a portion of the year 1838, he preached monthly for the congregation at Coffee Creek; and through his efficient labors the church increased from forty to over one hundred members. In the year 1839 he immersed about five hundred persons, and about four hundred the year following. Not all of these, however, were enlisted under his preaching alone; for he travelled much in company with his father, Jesse Mavity, Mordecai Cole, and the Littells—John T. and Absalom.

Among other important achievements of the year 1839 was the organization of the churches at Driftwood and Brownstown—churches which still continue to enlarge their borders, and through the instrumentality of which, many a "mouldering heap," in the cemeteries hard by, will give up its inmate at the first resurrection.

These years—from 1838 to 1840—were the most successful of his whole ministry.

At the close of this period his usefulness as a preacher was seriously impaired, and for a while entirely destroyed, by his becoming entangled in the affairs of this life. By close economy and hard labor in his cabinet shop he soon acquired considerable means, which he invested in a steam flouring mill. In this enterprise he had a partner to whom he intrusted the management of the business, while he, for the most part, gave himself to the word. Under this arrangement the firm became involved in debts; and the great financial crisis of 1840 coming upon them, in that situation, rendered them completely bankrupt.

Up to that time his preaching had been almost gratuitous, having received only about *fifty dollars* during the last *six years* of his ministry. He, therefore, had no reason to look in that direction for pecuniary aid.

Under these circumstances, and in view of the commandment to "provide things honest in the sight of all men," he determined to quit preaching, and labor with his hands, at least until he could pay off all his debts. Accordingly he went to work as a house-carpenter, and by extraordinary exertions was fast liquidating the claims against him.

But the brethren, especially those of Jackson county, were unwilling for him to abandon the evangelical field. They held that such a course on his part would either produce the impression that his faith had been shaken, or reflect upon his brethren for not giving a more liberal support to one who had made so many sacrifices and manifested so much zeal in the work. Therefore the churches at Driftwood, Brownstown, Pea Ridge, and Indiana Creek, met "in co-operation," and agreed that if he would resume the preaching of the word, as evangelist of Jackson county, they would remunerate him sufficiently to enable him to continue the payment of his debts. To this agreement he became a party; and since that time —October, 1841—he has been (save one year) continually before the public as a minister of the gospel.

From his journal of proceedings for the year 1842 it is ascertained that he preached for the four churches above-named, and also at Friendship, Leesville, and Leatherwood, in Lawrence; Coffee Creek and Paris, in Jennings; Sand Creek and Columbus, in Bartholomew; Harrodsburgh, in Monroe; and Canton, in Washington county. The record also reveals the fact that during the year two hundred and seventy-eight persons were added to these several churches.

He continued his labors in Jackson until the Fall of 1844, during which time the disciples in that county were greatly multiplied. At other points also he held important meetings, among which was one at Mill Creek, in Washington county, where fifty-five were added under his preaching alone.

His health failing in the Fall of 1844, he removed to Salem, where he was employed during the year 1845 as a clerk in the dry-goods establishment of J. B. Berkey.

When he entered the ministry the second time in 1841, he determined to seek some further scholastic attainments—at least to acquire the art of using with propriety the English language. Therefore when he engaged to preach for the churches in Jackson county, he also made arrangements to spend a portion of his time in a school taught by a brother Richard Fisher. His main study was Kirkham's Grammar, with which he became quite familiar. He also acquired some further knowledge of the subject by attending the lectures of Dr. H. T. N. Benedict, of Bloomington, who was traversing the country as a teacher of the English language.

Subsequently he fell in with a brother Newton Short,

by whom he was induced to begin the study of Greek. In order to encourage him, his patron gave him a Greek Testament, grammar, and lexicon, and also taught him the alphabet. After this humble beginning he continued for two or three years to wrestle with the declension of nouns and adjectives, and to grope his way slowly through the labyrinth of the verb. He obtained all the information he could from every scholar he chanced to meet; and aside from this he had no assistance until he removed to Salem in 1844. There he placed himself for a few months under the instruction of Prof. John I. Morrison, formerly of the State University; and by this means he was enabled to read the original text with tolerable proficiency.

Only a few years ago he began the study of Hebrew, which subject, like the Greek, has been pursued under many difficulties and mainly without a master. He does not profess to be proficient in either language, but he has learned a sufficiency of both to be able by means of his lexicons to determine in most cases the true meaning of the Scriptures. Thus it appears that he has pursued an *irregular* course—not *thorough* by any means, but surpassing in *length* even the curriculum of the German Universities!

On the first of January, 1846, he resumed his labors in the ministry, engaging to preach for the churches at Greensburg, Milford, Clifty, and Clarksburg, in Decatur county. These congregations he found in a weak, lukewarm condition; but at the end of two years he left them zealous, prosperous, and happy. While employed in Decatur he also reached over into Franklin county, where he organized a church of some forty members. This was in a community previously under the influence of the United Brethren, several of whom entered into the new organization.

In the Spring of 1848 he commenced preaching monthly

for the churches at Salem, and New Washington, Clarke county, reserving the remainder of his time for holding protracted meetings at various points. For the space of three years he successfully served the church at New Washington. With the exception of one year he has preached one-fourth of his time at Salem since 1848. During this long period the church has passed through many vicissitudes, has experienced many expansions and contractions; but it still listens with unabated interest to the instructions of its long-tried pastor.

In March, 1851, he held a meeting, in New Albany, which resulted in several additions, and gave such satisfaction to the congregation that they employed him to visit them once a month for one year. During the next year he preached for them three-fourths of his time, and half his time during the year following. In the three years about one hundred and twenty-five were added to the congregation, which was otherwise greatly strengthened.

In the meantime he also organized a new church at Georgia, on the Ohio and Mississippi Railroad. This was composed largely of those who had formerly been Baptists.

During the years 1855–56 he served the churches at Milroy, in Rush, and Clifty, in Decatur county.

In November, 1858, he returned to his old field of labor at Driftwood, where he has since continued to preach once a month Through his zealous ministry nearly the whole community have been converted to the faith of the gospel.

About this time a rather remarkable meeting took place at Courtland, Jackson county. The Methodists, Baptists, and Disciples of that locality had united their means and erected a union meeting-house. All parties claiming a share in the dedication, Elder Wright was invited to represent the Christian element on that occasion. Arriving at the appointed time, and finding that the building would not be completed for several days, he determined to have a few *valedictory* exercises in the old house of worship. He accordingly delivered four discourses on the subject of Christian Union, at the conclusion of which one of the class-leaders arose and expressed his determination to embrace the Reformation. He paused long enough, however, to deliver a powerful exhortation to the members of his class, about twenty of whom—all but one or two—took their stand with him on the Bible alone. Thus, while the workmen were finishing the union *house*, Elder Wright, as a workman that needeth not to be ashamed, was preparing a united *people* to occupy it! Through the increased moral power resulting from this more perfect union, not less than forty or fifty others were brought into the heavenly family before the close of the meeting.

But it is not designed to enumerate even a tithe of the meetings which he has held with signal advantage to the cause of reform; and perhaps those already referred to are sufficient to illustrate, with justice to himself, the manner in which he has been employed, and the success that has attended his efforts for the last thirty years. A line indicating all his travels would pass through, at least, the counties of Decatur, Rush, Franklin, Bartholomew, Jennings, Johnson, Morgan, Monroe, Owen, Lawrence, Jackson, Martin, Washington, Jefferson, Floyd, Greene, Davis, Sullivan, Clark, Scott, Orange, and Harrison. Indeed, his field has embraced almost the whole of southern or southeastern Indiana, which district he has traversed again and again; for it has been his custom not only to plant, but also to revisit and confirm. He has organized many new churches, set up many altars that had fallen down, and, from the data at hand, the number of his proselytes cannot be much less than five thousand.

But Elder Wright has rendered important services in another department. He is emphatically "*the* disputer"— if not "of this world," at least of the State of Indiana. It is as a debater that he has especially distinguished himself, though he was a weak opponent in the beginning. In a brief sketch like this, his numerous discussions cannot be dwelt upon; but justice demands that they shall, at least, be enumerated as follows:

1. His first was with a Methodist preacher by the name of John Bailes. It occurred at Martinsburg, about the year 1835.

2. His next debate, which was on *slavery*, also took place at Martinsburg, in 1836. His opponent was one Dr. Suggs, an Englishman, who is said to have had a liberal share of the braggart spirit for which his countrymen are remarkable. In this respect Elder Wright was also fully up to the *American* standard; and conscious of Yankee superiority and the justice of his cause, he accepted the disadvantage of affirming a negative, viz., that "American slavery is *not* according to the revealed will of God." This he was compelled to do, or be reproached with "backing out;" for the Doctor, with genuine English obstinacy, insisted upon the proposition in that form as a *sine qua non*. The moderators decided in favor of freedom.

3. At the same place and within the same year, he had a sharp engagement with a Mormon apostle, by the name of Emmet.

4. His next collision with one of the contrary part was at Brownstown, Jackson county, in 1839. It was an insignificant, extempore affair, in which he was opposed by the Rev. Philip May, of the M. E. Church.

5. This was followed by a regular discussion with a Methodist preacher by the name of Walker. The subjects

discussed were, "The Influence of the Holy Spirit in Conversion and Sanctification," "Infant Baptism," and "Immersion." The debate began at Leesville, Lawrence county, August 1st, 1842, and continued three days. Before leaving the ground, Elder Wright immersed twenty-two; and before the approach of Winter he immersed more than one hundred and fifty in that immediate vicinity.

6th. On the 27th of June, 1843, he met Erasmus Manford, the Universalist editor, in a discussion which took place at Columbus. On this occasion, his antagonist had the advantage of him in education and experience; and it is the part of candor to express the opinion that the result was against him.

7. In the Spring of 1846, and near Clarksburg, Decatur county, he had a sharp but irregular contest with the Rev. Williamson Terrell, a Methodist itinerant. The substance of this debate, with the causes that led to it, has since been published by Elder Wright, in a pamphlet of sixty-six pages.

8. In October, 1848, he debated five days with Mr. —— Foster, (Universalist,) at New Washington, Clark county. This time he was more successful than in his former discussion of Universalism. At the close he immersed about fifty persons; and it is said that " the final holiness and happiness of all mankind" was not again preached in that place for several years.

9. His ninth engagement was at Salem, in 1850, with a travelling phrenologist, who, in harmony with that whole race, was inculcating infidel sentiments.

10. From the 2d to the 10th of August, 1859, he debated, at Palmyra, with Dr. E. E. Rose, (Methodist,) on the following ten propositions:

First. Does the Holy Spirit ever operate, in the conviction, conversion, or sanctification of a person, apart from the revealed or written word of God? Affirmative, Rose.

Second. Did the baptism of the Holy Spirit cease with the death of the apostles? Affirmative, Wright.

Third. Has the Church been one and the same under both the Old and New Testaments, and children of believing parents entitled to membership and baptism therein? Affirmative, Rose.

Fourth. Is immersion the one only apostolic baptism? Affirmative, Wright.

Fifth. Is sprinkling or pouring apostolic baptism? Affirmative, Rose.

Sixth. Is immersion a necessary condition of justification or pardon? Affirmative, Wright.

Seventh. Is the Methodist Episcopal Church, as such, a part of the Church of Christ? Affirmative, Rose.

Eighth. Is the Church of Christ, which is frequently called "Campbellite," in its organization and form of government, the Church of Christ? Affirmative, Wright.

Ninth. No church or council has a right to make a discipline or creed for the government of the Church of Christ. Affirmative, Wright.

Tenth. Is it the will of God that all Christians should be visibly united in one body? Affirmative, Wright.

11. In 1860 he again debated with Dr. Rose, at Worthington, Greene county. The propositions were almost the very same.

12. In November of the same year he had a discussion with Nathan Hornaday, at North Salem, Hendricks county, on the following propositions:

First. Has the kingdom of God, spoken of by Daniel, ii. 44, been set up or organized? Affirmative, Wright.

Second. Does the soul of man survive the death of the body, and remain conscious after the death of the body? Affirmative, Wright.

Third. Do the Scriptures teach that the "everlasting

punishment" of the finally impenitent will be utter extinction? Affirmative, Hornaday.

13. His last public debate, in which he was opposed by Rev. T. S. Brooks, (Methodist,) began August 1st, 1861, and continued seven days.

Thus ends the long chapter of his public discussions, which, in connection with what precedes it, will exhibit to the reader the part which Elder Wright has performed in the current Reformation. For thirty years he has endured "hardness as a good soldier of Jesus Christ;" and, through the kindness of the Heavenly Father, he still stands upon the walls of Zion, clad in the full armor of God, and brandishing with a strong arm "the sword of the Spirit."

Elder Wright is a small, sinewy man, black-haired, black-eyed, and of a rubicund complexion. His form, his features, his dress, his gait—every thing about him indicates that he is, in a good sense, a *busy-body*, a man of *deeds*, as well as pretensions not a few. He is never weary in well doing, and whatever his hands find to do he does with his might.

His mind is well-balanced and well-informed, especially upon theological subjects. He sees a point readily and clearly, and reasons forcibly from cause to effect. In phrenological terms firmness is large, combativeness larger, self-esteem largest.

He is rather original and profound in his mental operations, hence the fact that he has preached for the congregation at Salem during the past sixteen years, without exhausting his intellectual resources. He is far from belonging to that class of preachers who deliver a few discourses with great effect, and after that have no more that they can do.

His manner of preaching is plain, straightforward, energetic, authoritative. He speaks with tolerable fluency, yet he is not rich in language; and his gestures are impressive rather than pleasing. He deals exclusively in facts, and carries his point by sheer force of logic. Though not harsh and repulsive in his elocution, yet he is destitute of pathos, and ordinarily incapable of delivering a touching exhortation.

In debate he is prompt, discerning, perfectly candid, and mild even to a fault; therefore he contends more successfully against an able opponent than against a deceitful quibbler. From the number of public discussions in which he has been engaged, it would be inferred that he is not only combative, but habitually aggressive. Such, however, is not the case; for in the most, if not in all of his regular debates, he has been the challenged party.

In the world as in his profession, he shows "uncorruptness, gravity, sincerity." Though in every respect a *positive* man, yet he is humble, frank, affable, and therefore popular, especially among the common people. Wherever he has gone preaching he has a host of friends, with whom his example avails not less than his precepts.

Poor in this world's goods, yet rejoicing in prospect of a heavenly inheritance, he still proclaims the glad tidings of salvation, resolved to devote the remainder of his days to the advocacy of the principles for which he has so long plead, and which he is fully persuaded will eventually prevail over the whole earth.

B. K. SMITH.

ELDER BUTLER KENNEDY SMITH was born in Spartansburgh District, South Carolina, on the sixteenth day of September, 1807. When he was an infant his father disposed of his possessions in South Carolina, intending to emigrate to Indiana Territory; but, changing his purpose, he settled in the adjoining District of Union, where Butler K. spent the happy days of his childhood.

In the Spring of 1817 his father carried out his long cherished design of removing to the Northwest. In April of that year he reached Indiana, and soon after entered land on the head waters of West river, in Wayne county. Here in the wild woods—theirs being the extreme frontier house for a long while—Butler K. passed the remaining years of his minority.

In a country like that there could be no such thing as a school; consequently he never suffered from that "weariness of the flesh" which is produced by "much study." He had been taught to read before leaving his native State; and with this ability he gleaned what information he could from the few books owned by his father, and from the newspapers, which at long intervals found their way into the neighborhood. In the course of a few years, however, a respectable school was established, in which he acquired a pretty thorough knowledge of arithmetic, and was shown a little way into the symbolic mysteries of algebra. This, with the general knowledge since gathered by the wayside, is the sum total of his education.

The circumstances surrounding him were equally unfavorable to moral and religious culture. It was only occasionally that a Methodist itinerant left an appointment in the neighborhood; and the nearest Baptist church, of which both his parents were members, was ten or twelve miles distant—entirely beyond his range. At a distance of three or four miles there was a Society of Friends, whose meetings he frequently attended, but without once hearing a discourse exceeding five minutes in length. His religious training devolved, therefore, on his parents, by whom he was thoroughly indoctrinated according to the creed of the Calvinistic Baptists.

In the course of a few years a couple of Baptist missionaries established a station at his father's house; and from that time he heard one or more of the "five points" expounded every month. Under this preaching several persons professed to have "obtained a hope," and among the number was Carey Smith, the eldest brother of Butler K. These fresh recruits, together with a few old soldiers of the cross—nine in all—were organized as a "Baptist Church of Jesus Christ," which was christened "Bethlehem." William Smith, the father of B. K., was made deacon, and Carey was ordained as pastor, with license "to preach and exhort wherever God in his providence should cast his lot."

Thus a *church* was brought near to Elder Smith, but from the *gospel* he was as far removed as ever. He strove to enter in at the straight gate, but all his efforts were ineffectual. By constant exertion he worked himself into the belief that he had obtained what his parents and brother denominated a "trembling hope;" but his "experience" being unsatisfactory, his "hope" was evanescent. He finally reached the following conclusions, which are stated in his own language:

1. That I was one of the non-elect. Such being the

case, the present life was all I could promise myself any enjoyment in; consequently the less I thought about a future state the better.

2. If I was of the elect the Lord's time for effectually calling me had not yet come; consequently any effort, on my part, to forestall the divine arrangement would be useless, if not sinful.

3. That the whole matter of religion was but a farce, gotten up by priest-craft to gull the superstitious and weak-minded.

Such being his convictions, the Bible was laid aside, and Burns' Poems became his favorite pocket companion. In "Holy Willie's Prayer," "Kirk's Alarm," "Ordination," and "Holy Fair," he specially delighted, because of the clear light in which they exposed the absurdity of the Calvinistic theory. A decent self-respect and the early counsel of his parents kept him from descending to gross immoralities; but, for a long while, the fear of God was not before his eyes.

In the Fall of 1823 or '24 his brother Carey, mounted on a sorry nag and an old weather-beaten saddle, set out on a preaching tour through Kentucky and other Southern States. In Kentucky he fell in with "The Christian Baptist," with which he was so well pleased that he ordered two copies of the work, as far as published, to be sent to Indiana, one to his own address, the other to that of his father. Thus his apparently unpromising mission was the means of introducing the primitive gospel and the ancient order into Wayne and other counties of Eastern Indiana.

He lived to see many churches grow up under the labors of himself and others. Finally he went on a mission to the South, under the special patronage of Elder A. Campbell, and fell a victim to the Southern climate soon after reaching his field of labor. He died at Fayette,

Miss., on the 27th of January, 1841, in the forty-first year of his age, and about the eighteenth of his ministry. He was among the very first of the pioneer preachers of Indiana, but his career was of short duration, and confined to the day of small things.

By the reading of the "Christian Baptist," Butler K.'s objections to Christianity were removed one by one. Gradually the fog of false teaching and consequent skepticism rolled away, and he saw once more the water of life, with full assurance that he might approach and partake freely. But on the principle embodied in the old adage, "A burnt child dreads the fire," he approached very slowly and cautiously. It was not until the Spring of 1832 that he obeyed the gospel, being baptized some six miles southwest of Indianapolis, by an aged and semi-reformed Baptist preacher by the name of William Irvine —*alias* " Uncle Billy."

Prior to this event, however, some changes worthy of note had taken place. For the purpose of establishing themselves in the business of blacksmithing—which trade was a kind of heirloom in their family—he and his brother Carey had removed to Indianapolis, at which place they arrived on the 1st of February, 1829; and, on the 17th of November, 1831, he had married Miss Sarah Bristow, the third daughter of Peyton Bristow, Esq., of Marion county.

At the time of their removal to Indianapolis, there was at that place a Baptist church, which had reported itself to the "Christian Baptist" as reformed; but it was still so far from the ancient order that Carey Smith refused to unite with it, and attached himself to a congregation in the country designated by the significant name of Liberty church. At the period of Butler K.'s immersion, the said Liberty church was arraigned before the Indianapolis Association on the charge of heresy, and the so-called

Reformed church was taking an active part in the prosecution. Therefore the little church which was organized in the "Bottom," (or six miles from town on the Bluff road,) and of which Elder Smith and his wife were original members, did not report itself to the Association, but assumed an independent form of government, adopting the New Testament as its constitution or creed. They also recognized the principle of weekly communion; and, as far as they understood it, conformed in all things to the order observed by the primitive churches. In this faithful little congregation he retained his membership until the 12th day of June, 1833, on *which day was organized "The Church of Jesus Christ at Indianapolis, Indiana."* The organization was effected at the house of a brother Benjamin Roberts, Peter H. Roberts and John H. Sanders being chosen as the first overseers.

When the disciples met together on the next "first day of the week to break bread," *not an officer of the church was present.* But there were a faithful few who were not ashamed of the gospel; and there were quite a number of spectators, anxious to see how those "Campbellites" would conduct a meeting without a preacher.

For a while it was conducted in the most approved Quaker style. Not one of the members present had ever spoken in public, and every one's "tongue seemed to cleave to the roof of his mouth." When the suspense became intolerable, Elder Smith went forward, took up a collection of Baptist hymns—there was then no Christian hymn-book—and began to search for a suitable song. The prayer that he was soon to make in public was pressing with mountain weight upon his mind; and, fearing that he might make a failure, he selected the familiar hymn beginning with a *definition* of prayer especially favorable to him on that occasion, viz. :

"Prayer is the soul's sincere desire,
 Uttered or *unexpressed.*"

This hymn he read and lined out as it was sung, thinking by that means to throw off his embarrassment before the arrival of the critical moment. But the last stanza being ended, his heart failed him, and he sat down, overwhelmed by a sense of dizziness and blindness. One or two other brethren attempted to lead in the exercises, but each and all failed precisely where Elder Smith had failed. Thus the first meeting adjourned, the loaf being unbroken, not a single prayer having been offered.

This mortifying failure taught the disciples that elders and deacons alone were not to be depended upon; but that it was the duty, as well as the privilege, of *all*, "to offer up spiritual sacrifices acceptable to God by Jesus Christ." Realizing this, and seeing clearly that the church would go to ruin if such abortive meetings were permitted to recur, Elder Smith added to his faith *courage*, and at once stepped forward into the front rank of that little faltering band.

To obviate the difficulty growing out of the absence of the officers, two more elders and as many additional deacons were appointed. Of the latter, Elder Smith was made one; though he still retained the office of sexton— sweeping, warming, an dilluminating the old school-house, which was the *pro tempore* "Christian chapel." Ever faithful and punctual in his attendance, he gave the sacred emblems to the disciples; and in the absence of *all four* of the elders, he officiated at the table.

In a short time he became one of the overseers of the congregation, which position he occupied until Elder L. H Jameson was installed as pastor of the congregation, in October, 1842. At that time Elder Jameson was ordained as an evangelist, Ovid Butler as bishop, and some three other brethren as deacons. His last official act, as an elder of that congregation, was to preside over the Presbytery which officiated on that occasion.

Shortly afterwards he was himself ordained as "an evangelist at large;" and thus released from all personal responsibility as to the management, government, and edification of the Indianapolis church.

In his watchful care over that congregation, and his zealous efforts to extend its borders, he had greatly neglected his own business, and had consequently lost very much of the liberal patronage he once received. Moreover, his location at that central point, and his position as elder of the church at the capital, enabled him to form but too many acquaintances, and constrained him to receive but too many calls from his brethren in different parts of the State. His house was for many years a Disciples' Inn, and his stable was usually well filled with horses not his own.

Owing to these combined causes he became greatly involved in debt; and finally had to dispose of his town property (that would be a fortune to him now) at a great sacrifice, and remove to a farm several miles in the country. There he worked hard to retrieve his former losses; and in the course of a few years, frowning poverty was succeeded by smiling plenty. During these years of severe manual toil he did not wholly forsake the word of life; but on almost every Sunday he rode away from one to ten miles, preached one or two discourses, and returned the same day.

Early in the year 1849 he was solicited by the co-operation meeting to evangelize in the county of Johnson. This call he accepted; and, in April, entered into his new field at a salary of three hundred dollars per annum. The principal churches composing the "co-operation" were at Franklin, Mount Auburn, Edinburg, and Williamsburgh.

For these, and in destitute places, he labored with such success, that he was employed to evangelize another year in connection with Elder Ara Hollingsworth.

Anxious that he should devote his whole time and attention to the work of the ministry, his brethren, at the commencement of the second year, urged him to lease out his farm for a term of years, at the same time making him verbal and indefinite promises of a liberal support. Yielding to their requests, and abandoning the farm—his only sure base of operations—his supplies were soon cut off; and by the close of the year he found himself reduced almost to absolute want. But this return of financial embarrassments only exemplified still further the apostle's declaration that "all things work together for good to them that love God." By the irresistible force of circumstances he was compelled to visit other and distant points, where he hoped to find more liberality, and at least equal opportunities of doing good. In this way he made himself known to many brethren who, perhaps, would never have heard of him had he continued a successful tiller of the soil. Thus his area of usefulness was widely extended; and he was forced to fulfill the hitherto unfulfilled conditions of his commission as "evangelist *at large.*"

Though his labors were arduous, he fared sumptuously every day, and so far as himself was concerned he could have enjoyed this itinerant service very well. But every dainty morsel was robbed of its relish by the recollection that his wife and children were subsisting on the cheapest and coarsest fare; and as he sat by the fireside of the thrifty farmer—father, mother, sisters, brothers, all present, the happy circle unbroken—his mind was filled with sad thoughts of a very different scene beneath his own distant roof. But remembering the words, "He that loveth *son* or *daughter* more than me is not worthy of me," he sustained the cross, and continued to point the people to Him whom, for their sakes, the cross sustained.

Having spent some two years in these desultory labors, he was invited to take the pastoral charge of the congregation at Harrison, in Dearborn county. This call he accepted, and removed to Harrison in the Spring of 1853. The congregation at that place gave him three hundred dollars for half his time, and two churches in Kentucky gave him the same amount for the remainder. Thus he received a salary of six hundred per annum, which was more than sufficient to supply the temporal wants of his family. At this point he spent two of the happiest years of his life, the success of the gospel being not the least cause of his rejoicing.

In May, 1855, he returned to his farm near Indianapolis, where he has continued to reside. From that time to the present he has preached regularly for some two or three congregations, and has gone hither and thither throughout Central Indiana, preaching the gospel of the kingdom, establishing new churches, edifying old ones, healing dissensions, and provoking to love and good works.

In addition to his preaching he has exerted a considerable influence, and become somewhat distinguished as a writer. He wields a vigorous pen, which, for the last fifteen or twenty years, has been industriously employed in contributing to the various Christian periodicals.

He is now, and has been from the beginning, a *punctual* and *working* member of the Board of Directors of the N. W. C. University. He also acts a prominent part in the management of County, District, and State Meetings; and is well known as a true friend of education, an active and liberal supporter of missions, both home and foreign, and of every institution, human or divine, which tends to the physical improvement, mental illumination, or spiritual elevation of his race.

Of the personal appearance of Elder B. K. Smith, no written description is necessary. By one glance at the portrait accompanying this sketch, the inquirer will obtain a better idea of that than it is in the power of words to convey. Like the ancient Eli, he is "an old man and *heavy*." He has too much sound sense to attempt to adorn such a person as his with fine clothes; therefore he dresses in very plain style, his main object being to give the respiratory organs full play, and to guard against the suffocating effects of heat.

His mental machinery is not of the most ponderous kind; but his inexhaustible supply of physical force runs it at a furious rate. Impelled by this bodily vigor, his mind easily surmounts obstacles which would be insuperable to a superior intellect inhabiting a frailer tenement. But the Lord has given him more than one talent, though he may not have given him five. Such are his abilities, natural and acquired, that when the Master comes to reckon with his servants, he may truly say, "Lord, thou deliveredst unto me *two* talents; behold, I have gained two other talents besides them." He is a bold, original thinker, who attempts the solution of the most intricate problems in theology, and who usually throws some additional light on subjects the most difficult to elucidate.

He is an edifying, stirring speaker—fluent, impressive, and oft-times affecting even to tears. His voice is deep and powerful, but under perfect control; his gestures are natural, and therefore appropriate; his countenance glows with animation; and his whole manner is so earnest as to force upon his hearers the conviction that "from the abundance of the heart the mouth speaketh." He is fond of doctrinal subjects; but he faithfully reminds his brethren of the practical precepts of the gospel. He opposes at all points those who resist the truth; yet in so doing he does not assume the authoritative air of the Saviour when he said, "O generation of vipers," but rather that sympathetic mood in which he exclaimed, "O Jerusalem, Jerusalem, thou that killest the prophets, and stonest them that are sent unto thee."

In all things he endeavors to please him who has called him to be a soldier. Therefore he does not suffer himself to become much entangled in the affairs of this life; but the affairs themselves—especially his own—are apt to become greatly entangled. He is not remarkable for the possession of great tact, or superior business qualities; and his *bump* of order would hardly be found by the clumsy fingers of some pseudo-phrenologists.

He is a man of warm and generous emotions—kind, forgiving, tender-hearted, ardently attached to his family and friends. Above all other objects he prizes "the kingdom of God and his righteousness"—

> "The church our blest Redeemer saved
> With his own precious blood."

For it he has toiled and suffered, denying himself the pleasures, the riches, the honors—all the "vain pomp and glory of this world." In its service he is fully resolved to spend the remainder of his days, with a firm reliance on the promise, "They that be wise shall shine as the brightness of the firmament, and they that turn many to righteousness as the stars forever and ever."

BENJAMIN F. REEVE.

Elder Benjamin F. Reeve was born in Prince William county, Virginia, on the 28th of October, 1798. He is of Welch descent with a slight mixture of Scotch and Irish. Tradition has it, that, very early in the history of this country, four brothers by the name of Reeve emigrated from Europe and settled in four different and distant parts of what is now the United States; and that from the said brothers have descended all of that name in America.

Near the beginning of the present century his grandfather, Asa Reeve, removed from Virginia to Fleming county, Kentucky, where he died more than forty years ago. He was a most zealous Methodist, and the most of his family embraced the faith in which they were brought up. Two of his sons became Methodist preachers, but Benjamin, the father of Benjamin F., never made any profession of religion; and especially did he not receive the doctrines of the Methodists. He rejected all creeds, human and divine, and made one for himself, which contained only a single article, namely, *Whatsoever things are honest.* He was careful to observe but one commandment: "*Thou shalt not steal.*" He employed in his family but one exhortation: "*Let us walk* HONESTLY, *as in the day.*" With him, as with multitudes now, *honesty* constituted the whole of religion: upon it hung all the law and the prophets; as if the Messiah had said to his apostles, "Go ye into all the world and preach *honesty* to every creature. He that deals honestly according to the decisions of his own mind

shall be saved, but he that defrauds in any matter shall be damned." This being his faith, he sought to implant no other in the minds of his children, who therefore grew up as free from religious bias as it is possible for human nature to be.

When Elder Reeve was six years old his father removed from Virginia to Kentucky, and settled in Mason county, about six miles below Maysville and near the Ohio river, whose waters were then disturbed only by the light canoe of the Red Man and the clumsy keels of the Whites. When quite young he was sent to school until he learned to spell, read and write with tolerable proficiency. When sufficiently old to work, he employed his time mainly in agricultural pursuits, yet he went to school more or less each winter until he arrived at manhood. He then attended a kind of high school for a year or two, in which, by diligent application, he acquired what was then regarded as an excellent English education.

Soon after completing his studies he was married to Miss Elizabeth D. Driskell. She subsequently followed him into the Reformation, and has long since preceded him to the Spirit land.

After his marriage he engaged in the business of teaching, which he prosecuted successfully and exclusively for fifteen years. At the expiration of that time he abandoned the profession, having demonstrated by actual experiment that, by teaching, he could make no more than a bare living for himself and his family.

The religious element of the community in which he lived was composed principally of Methodists, Baptists, and Newlights. The meetings of these several denominations he attended quite regularly from his boyhood to his thirtieth year. This he did, not for the purpose of ascertaining the will of God and doing it, but merely to listen to the extravagant logic of the preachers, and find agreeable companions with whom to while away the sluggish hours of the Sabbath. The pious quarrels indulged in by those three religious orders, with reference to election and free grace, and sundry other matters set forth in their creeds, were not well calculated to influence, in the right direction, a mind early taught to criticise the strife and divisions existing among the professed disciples of the Prince of Peace. Under such circumstances he made little or no progress toward the kingdom. So disgusted was he with conflicting doctrines, that he never seriously thought of searching out the narrow way. He knew but little about religion, and, if possible, cared less. With some of the more interesting portions of the Old Testament he had a slight acquaintance. He had read of the creation, of Noah and his ark, of David and Goliath; he was familiar with the story of Joseph and his brethren, and had some skeptical recollections of Sampson and his foxes. But to his understanding the seal of the New Testament had scarcely been broken. In his mind those wondrous things which the angels desire to look into had awakened no interest. He was truly without God and without hope in the world. Who can contemplate his spiritual condition at that time, and the causes which mainly led to it, without being convinced that a divided church is opposed to the spiritual welfare of man, as well as to the revealed will of God?

The first book of a religious character he ever read with any interest or seriousness, was the published debate between Alexander Campbell and W. L. McCalla. Having as yet no preference for this denomination or that, he gave the work an unprejudiced perusal, being just as willing at that time to be a *McCallaite* as a *Campbellite*. From it he obtained some substantial knowledge of religion, and he closed the book with the impression that the Bible is less contradictory than the sects, and that, like any other book, it may be studied and for the most part understood.

About the year 1828 the three denominations mentioned above imported into the neighborhood three preachers, one of each order, and each an able defender of the dogmas of his church. Many things were then done through strife and vain glory. Meetings were so frequent that opportunities were afforded of hearing one of the three champions every Lord's day. From the very first Elder Reeve attended these meetings, and he soon became a deeply interested listener, having now learned how to compare the views of men with the word of God. They mainly discussed the subjects of Baptism, Calvinism, and the Divinity of Christ. He hearkened diligently to them all, until he understood clearly their positions and the differences between them. On Baptism the Baptist and Newlight opposed the Methodist; on Calvinism the Methodist and Newlight opposed the Baptist; and on the Divinity of Christ the Baptist and Methodist opposed the Newlight. It was, therefore, a remarkable, triangular, and unequal contest, there being two against one on each of the subjects.

In addition to these discussions, the doctrine of the Reformation was beginning to be preached in that community, though as yet, it had made no breach in the walls of sectarianism. In the midst of all these circumstances, Elder Reeve desired greatly to know which of all the doctrines was true, or whether all were alike false. To satisfy himself, he resolved to try the whole matter before the apostolic jury.

Baptism being put on trial first, he took up the New Testament and read it through with special and exclusive reference to that subject. Wherever the term occurred, or wherever the subject was alluded to in any way, there he paused, scrutinized, and analyzed as closely as possible

He examined well the locality of "Enon near to Salim," and weighed well the reason why John was there baptizing.—Jno. iii. 23. He hears John say, "I indeed baptize you *with* water," and he resolves to discover if possible how he does it. Presently a subject approaches. It is Jesus coming "from Galilee to Jordan unto John to be baptized of him."—Matt. iii. 13. He watches with intense interest and perceives that John baptizes *in* water; for "Jesus, when he was baptized, went up straightway *out* of the water." He observes the passage of our fathers through the sea, and finds that they were baptized unto Moses *in* the sea—not *with* it. He seeks diligently the "spray" by which, the preachers affirmed, they were sprinkled on that memorable occasion. He finds to his astonishment that the waters are frozen in the heart of the sea, and that they are "a wall (of ice) unto them on the right hand and on the left."—Ex. xv. 8 and xiv. 22. He follows the chariot over the desert toward Gaza, to witness the baptism of the eunuch. As they go "down both into the water," he vainly strives to discover some similarity between the action of Philip and that of the man who administers this ordinance, standing on a soft carpet with a basin of water in his hand. He closely observes the Saviour when the little children are brought unto him. He sees him put his hands on them; he hears a blessing pronounced over their innocent heads; but not a thing does he see or hear relative to baptism. He goes to the jail at Philippi, and inquires after the jailer's "house"—the little ones that were said to have been baptized upon their father's faith. He finds that they are all of sufficient age *to believe in God.*—Acts xvi. 34. He asks Paul and Silas as to the number, the ages, and the names of Lydia's children, but they return no answer.

These researches he made impartially, being as willing to find authority for Sprinkling or Infant Baptism, as for any thing else. Having heard so much about these outside of the Bible, he was not a little surprised to find, *in* it, no trace of either the one or the other. He read the Testament through again in the same manner and with the same result. The doctrine so eloquently advocated by the Methodist brother in opposition to the Baptists and Newlights, was not written in the book of God.

Returning one evening from school he stopped at the village where several persons were assembled, and among them a certain class-leader who knew that he was searching the Scriptures. Being interrogated by the brother as to the result of his investigations, he replied, that if he had not previously heard, from men, of Sprinkling and Infant Baptism, no thought of them would have ever entered his mind in all his reading of the New Testament. The official assuming a contemptuous air and giving expression to some taunting remarks, Elder Reeve handed him a Testament, which at that time he always carried in his pocket, and requested him to "put his finger" on the passage, which, of itself, would have originated such an idea. He took the book reluctantly, but instead of pointing out the passage, he began to talk of Lydia and her "household." He has often made the same demand of the advocates of those doctrines, but no one has ever met it. He is therefore profoundly impressed with the difference between finding a doctrine *in* the Bible and proving one from the Bible The latter practice he regards as a fruitful source of errors and *isms*.

The first subject being disposed of he again read the Testament through with an eye single to Eternal and Unconditional Election. On the first reading he was fully persuaded that the way of salvation is open to all—that "in every nation, he that feareth him, and worketh righteousness, is accepted with him."

He then took up the remaining subject—the Divinity of

Christ—in the same manner, but with less success. On the first reading, he felt that he knew but little about it; on the second, less; and on the third, still less. Though the term "divinity" was freely used in the discussions of that day, yet the question in hand was more properly the *eternity* of Christ—was he co-eternal with the Father, or did he derive his existence from the Father? This was the subject which to Elder Reeve grew more and more obscure. But that Jesus Christ is the Son of God, he found abundant evidence in the Scriptures. With this great, central truth he contented himself; and beyond that, after the third reading, he sought not "to penetrate the vail."

By the time he reached his conclusions on the subjects before mentioned, the doctrine of the current Reformation was being extensively taught in that community, not only by disciples, but also by many Baptist preachers. Among these was Jesse Holton, a most excellent man, in whom the people had very great confidence. He afterwards came completely over to the Bible alone, and continued a steadfast disciple till he entered into his rest. By this devout man, in the Summer of 1829, Elder Reeve was immersed, with an intelligent understanding that it was an act in order to the remission of sins. Thus was he *born free*, though he afterwards united with a Baptist congregation known as Bracken church.

In 1830 or '31, this church divided. Of some hundred and fifty members, all went into the Reformation except about thirty. The old house of worship was held as common property, the Baptists occupying it one-third of the time.

Soon after this division B. F. Reeve and Daniel Runyon were selected as elders. In the Summer of 1832, they were formally ordained—Elders D. S. Burnett, John Smith, and Guerdon Gates officiating.

In the Spring of 1833 he removed to Indiana, and settled, where he now resides, in Noble township, Rush county. That county has been the principal field of his labors. He has worked in only a small portion of the great vineyard; but he has cultivated that portion well. When he came to that county the Christians were few in number and everywhere spoken against. But the face of the western country has scarcely changed more, in the last quarter of a century, than has the religious phase of Rush county. It is no vain boasting, but the statement of a well-attested fact, to say that the despised few have been so multiplied that they now far outnumber any other denomination—that they have more and better churches, sustain in the field more preachers, do more in the cause of education, and exert more influence in every way over the public mind. To bring about this happy state of affairs, no one has done more, perhaps, than Benjamin F. Reeve. To realize the good that he has accomplished, that interesting region must be seen *as it is* by one who recollects it *as it was*.

Upon his removal to that locality, he united with the Flat Rock church; and for *twenty-eight years* has been one of its bishops, and its principal instructor in word and doctrine. During this long period, Flat Rock has been one of the largest and most influential churches in the State. It now has over two hundred members, and it has seldom had less. It has sent whole colonies to various portions of Indiana, while many have gone from it to the far West, carrying with them the "incorruptible seed."

In addition to his labors at Flat Rock, he has rendered efficient service to the neighboring churches, sometimes visiting them monthly. When the system of county co-operation was adopted throughout the State, he travelled and preached over a small district for about three years. His labors were attended with great success.

During his ministry he has been especially useful as an immerser. Possessing great strength of body, caution, and self-possession, he has usually been called on to immerse the obedient wherever he has been present. He baptized his first subject in June, 1833; since which time he has immersed hundreds, if not thousands, without the slightest accident to any. On one occasion he buried thirty-six without coming up out of the water.

He has also enjoyed great popularity among the young men and maidens, very many of whom he has united in the bonds of matrimony.

He has himself been twice married. His first wife died in 1839, and in the following year he was married to Elizabeth B. Lower, who still survives.

In view of the important results which he has accomplished in behalf of primitive Christianity, it may be well to consider the means by which those results have been obtained. It may be safely affirmed that they have not been brought about by *extraordinary exertions as an evangelist*. Many men, who have done less good, have preached more, travelled farther, and experienced greater hardships. Though he has preached a great deal, he has never given himself wholly to the word. Much of his time has always been devoted to secular pursuits. Upon these he has relied for the support of his family, and, until quite recently, he never received any remuneration for his services in the gospel.

For several years he was a member of the Board of Managers of the White Water Canal. From the organization of the North Western Christian University, he has been a punctual and highly efficient member of its Board of Directors, and Business Committee. In the township in which he resides he has served as justice of the peace for thirteen consecutive years; and for the last twenty years he has been engaged in settling up estates, and acting as guardian of minor heirs. At this time he is executor of five different estates, and the guardian of six families of children. He has sometimes had more of such business on hands, but seldom less. In this capacity he not only *guards* the dollars and cents, but also superintends the moral and intellectual training of those entrusted to his care. During five sessions he has been honored by the people of Rush county with a seat in the State Legislature; two terms in the House—from 1836 to 1838—and three years in the Senate, from 1841 to 1844. Although not wealthy, he has, by judicious management of his worldly affairs, and by hard manual labor, placed himself in a condition to live easily and independently during the remnant of his days.

It may be affirmed with equal safety, that his success in the ministry is not owing to the possession of *extraordinary ability*. True, he is a workman that needeth not to be ashamed, and one fully competent to officiate creditably in any pulpit; yet he is not generally regarded as a *great* preacher. But in the little circle in which he has quietly labored, it is universally conceded that "brother Reeve is the *safe* preacher." This expression, which has become almost proverbial in Rush county, reveals the secret of his success. He has accomplished his work by being emphatically a Book man; by always meeting the opposer with a "thus it is written;" by taking heed to himself and his doctrine; by avoiding, as a preacher, all superstitious notions, speculative theories, "vain babblings," and "foolish and unlearned questions;" by teaching the people the pure word of God; and by being, himself, "an example to the believers in word, in behavior, in charity, in spirit, in faith, in purity."

Besides these excellent traits as a preacher, he possesses admirable qualities as a bishop. It is in this office, rather than the ministry, that he stands pre-eminent. There is scarcely a single particular in which he does not conform to the standard given by Paul to Titus. During the twenty-eight years that have elapsed since he became bishop of Flat Rock church, no serious difficulty of any kind has occurred in the congregation; and the cause of primitive Christianity, in that community, has been saved from the disgrace which often arises from contentious elders and disputing brethren. This calamity he has prevented by permitting to be brought before the church no question which was calculated to divide it, or seriously disturb its harmony; by not assuming, as too many bishops do, a dictatorial attitude; by causing the church to feel its responsibility, and thus, in a great measure, govern itself; and by not being determined to thrust himself forward as a preacher, but by being always willing to speak or refrain from speaking according to the will of those whom he served.

Still proceeding in this way the pleasure of the Lord continues to prosper in his hands; and never, while he stands at the door, will grievous wolves enter in to devour his flock. A little longer shall he "feed the flock of God, taking the oversight thereof, not for filthy lucre, but of a ready mind." Then shall the chief Shepherd appear, and he shall receive a crown of glory.

From this brief sketch of his life and services let at least one important conclusion be drawn, namely, to advance the interests of the Redeemer's kingdom, it is not necessary to travel into Asia, or possess the mental acumen of the apostle Paul. Ordinary ability, employed with discretion in the pulpit, and prudence in the bishop's office, may establish the claims of the ancient gospel in any other county, as, by such means, they have been established in the county of Rush.

In the personal appearance of Elder Reeve there is nothing remarkable. He is rather heavy set, hardly up to the average height; and his whole contour is indicative of great strength, activity and endurance. He has a keen gray eye, light hair, and a highly nervous temperament.

He is a thoughtful, well-informed, common-sense man; not disposed to consider things abstractly; but of a practical and business turn of mind.

His dress is plain and neat, correctly representing him as a well-to-do farmer.

He is easily approached, very lively in conversation, and hospitable to a fault. For many years his house has been the preacher's home; and every good and great enterprise finds in him a "cheerful giver."

He preaches the simple gospel in very simple style. His action is not that of an orator; but his ideas are good, his language well chosen, and his delivery impressive.

When death claims him the world will be minus an obliging neighbor, a patriotic citizen, a patron of learning, a true philanthropist, and an exemplary Christian.

JOSEPH W. WOLFE.

Elder Joseph W. Wolfe was born in Frederick county, Virginia, April 19th, 1810. Like most persons of that day his advantages for obtaining an education were very limited. He was sent to school three months in the year 1817; and about nine months in the following year. On the 3d of April, 1819, he left Virginia and removed to Sullivan county, Indiana, where he still resides. Arriving at his western home on the 1st of the following May, being a little more than ten years of age, he soon discovered that he was by no means the *only wolf* that had emigrated to that locality; for at that time Sullivan county was but sparsely settled; the howling of wolves was heard more frequently than the sound of the gospel, and far more numerous than school-houses were the wigwams of the Indians. Here among savages both human and inhuman, he grew up, toiling daily in forest or in field; nor until eighteen years of years of age had he any further opportunity of attending school. During the years 1828–9 he again went to school for about six months; and, by a diligent improvement of his time, he mastered the Spelling Book; learned to read and write, and *"ciphered"* to the rule of three in arithmetic. His education was then regarded as complete; for by the people of that day, geography, English grammar, and indeed all things beyond the rule of three were deemed of no practical utility.

Unlike most of our modern students, he did not confine himself within the narrow bounds of "man's wisdom,"

T. Sinclair's lith. Phila.

Very Respectfully
Jos. W. Wolfe

but diligently inquired after "that wisdom which cometh down from above." He soon found and appreciated the great truth, too often overlooked by young men, that "the fear of the Lord is the beginning of wisdom and to depart from evil is understanding." Accordingly, on the 2d of August, 1828, he was immersed into Christ, and on the first Lord's day of September following, united with the Baptist church at Maria Creek, Knox county, Indiana.

A little prior to this time, the light of the Reformation began to dawn on that vicinity. Influenced by the writings of Barton W. Stone, Alexander Campbell and others, the principal Baptist ministers preached, with Paul, that "faith cometh by hearing, and hearing by the word of God. While they insisted on faith and repentance as essential antecedents of baptism, they no longer taught the people that they could not be baptized without a previous assurance of pardon. *Elder Wolfe declares that, had it not been for these modifications of the orthodox gospel, he would never, perhaps, have united with the church, and that he certainly would not have done so at that time. Happily for him and the thousands that have been saved through his instrumentality, these modifications were made; but alas! in how many cases have they *not* been made! Who but God can estimate the influence, nay the *souls* that have been lost because of them that have hesitated to preach the simple gospel through fear of being called heterodox?

But to the new doctrines proclaimed from the pulpit, many of the members seriously objected; and previous to his immersion he was required to relate an "experience." He stated that he had "heard the word;" that he believed that Jesus is the Christ; that he had repented of his sins; that he hated iniquity; loved righteousness; and desired to be baptized. The fact that he loved righteousness and hated iniquity was regarded as proof, strong as holy writ, that God had blotted out his transgressions; and they accordingly proceeded to baptize him "because of" the remission of sins. Thus he became a Baptist; but the gate had well nigh proved too straight for him.

Soon after his union with the Baptist Church, the creed question was greatly agitated in the congregation at Maria Creek. Many of the members were much dissatisfied with the Baptist Confession of Faith, especially to that part of it which relates to the doctrine of eternal election. So high did the excitement run, that at every monthly meeting some one would move that the creed be read, which being done, the debate began, almost every male member taking part in the discussion. In the midst of this excitement, Elder Wolfe and seventeen others requested to be organized as a separate congregation, at Shaker Prairie, in Knox county; but they were unwilling to be organized on a creed unless that creed should be expressed in Bible terms. To obviate the difficulty, the church appointed Elder Wolfe and their pastor, Elder B. W. Fields, as a committee to prepare a satisfactory creed. At the next monthly meeting they reported one, which began as follows:

"Preamble.

"We believe that the Scriptures are divinely inspired, and the only infallible rule of faith and practice:—Therefore we declare to the world our faith in the following manner, viz.:

"1st. We believe 'There are three that bear record in heaven, the Father, the Word, and the Holy Ghost, and these three are one.'

"2d. We believe 'There are three that bear witness in earth, the Spirit, and the water, and the blood: and these three agree in one.'

"3d. We believe that 'In the beginning was the Word, and the Word was with God, and the Word was God.'

"4th. We believe that 'All things were made by him, and without him was not any thing made that was made.'

"5th. We believe that 'The Word was made flesh and dwelt among us, and we beheld his glory, the glory as of the only begotten of the Father, full of grace and truth.'

"6th. We believe that 'Every spirit that confesseth that Jesus Christ is come in the flesh is of God.'

"7th. We believe that 'Every spirit that confesseth not that Jesus Christ is come in the flesh is not of God.'

"8th. We believe that 'God hath appointed a day in the which he will judge the world in righteousness by that man whom he hath ordained; whereof he hath given assurance unto all men in that he hath raised him from the dead.'"

Other articles followed in the same style, but this will suffice as a specimen.

After due deliberation, this singular creed was pronounced unexceptionable; and on it the church at Shaker Prairie was organized, in the year 1830. They elected their officers; chose B. W. Fields as their pastor; and entered upon a short career of peace and prosperity. But ere long a serious question arose among them, viz.: Why should they adopt as their creed a few passages of Scripture, and not the whole Bible? Then again was discussion, until, finally, they unanimously decided to erase all their creed save the first sentence. This was done by Elder Wolfe, as clerk; and to the fragment saved he added the words, "which we adopt as our creed and Book of Discipline;" so that the instrument, thus amended, read as follows: "We believe that the Scriptures of the Old and New Testament are divinely inspired, and the only infallible rule of faith and practice—which we adopt as our creed and Book of Discipline."

By this time the Annual Baptist Association was drawing nigh, and the church appointed Elders Wolfe and

Fields to prepare a letter to that body, setting forth the fact that they had discarded the Baptist creed, and adopted the Bible in its stead. The letter having been prepared, presented to the church, and approved, Elders Wolfe and Fields and brethren James Boyd and Jacob Wolfe were appointed as delegates to bear it to the Association. This body met in September, 1830, at Indian Creek church, Sullivan county; and no sooner was the letter presented than a motion was made to eject the delegates from the Association. Elder Fields obtained leave to explain their position; and, for an hour and a half, proceeded to show, 1st. The right of congregations to choose their own creeds; 2d. The perfection of the Divine creed; 3d. The duty of Christians to adopt it; and, 4th. That it was antichristian to be governed by any other. At the close of his address, finding his auditors irritated rather than convinced, he and his fellow-delegates withdrew from the Association. Thus ended the connection of Elder Wolfe and the congregation at Shaker Prairie with the Baptists; and thus was furnished at least one undeniable evidence that human creeds are schismatical.

Then began the brethren at Shaker Prairie to meet on every Lord's day to break bread; and the Lord, from time to time, added unto them "the saved." Then, too, began persecution—not such as once filled prisons, fed ravenous beasts, and illuminated with human torches the gardens of Nero—but such as *reviles* one, and says all manner of evil against him falsely for Christ's sake. The Baptists stigmatized them as "Campbellites," and closed their doors against them. The Methodists organized a class among them, and pronounced them heterodox; while, by the orthodox generally, it was industriously asserted that they denied the Divinity of Christ, and the operation of the Holy Spirit, and that all they required of any one in order to membership was simply to be immersed—misrepresentations which, though corrected a thousand times, continue to be repeated by very many even to this day. "But step by step," says Elder Wolfe, "we advanced on our glorious platform, gaining ground on all opposers." As the means by which this was accomplished he adds, "Every member of us acted as a preacher. We carried our Testaments into our cornfields, and read the word at every interval." *Thou who hast been wont to rely only upon the preacher for progress, "go thou and do likewise."* Fired by such zeal, and instructed by Elders B. W. Fields, M. R. Trimble, and others, the church steadily grew in grace and in numbers; so much so that in less than two years they had increased from eighteen to twenty members; and in 1838 they numbered a hundred and twenty, as did the disciples at Pentecost, while the persecuting church at Maria Creek went down almost to zero. Let the history of this church serve as an index of what might, by proper effort, be accomplished by the Reformation. If every disciple would labor with equal zeal, there would be reason to hope that, ere long, human creeds would be driven from the church; the walls of sectarianism razed to the ground; and the people of God united on the one foundation of the apostles and prophets, Jesus Christ himself being the chief corner stone. Then indeed would the doubting world believe that God has sent his Son to seek and to save that which was lost; and the kingdoms of this world would speedily become the kingdom of our Lord and of his Christ.

In the Christian meeting-house at Shaker Prairie, on the 6th of May, 1839, Elder Wolfe was ordained as an evangelist by Elders B. W. Fields, John B. Haywood, and Albert P. Law, all of whom now "rest from their labors." He immediately began to thrust in his sickle with those that were already

> "Shouting and singing in the open fields
> Their harvest hymns."

His first labors were confined chiefly to his own and the adjacent neighborhoods. There he not only preached on Lord's days, but held night meetings at various points through the week, and, imitating the great apostle to the Gentiles, he taught the people publicly and *from house to house*—a style of preaching now too nearly obsolete. Afterwards he preached for several churches in more distant parts of Sullivan and Knox counties, until January 1st, 1840, when he took a district embracing these counties in Indiana, and the counties of Lawrence and Crawford in Illinois. In this district, which contained about fifteen congregations, he became a regular "circuit-rider," but, unlike others of that class, he was subject to no "bishop" save the Shepherd and Bishop of his soul. From May 5th, 1839, the date of his ordination, to the close of that year, he had persuaded seventy persons to obey the gospel, and, encouraged by this success, he entered upon the work of his district with large hope and much zeal. This being the year of General Harrison's election to the Presidency, the people were wild with political enthusiasm. The world thought but little of the Church, and, what was equally embarrassing, the Church thought too much of the world. But, undiverted from his purpose, Elder Wolfe still urged the people to moderation, and besought them to make their *own election* sure. The result of his labors this year was four hundred and twenty-six additions by immersion, plus a considerable number by letter and otherwise. This result was effected at great personal sacrifice; for though he was performing such excellent service for the churches, they gave him but very little support. This year he consumed what little money he had and most of his personal property. His supply of clothing was also nearly exhausted; hence he had to abandon his circuit and return to the cultivation of the soil for the support of himself and family. During the next year, refusing numerous invitations from abroad, he preached on every Lord's day, and sometimes on Saturdays and Mondays, to the home congregation, visiting only a few other churches at such times as the farmers had most leisure. The accessions were one hundred and forty-six by immersion and thirty-two from other churches, a deficiency of two hundred and eighty compared with the year before. Had he been properly sustained, instead of a deficiency there would no doubt have been a greater number of additions; for this year there was no political excitement. Therefore, if these two hundred and eighty persons are lost, will not the brethren of that district, when they stand before the great white throne, reproach themselves severely for their illiberality in supporting the gospel?

Having, by the labor of his hands, provided for the wants of his family, he, in 1842, again entered the harvest in which the laborers are few. This year he agreed with four congregations to visit each once a month and hold a two days meeting. Under this arrangement he immersed two hundred and sixty-five, and *received for his services seventy dollars, inclusive of sundry articles of food and raiment.*

In 1843 he preached for fifteen congregations, and occasionally in destitute neighborhoods, adding to the several churches three hundred and sixty, and receiving for his labor one hundred and thirty-three dollars in cash and produce.

During about two thirds of the year 1844 he preached for the churches at Lawrenceville and Russellville, Illinois, and Bruceville and Shaker Prairie, Indiana. He added to the kingdom more than two hundred and fifty, and received one hundred and fifty dollars in cash; while the brethren at Shaker Prairie, in addition to their portion of the money, gathered his crop of corn, prepared wood for his family, and cheered his heart by several substantial presents. This year, in connection with Elder John E. Noyes, he held a series of protracted meetings at various points in Indiana and Illinois, a short account of which may serve to illustrate the power of both Elder Wolfe and the truth in those days.

They began at Bruceville, Knox county, being assisted at this place by Elder B. W. Fields. The arrangement was that Elder Fields should preach each day at nine o'clock, A. M., Elder Noyes at three P. M., and Elder Wolfe at night. At the close of the sermon on the second night, eighteen persons came forward to confess the Lord before men. An exhortation was given, and three others came. Thus they continued from day to day until sixty-nine were immersed. Several things conspired to make this a remarkable meeting. The weather was excessively cold; the ground was covered with snow, which afforded excellent sleighing; and vast multitudes of people were daily in attendance. The stream in which they baptized was covered with ice more than a foot in thickness. The opening made through this and the overlying snow, had a striking resemblance to a grave; so that the people had no difficulty in conceiving how they might be *buried* with Christ in baptism, and arise to walk in newness of life.

Leaving Elder Fields, they next held a meeting at Russellville, Illinois, which closed, after ten days, with forty-eight additions. They then removed ten miles west to a point on the Ambrosia river, where, in five days, they obtained sixteen additions. Next, on their return, they preached four days at Palestine and immersed eighteen. Their last joint meeting was held at Shaker Prairie, and resulted in twenty-two accessions, making one hundred and eighty-three in all.

At the close of this year, finding himself encumbered with debts and his farm in a bad condition, he became discouraged and thought of abandoning the work of an evangelist; but he was encouraged by his wife to persevere. Soon, however, the voice of that wife encouraged him no more; her heart sympathized with him, her prayers ascended for him only a little longer; for on the 26th of April, 1845, she died, leaving him with four children—the youngest four, the eldest eleven years old. Then to him were "the days of darkness," which in every man's life shall be many. He preached but little, save to the home congregation; and this year brought into the kingdom only about one hundred. At the close of the year he was married the second time; and again entering the field as an evangelist, during the years 1846–7, he added about four hundred to the Church.

In 1848 he was elected county commissioner for three years. This interfered but little with his preaching arrangements; and each year his labors were crowned by about two hundred accessions.

In 1851 he was elected clerk of the Circuit Court of Sullivan county, but still continued to preach with his usual success. Assisted by Elder Jas. Blankenship of Monroe county, he held several protracted meetings, at which about two hundred persons became obedient to the faith. But the principal achievement of this year was the planting of a church at Middletown in Vigo county. Here the missionary Baptists had then a large church, while there were but about half a dozen disciples in an unorganized condition. At this point he and Elder B. preached; organized a church; and obtained over sixty additions, among whom were several of the most efficient members of the Baptist Church. This gave to the Christian Church at that place great strength, which it has maintained, and steadily increased, to this day. On the

5th of January, 1852, having sold his farm, he removed to Sullivan, the county-seat, and entered upon the duties of his clerkship. This year he visited several congregations in the country; but labored chiefly for the church at Sullivan, preaching often at night after the toils of the day were over.

During the next three years his manner of life was much the same; only he preached more, held more protracted meetings, and induced greater numbers to obey the gospel. In 1855 he was reëlected clerk of the Circuit Court. In 1856 he turned more than two hundred from the broad to the narrow way, and planted one new church. During the three years following he preached regularly for four congregations, and averaged about one hundred and fifty accessions per year.

In 1858 he and Elder Jos. Hostetler held a protracted meeting at Providence, in Sullivan county, where there was a church recently organized and very feeble. The meeting continued ten days, and closed with eighty-five additions. One year later they held another meeting there. As at Samaria, the people with one accord gave heed unto what they spake; about forty others believed and were baptized, and there was great joy in that city. A few years previous to this, when Elder Wolfe first visited that point, there were but three or four disciples and a few United Brethren in all that region. The entire neighborhood was a very Sodom, in which ten righteous could hardly be found; having long been famous for horseracing, drinking, gambling, and almost every vice in the catalogue of crimes. At the conclusion of two years' labor among them the church at Providence numbered largely over two hundred; and the Sodom had been transformed into a Salem—a peaceable, a Christian community. So it remains unto this day, a monument more durable than brass, whose top touches heaven.

Although he has received but little from the churches, the proceeds of his farm and the emoluments of his civil office, have placed him above want. He has recently invested his small capital in the mercantile business, and has, in a measure, retired from the regular service. But still he is resolved to preach Jesus, as health may permit, until the Master shall say: "It is enough; come up higher;" and he now sings the living sentiment of his soul in this beautiful stanza:

> "E'er since, by faith, I saw the stream
> His flowing wounds supply,
> Redeeming love has been my theme,
> *And shall be till I die.*"

Such is a brief account of the life and services of Elder Joseph W. Wolfe, from which it will be seen that, among other good deeds, he has led back to the Shepherd's fold about four thousand five hundred persons that, like sheep, had gone astray.

Nature granted to Elder Wolfe the two great blessings for which the heathen poet taught his contemporaries to pray, namely, *a sound mind in a sound body*. Inured to labor from his early youth, his physical powers were well developed; and the hardships he experienced as a pioneer farmer eminently qualified him for the more severe trials of a pioneer preacher. He is six feet four inches high, and weighs about one hundred and seventy pounds. His frame is muscular, head very large, eyes pale blue or gray, hair and complexion light. His temperament is highly nervous, giving him a rapid utterance and quick movements.

His natural powers of mind are much above the average, and, had he enjoyed the advantages of a collegiate education, he would have occupied a high rank among the greater lights of the church. His mind is of the perceptive caste, observing closely and comprehending easily both men and things; yet he reasons forcibly by the best of all logics, *common sense.*

He is a man of great vivacity—plain in his dress, simple in his habits, frank in his demeanor, indulgent to his family, and obliging to his neighbors.

Though not ordinarily eloquent, yet he is a fluent, distinct, impressive speaker, very much like George Campbell in his lofty flights and impassioned exhortations. At such times he enunciates with wonderful rapidity, gesticulates violently, and is all aglow with animation. His language is respectable, though not elegant; and he presents the truth with great clearness and simplicity by means of apt illustrations. He usually deals in facts; and his discourses are generally argumentative, hortatory, practical. He never raves like a mad man, but always utters the words of truth and soberness like one who really believes that God "has appointed a day in which he will judge the world in righteousness."

In whatever he has undertaken he owes much of his success to his untiring industry. In the office or on the farm, whatsoever his hands found to do, he did with his might. Hence he has acquired a sufficiency of this world's goods, although the most of his time has been spent in the Lord's vineyard.

In the ministry, he has regarded neither winds nor clouds; but in the morning has sown the incorruptible seed and in the evening withheld not his hand. Thus, having spent his life in sowing to the Spirit, he shall ere long reap the harvest of life everlasting. For, with constitution impaired by exposure, oppressed by the weight of more than half a century, and robbed by death of a large portion of his family, he only waits the summons to join them "beyond the river"—

" 'Tis hid from view, but we may guess
   How beautiful that realm must be;
For gleamings of its loveliness,
   In visions granted, oft we see.
The very clouds that o'er it throw
   Their vail, unraised for mortal sight,
With gold and purple tintings glow,
   Reflected from the glorious light
      Beyond the river."

THOMAS J. EDMONDSON.

ELDER THOMAS JEFFERSON EDMONDSON was born in Sullivan county, Indiana, December 25th, 1816. In the Spring of 1817, his father, William Edmondson, removed with him to Monroe county, where he was brought up. He was the eldest of eight brothers, three of whom, George, Porter, and John, became ministers in the Cumberland Presbyterian Church. They were men of more than ordinary intellectual ability and moral worth, but of very frail constitutions. All three died of pulmonary diseases when they were comparatively young men. His father, who still lives, has never been a member of any church, but is an upright citizen, who has given special attention to the moral and intellectual training of his children, of whom he has had twelve, eight sons and four daughters. All, save three or four, have long slumbered beneath the sod.

His mother was a most devoted member of the Cumberland Presbyterian Church, and she studiously impressed that particular form of doctrine upon the minds and hearts of her children. Upon the faith of his mother he was sprinkled in infancy, and under her well-meant instructions he grew up with the rest.

From the first dawn of reason he seemed to be absorbed in thought. As he grew older he delighted to steal away from his brothers and spend his time in the forest with his rifle. He was also passionately fond of fishing, like those of old, who afterwards, in the provi-

dence of God, became fishers of men. As a school-boy, he was mostly remarkable for seldom seeming to study, yet always reciting well at the head of his class. In his own easy and peculiar way he made rapid progress, and soon mastered all the branches of the common-school.

He was of a roving disposition—not a man, like Pollock's, who thought "the visual ray that girt him in, the world's extreme." Through life his motto was *plus ultra* —more beyond—more knowledge to be acquired—still higher degrees of excellence and enjoyment to be attained in the Christian profession. Shut in by the hills of Monroe county, his expansive spirit was cramped and restless. Before he was twenty-one years old, therefore, he left the paternal roof, made a trip to Mississippi, and there acquired some knowledge of the men, manners, and institutions of the sunny South.

On his return home he commenced and prosecuted for some time the study of medicine; but he was destined to become a disciple of the Great Physician, and, according to his instructions, administer the "balm in Gilead." It was in the Fall of 1839 that he was brought under the influence of the gospel through the instrumentality of James M. Mathes. This excellent evangelist, then just entering upon his career of usefulness, was preaching once a month at a schoolhouse in the Edmondson neighborhood. On going one day to fill an appointment, he perceived, near the house, a man walking to and fro in the road, and seemingly engaged in profound meditation. When they met, the troubled stranger introduced himself as Mr. Edmondson, and requested an interview prior to the commencement of preaching.

In the course of this interview he presented his difficulties with regard to Infant Sprinkling, and several matters connected with the subject of conversion, saying, "If you can remove these difficulties from my mind, I will gadly obey the gospel, as I desire to make religion the basis of every thing. I am studying a profession, but before I enter upon it I want to be a disciple of Jesus— then I can build on a sure foundation." The preacher was successful in removing all his difficulties, and in giving him perfect satisfaction as to what the Lord requires one in his condition to do. It was therefore agreed between them that on the next day he should meet Elder Mathes at his appointment in Bloomington, and then and there obey from the heart the form of doctrine delivered to the world by the apostles.

Accordingly on the next day, which was Friday, he and his brother Porter attended the meeting at Bloomington. At the close of the discourse he went forward and publicly confessed his faith in the Great Messiah. The congregation immediately repaired to the water—a natural pool in Clear creek, a little south of the University— where, in the presence of a large concourse of people, he was buried with the Lord by baptism into death. It was an interesting, a solemn, an impressive scene. As he came up out of the water, while all hearts were softened for the impress of truth, he made some excellent remarks, which evinced not only his sincerity, but also his clear understanding of "the way, the truth, and the life."

About the first of November, 1839, he went to Bloomington on a visit to Elder Mathes, who had previously removed to that place for the purpose of attending the University. While there he was easily prevailed upon by his instructor in the gospel to give up the study of medicine and finish his education at the college, preparatory to engaging in the work of the ministry. He immediately went to live in the family of Elder Mathes, and entered the State University, then under the direction of that profound thinker Dr. Andrew Wylie. There he continued his studies until he acquired a respectable knowledge of the Latin and Greek languages, Mathematics, the Physical Sciences, Rhetoric, Elocution, Logic, Evidences of Christianity, and Metaphysics. He was a most laborious student, equalling—if he did not surpass—all his classmates in both thoroughness and dispatch. It is not improbable that, accustomed as he had been to labor in the open fields, he there laid the foundation of that fell disease which carried him, as it carries millions, to an untimely grave.

Early in the year 1840, while yet a student at college, he commenced preaching. On Saturdays and Sundays he would accompany Elder Mathes into the country, and would occasionally deliver a discourse—at first using notes prepared for him by his companion and tutor in the gospel. On this account he received the name of *"Timothy,"* or *"brother Mathes's Timothy,"* by which title he was for years extensively known. Often when the brethren abroad would request Elder M. to visit them, they would write, "Come, brother Mathes, and bring 'Timothy' with you; or, if you cannot come, send 'Timothy,' and we will be satisfied."

After leaving the university he gave himself wholly to the word, rose very rapidly, and soon became a very useful, widely-known, and popular preacher. For several years he had no particular location, but went everywhere preaching Jesus and the salvation that is through faith in his name and obedience to his commands. He was very successful in convincing the people of the correctness of the principles he advocated, and of the necessity of a return to the ancient gospel and the order of the primitive churches.

In the course of his travels he came to Madison, where, in 1843, he was married to Miss Sarah Ann Hutchinson, who became the mother of his three children. The eldest of them, a son, died at Columbus at the age of six years.

The other two, a son and a daughter, he left with his widow, never again to return to them, but in hope that they would come to him. Those two are still living somewhere in the far West.

After his marriage, and through the influence of that excellent man of God, Joseph Fassett, he located at Columbus, Bartholomew county, and became the pastor of the church at that place. He did not content himself, however, with feeding that one flock; but preached often in the country and at various points along the Madison and Indianapolis railroad. A portion of his time was regularly employed in serving the congregations at Edinburg, New Hope, and Greensburg.

At no time did he receive from all the churches under his care a sufficiency for his support; but he was always under the necessity of devoting a portion of his time to some secular business. Through this neglect on the part of the churches, and through bad management of his temporal affairs, he became involved in debt, by which both his happiness and usefulness were impaired.

He was a ready, keen, and powerful debater, though he never held but one regular public discussion. This was on the subject of Universalism. It took place at Franklin, Johnson county, on the 18th, 19th, and 20th days of January, 1844. His opponent was the great Universalist champion, Erasmus Manford, of Terre Haute, then editor of the "Christian Teacher."

The two propositions were the same that have long been stereotyped, one affirmative for each. The following short account of the debate is from the pen of one who heard it:

"This discussion, we are assured, did much good in Franklin and vicinity, in exposing the sceptical heresy of Universalism, and in the development and establishment of the truth as taught in the Bible. In this debate Mr.

Manford, though a practiced and wily debater, was no match for the youthful and philosophic Edmondson, who, though young and inexperienced in debate, yet having on the armor of righteousness and truth, laid hold on his opponent with a giant grip, and bound him hand and foot with the strong cords of reason, logic, and Scripture testimony." The writer of this flattering notice, it is true, was a great admirer of Edmondson and a zealous opposer of Manford, yet he is one whose skillful pen is not given to vain boasting but rather to words of truth and soberness.

The only other debate of his was an informal little affair that took place in the village of Leesville, Lawrence county. It occurred in the Summer of 1845, and on this wise:

Jacob Wright of Salem, and George Walker, a circuit preacher, had just concluded a discussion on the subjects of Baptism and the Influence of the Holy Spirit. At this discussion Edmondson was present, with other Christian evangelists; and the Rev. Philip May, another circuit preacher, was also present with others of his brethren. At the close of the discusssion—which was just before noon—some one of the Christian preachers announced that, at a certain hour in the afternoon, he would deliver a discourse at the place where they were then assembled. Mr. May immediately arose and gave notice that, commencing an hour earlier, he would preach, at the same place, on the subject of Baptism; at which time and place he would prove *from the Greek language* that sprinkling and pouring are scriptural *modes* of administering that ordinance. Dinner being over, all repaired to the grove, anxious to hear Mr. May prove what mortal man had never before established. By common consent Mr. Edmondson was appointed to follow the reverend gentleman, and reply to his Greek arguments. This Mr. May did not expect; indeed he was not aware that any one present understood the language in which God, for wise purposes, wrote through his amanuenses, and stereotyped through his providence, the precious record of His well-beloved Son. He therefore assumed considerable latitude and disclosed a great many things relative to the Greek language, that would certainly have been new to Demosthenes or Plato—the latter of which gentlemen especially, is supposed to have had a respectable knowledge of that tongue!

Mr. Edmondson busied himself in taking copious notes; and when the argument was concluded, he took the stand and began his review. Then came the tug of war—for Greek met Greek. He showed first of all that Mr. May was neither a classical scholar nor a reliable critic; that his assertions were altogether reckless and without foundation either in the New Testament Greek or in the Greek classics. His speech is said to have manifested great ability, profound research, and sound learning. It also abounded in good humor, wit, and pleasant sarcasm, which rendered his opponent very uneasy, and placed himself in the first rank of debaters. It was generally regarded by the people who heard it as a most triumphant vindication of the oft-assailed truth on that subject.

As a writer also, he attained to a high rank, and no doubt accomplished more good by his pen than by his tongue. Many of his articles were published in the "Christian Record," where they were read with profit by thousands. They are still in print to be read by thousands more, now that his tongue lies forever silent in the grave. The style, force, and tone of his literary productions may be best described by inserting a few extracts. The following are taken from his articles written for the Record under the broad caption, "Christian Obligations." After quoting some of the apostolic injunctions, such as,

"Do justly, love mercy, and walk humbly before the Lord," he says:

"A want of conformity to these moral precepts is the cause of a great amount of infidelity in the world. The moralist, instead of looking at the true evidence of Christianity, looks at the conduct of the lukewarm or ungodly professor, and concludes that the character of such is proof that the Bible is not adapted to the nature and wants of man, and consequently he is opposed to Christianity. He concludes that there is more divinity in human nature than there is in the authenticity of the Bible, and, therefore, he attributes the good qualities which some Christians possess, more to the organization of their nature than to the influence of the Bible; and hence he sets up in opposition to what he calls Christianity, some of its own moral precepts. Others set the moralist in opposition to the ungodly professor—not for the purpose of imitating him, but for an excuse to indulge in immorality and crime."

On the subject of prayer he writes thus:

"Prayer is indispensable to the life of the Christian. In fact, a prayerless Christian is, to my mind, an anomaly in the universe of God. It is like attempting to identify the ideas of opaque and transparent qualities in a simple substance, or to conceive of two substances occupying the same space at the same time. * * * * * It may be contended by some that if we possess the spirit of prayer, that will suffice without formal or vocal prayer. This argument might be brought with equal force against every commandment in the gospel. Some people bring the same argument against obeying the first principles of the gospel. 'Oh,' say they, 'God looks not at forms and outward ceremonies, but at the heart. He abhors the sacrifice where the heart is not found.' Thus people argue, and thus conclude to omit 'the sacrifice' altogether, or offer it on an altar that God has not erected, and thus the virtue of the sacrifice is lost, for 'it is the altar that sanctifieth the gift.' I could not make use of such an argument against an institution of heaven, except it were as an opiate to a guilty conscience, which was too weak to bear the wholesome and strengthening doctrine of Jesus Christ and his apostles. * * * * Is it not strange that, with the example of patriarchs and prophets—apostles and first Christians—together with the many precepts on that subject, individuals professing Christianity should never be known to pray?—no, not even so much as give thanks to Almighty God for the food they eat? Such, however, in some (I hope few) instances, is literally true. The devotion of the heart is too much neglected. How many are there who are raising up children, bound with them to the grave and to the bar of God, who have never been heard by them to pray or give thanks to God for any of his blessings which he bestows so profusely upon us! Are there not bishops of churches whose duty it is to watch over the souls of the flock, who never pray in their families or read the word of God to them?" This long extract on prayer will not be injurious to the readers of these sketches—to the disciples of this present day.

In more lively style, he treats directly of some of the bishops, as follows:

"What would you think, Christian reader, notwithstanding the importance of the office of the Christian bishop, were I to tell you that I know of a Christian (?) bishop of whom I have been told by one of the flock of which he was appointed to take the oversight, that he came to *see* the flock—not to feed—*five times in forty-two weeks?* Such indeed is the fact. *Query: Will such a shepherd receive a crown of glory that fadeth not away?* * * * * What would you think were I to tell you of another bishop who undertakes to justify play-parties, and proves the sincerity of his advocacy by having one at his own house, thus setting an example to the flock? A church of Jesus Christ, the light of the world, in the habitual practice of such parties! Such a scene! A spectacle that would make angels weep, the devil smile, wicked men rejoice, and fill the hearts of the pious children of God with sorrow.

"Suppose a church having such a bishop as we have described should ordain an evangelist, and send him out to preach the gospel; and his labors are blest by the conversion of many who hear his voice; and when he returns home to report his success to his brethren, and thus fill their hearts with joy, there accompany him a young disciple, one of his late converts, whose heart is filled with zeal and love to God; and when they arrive at the bishop's house about nightfall, where they expect to tarry all night, they hear the voice of male and female engaged in singing, with much animation. 'Ah,' says the new convert to himself, 'I shall have a pleasant evening with these disciples, who have met together at the bishop's house to sing the songs of Zion." But to his great mortification, when he arrives at the house of this shepherd of the flock of God, he finds a company of male and female disciples going round in a ring, singing—

> "Old sister Phebe, how merry were we
> When we sat under yon juniper tree,"

* * * * while the bishop, with a smile on his countenance, and his sober companion by his side, sits and looks on, well pleased to behold the zeal and devotion of these young disciples, the flock of his care! What would be the feelings, on such an occasion, of the young disciple whom we have described?"

Elder Edmondson possessed also considerable poetic talent. He never spent much time in its cultivation or exercise, yet he wrote some very respectable pieces, mostly of a sacred character and plaintive tone. The following is a specimen from the "Christian Psalmist:"

KEDRON'S GLOOMY VALE.

"Among the mountain trees
   The winds were murmuring low,
And night's ten thousand harmonies
   Were harmonies of woe;
A voice of grief was on the gale,
It came from Kedron's gloomy vale.

It was the Saviour's prayer
   That on the silence broke,
Imploring strength from heav'n to bear
   The sin-avenging stroke:
As in Gethsemane he knelt,
And pangs unknown his bosom felt.

The fitful starlight shone
   In dim and misty gleams;
Deep was his agonizing groan,
   And large the vital streams
That trickled to the dewy sod,
While Jesus raised his voice to God.

The chosen three that stayed,
   Their nightly watch to keep,
Left him through sorrows deep to wade,
   And gave themselves to sleep:
Meekly and sad he prayed alone,
Strangely forgotten by his own.

Along the streamlet's banks
   The reckless traitor came,
And heavy, on his bosom, sank
   The load of guilt and shame:
Yet unto them that waited nigh
He gave the Lamb of God to die.

>   Among the mountain trees
>   The winds were murmuring low,
>   And night's ten thousand harmonies
>   Were harmonies of woe;
>   For cruel voices filled the gale
>   That came from Kedron's gloomy vale."

Leaving the reader to judge, from these specimens, of the character of his writings and their probable influence upon the minds and hearts of men, we proceed to give the sad remainder of his history.

He continued to labor at and around Columbus, in the manner above-described, until early in the year 1854, at which time he was called, by a co-operation of several churches in Lawrence county, to labor for them as an evangelist. He accepted this call, and for a few months prosecuted the work with good success; but his health failing him he was compelled to retire from the pulpit. He then returned with his little family to Columbus, where it was soon discovered that Consumption, that merciless destroyer, had marked him for his victim. Every effort was made by himself and his friends to stay the progress of the fearful disease, but it was all in vain. In a little while he went down lamented to the grave, whither descends every thing good and beautiful on earth. The subjoined extract is from his obituary notice, written by J. M. Mathes, and contained in the October number of the Christian Record, for the year 1855.

"A MIGHTY MAN FALLEN. We learn by a letter from brother C. C. Alden that our beloved brother and fellow-laborer, Elder Thomas J. Edmondson, fell asleep in Jesus, on Lord's day morning, August 19th, 1855. The disease was consumption, of which most of a large family of brothers and sisters have died. Brother Edmondson died at his residence in Columbus, Indiana, leaving a wife and two small children to mourn his departure. For several weeks before his death he suffered greatly, but he bore it patiently, and calmly awaited the moment that would admit him through the vail of mortality to the pleasures and glories of a better world."

Physically, as well as mentally and morally, Thomas J. Edmondson was a noble specimen of his race. He was six feet two inches high, and weighed about one hundred and eighty pounds—was well built, finely proportioned, and possessed of great power and activity. In his youth and early manhood, he was passionately fond of athletic exercises; and at three jumps or hops he had but few equals.

He had rather light hair, mildly-beaming blue eyes, and "the look of heaven upon his face which limners give to the beloved disciple."

His was a fine head, especially in the moral and intellectual departments; the moral, perhaps, predominating. He had an excellent memory and very great power of concentration. Every intellectual ray he could bring to a complete focus. The thoughtfulness of his youth so increased with his years that he became subject to fits of entire abstraction. Often has he been known to take his bucket, when in such a state of mind, and proceed to the *barn* instead of the well, for water. He was not a servile, but an independent thinker, whom no human creed could shut out from "the light of the knowledge of God."

In the pulpit he was rather a philosopher and logician than an orator, though he was a very pleasant speaker. His voice was charming, full of melody, silvery and sweet. He was an excellent singer, and greatly delighted in singing the songs of Zion. He had a fine flow of language, and his delivery was calm and dignified; never stormy and impetuous. He always treated his opponents with fairness and candor; and although he made no compromise with sectarianism but rebuked it with all authority, yet he was generally mild and conciliatory, never abusive. He was a bold, frank, and earnest speaker, yet he sometimes seemed to lack energy to stir, and pathos to touch the hearts of his hearers. In fact he delighted to stand upon the firm basis of proposition and proof, and to sway his audience by the force of logic and testimony, rather than by appeals to their sympathies, their passions, or their prejudices. Like Paul, he "*reasoned* of righteousness, of temperance, and of judgment to come," and when he finished his argument the Felixes trembled and felt that *it must be so.* His poetic imagination enabled him to make a good exhortation, and, when excited, his descriptive powers were very fine.

He was most amiable in disposition, eminently sociable, and by no means destitute of humor. Though slightly inclined to melancholy, he relished an innocent joke, and often indulged in a hearty laugh. In attachment he was strong as David; in friendship as true as Jonathan; and in death as unfortunate as righteous Abel, cut down at the altar of God.

> "How beautiful it is for man to die
> Upon the walls of Zion! to be call'd
> Like a watch-worn and weary sentinel,
> To put his armor off, and rest—in Heaven!"

NORTHWESTERN CHRISTIAN UNIVERSITY

BY A. R. BENTON, PRESIDENT OF THE FACULTY.

ITS ORIGIN.

THE idea of founding an institution of learning of the highest order was entertained, for many years, by leading minds in the Christian Church, before the work was consummated in the founding and organizing of the Northwestern Christian University—a view of which is presented in this volume.

It was plainly perceived by the prominent men among the Christian brotherhood in Indiana, that the prosperity of the Christian cause, as intrusted to their hands, was very intimately blended with the cause of education; hence, this subject was much discussed in the earlier Indiana State Meetings until the October Meeting in 1849, when definite action was taken in regard to the enterprise.

That meeting, aiming at the establishment of an institution of learning of the very highest grade, adopted the following resolution:

"That a Northwestern Christian University be founded at Indianapolis, as soon as a sufficient amount of funds can be raised to commence it; and that a committee of seven be appointed by this meeting to take the preliminary steps in reference to the founding and endowing of such an institution."

Such was the unostentatious origin of the University, which is evidently destined, under the favor of God, to take rank among the first of the noble educational establishments of our country.

LIBRARY
OF THE
UNIVERSITY OF ILLINOIS

To that State Meeting, acting under the impulse of Christian liberality and zeal for education and religion, we owe the inception and inauguration of this enterprise.

ITS HISTORY.

The Committee appointed by the State Meeting, in accordance with the foregoing resolution, obtained from the Legislature of the State an act of incorporation, liberal in its character, and which contemplated a University, composed of colleges of literature and science, law and medicine. The charter was approved, January 15, 1850, and thus became a law.

On the 5th of the ensuing March the commissioners named in the charter held their first meeting, and appointed a Board of Commissioners, whose duty it was to make prompt and efficient provision for procuring stock, in order to build and endow the University. Under the auspices and direction of this Board, the work of procuring subscriptions for the stock of the University was vigorously prosecuted until June 22, 1852. At this time, it appearing that seventy-five thousand dollars had been subscribed—the minimum amount named in the charter—an election of directors was ordered, as provided by the charter, and the commissioners adjourned *sine die*. The first Board of Directors was elected July 14, 1852, and convened on the 27th of the same month for the transaction of business.

The site of the University building was selected in September, 1852, and the contracts for the building were let in July of the following year; and at the May Meeting, 1855, the building was reported to the Board as completed.

On the 9th of April, 1855, a preparatory school was opened in the University under the direction of Professor A. R. Benton, and continued until it was incorporated with the college, which was ordered to be opened on the 1st of November, 1855.

The Faculty at the opening of the College was composed of Professors John Young, A. R. Benton, and J. R. Challen, to which number G. W. Hoss was added the following year. At the meeting of the Board of Directors in June, 1858, John Young having resigned his professorship, R. T. Brown was chosen to fill his place, and S. K. Hoshour was elected President of the Faculty of the University.

In January, 1859, Madison Evans was elected Principal of the Preparatory and English School, in place of J. R Challen, who had resigned. Up to this time, and until the Summer vacation of 1861, the Principal of the English Department was assisted at different times by Mr. and Mrs. L. H. Jameson, Mrs. E. J. Price, and Mrs. N. E. Burns.

At the July session of the Board, 1861, in view of the condition of the country, and the necessity of retrenchment in the expenses of the University, it was decided to diminish the number of instructors, and consequently a partial reorganization of the Faculty became necessary. In accomplishing this change A. R. Benton was elected President of the Faculty, which now consisted of S. K. Hoshour, R. T. Brown, G. W. Hoss, A. C. Shortridge, and the President-elect.

This organization of the Faculty continues at this time.

The attendance at the University has always been very creditable in numbers and in the character of its students. The average yearly attendance in the Literary Department has been nearly two hundred, and in the Law Department about thirteen annually. The whole number of graduates for seven years has been forty-two. Thus it will be seen that the University has enjoyed a remarkable degree of prosperity in the influence it has been enabled to exert; and nothing is now wanting but the return of peaceful times and the continued co-operation of its friends, to give it a pre-eminence among similar institutions.

LAW DEPARTMENT.

The propriety of establishing a Law Department was discussed very early in the history of the University, and several classes were instructed by Professor John Young previously to its being organized in its present form.

As at present constituted under the Professors, S. E. Perkins, LL. D., Judge of the Supreme Court of the State, and David McDonald, LL. D., it bids fair to become a valuable and popular department of the University. It designs to furnish as thorough and as extensive a course of legal study as any college in the West, together with a practical application of the things taught.

BUILDING AND ENDOWMENT.

The University building has been projected on a scale of unrivaled magnificence for a college building, thus indicating the enlarged and comprehensive designs of its projectors and founders.

Its location in the northeastern part of Indianapolis, in a *campus* of twenty-five acres of primitive forest trees, is unsurpassed for beauty, and convenience to the citizens of this State and of the Northwest.

The building is modeled after the Collegiate-Gothic style of architecture. It is made of brick, with the quoins and coping of stone, and constructed in the most artistic and durable manner—a fit type of its prospective career in the noble work to which it has been consecrated.

The west wing of the edifice is completed, and furnished

with accommodations for about three hundred students. The remainder waits for the liberality of its friends to bring it to completion.

The endowment of the University is projected on the basis of a joint-stock-company, in shares of one hundred dollars each, one third being paid over to the Company, and the remaining two thirds at the option of the subscriber, being retained as a permanent loan from the Company, the interest of which is to be paid annually.

According to this plan, funds enough have been obtained to erect a building, and to constitute the nucleus of a permanent endowment fund.

With the increase of this endowment will come an increase in the number of professors, and provision of the *matériel* of education in every department of study. The finances of the corporation are managed by the President of the Board of Directors, which responsible position has been successively filled by Ovid Butler, Esq., Elder Elijah Goodwin, and Jeremiah Smith, Esq.

NAME AND DESIGN.

The adopted name—Northwestern Christian University—was designed to be descriptive rather than geographical, and intended to stamp on its front its peculiar characteristics.

It is not unusual to give a local name to an institution of learning, as being most convenient in order to distinguish it from others, and to fix its location. In the name adopted for the University it was intended doubtless to embody its spirit and design, rather than to give it geographical distinction.

It is a truth recognized by all correct observers, that nature, society, and experience, as well as books, are powerful instructors. Thus while the University aims to give literary culture to all, East, West, North and South, yet it would imbibe and communicate that spirit of enlargement in which it was originated, and which is most aptly symbolized by the broad savannahs and the sweep of majestic rivers in the Northwest. Besides, that seething activity and ardor of enterprise, so peculiar to these States, devoted to individual freedom and development, is the spirit in which the University is designed to work, and which is indicated by its characteristic name.

It is not pretended that new ideas, with respect to the routine of college study, have been originated; for the course of literary study in the University is essentially the same as in other institutions of a similar grade—a course which is the result of the cumulative experience of the past, and in accord with the power and wants of the human mind.

In this respect no useful originality of plan is claimed, and if possessed of any superiority, it must be in the execution of its plan.

Whatever originality of design there may be, pertaining to the institution, it will be found in its provisions for Biblical study, and for female education in the classes of the University.

Its motto is, "the Bible the best classic," and its aim is to consecrate the vigor of enterprise and fervor of spirit peculiar to our time to the Lord. Hence, the Institution has the name Christian, by which, while it seeks to make no invidious distinction between itself and others, it recognizes its obligations to teach the Christian religion in the morality, facts and promises thereof. This, by the terms of the charter, is made an imperative duty, and in practice is effected by instruction in regular classes of the University.

Thus the Bible is made a text book—ignorance of which

is a foul reproach to graduates of Colleges, in a land of Christian civilization and influence.

Without it, impulse and passion may prevail with uncontrolled sway, but with it alone, *principles* of action, originating in a sense of duty, are best inculcated and enforced.

This daily contact of Divine truth, this personal and direct approach to the heart, is unquestionably the most potent means in forming character after the Divine model, and in fixing as principles of action the precepts of the Bible.

Another design of the University is somewhat novel, though by no means untried and impracticable.

The charter of the University opens it to both sexes, to be taught in the same classes, and to be graduated with the same honors.

This plan cannot be regarded altogether as an experiment, for in the High Schools of our country it is found practicable, and not attended with the evil consequences so much deprecated by those with whom this system has found little favor. It is a deplorable fact, that female education, in those branches that especially invigorate and strengthen the mind, labors under the reproach of inefficiency; and every effort to remove this opprobrium should be hailed with joy by every friend of sound scholarship. Hence for many years the most judicious educators have been devising plans, by which the moral restraints, the intellectual competition, and the refining influence of the sexes, may be reciprocally enjoyed in the school-room.

With sound philosophy on its side, and no countervailing experience to dissuade from the attempt, the University proposes to give to both sexes the advantage of the most enlarged and liberal culture.

ITS WORKS AND ITS WANTS.

It has already been shown from the statistics of the University, that the Institution has enjoyed a large measure of popular favor and patronage. Its growth has been healthful and uniform, with nothing to disturb its discipline or to mar its internal peace. The liberal spirit in which its administration has been conceived and conducted has conduced to this result.

Whatever of external agitation may have prevailed, the harmony and peace of College operations have never been disturbed. If, too, we compare the prosperity of the University with that of other Colleges, we have no cause of discontent or discouragement.

The number to be educated at College is limited by the educational spirit and pecuniary means of our people. For its past prosperity its friends have much reason to be thankful. This is due, in a large measure, to the liberal and enlightened policy of its Directors, which, as it is better known, will be more heartily approved.

From the partial praises we have thus bestowed on the University, we would not have any one infer that it has no *wants*. It does need a larger Endowment fund, in order that it may have a larger Chapel building and a greater number of Professors. In order to give this University that prominence which was contemplated by its founders, it will be necessary to increase its Endowment fund. In addition to the chairs of instruction already provided, there is pressing need of a Professor of Biblical Literature, who shall make that work a specialty, with reference to the wants of young men entering the ministry. This, with another Professor in the Literary Department, and with greater *matériel* of education in the Library, Apparatus, and Cabinet, will place the Institution in the very front rank of Colleges. A Medical Department, too, is demanded, and is under consideration, to be organized, it is presumed, before the lapse of many years.

The public men, the incidents of whose religious lives are here recorded, together with many brethren in private life, who have labored even more efficiently than the former in carrying the University thus far toward completion, here see the culmination of their efforts in the cause of education in this State. It remains for their later contemporaries, and for their children, in the same spirit of Christian liberality and faith, to carry forward the work which has been so auspiciously begun.

INDIANAPOLIS, *October* 4, 1862.

www.ingramcontent.com/pod-product-compliance
Lightning Source LLC
Chambersburg PA
CBHW022102300426
44117CB00007B/553